HOW TO AVOID A HAPPY LIFE

First published 2024 by
FREMANTLE PRESS

Fremantle Press Inc. trading as Fremantle Press
PO Box 158, North Fremantle, Western Australia, 6159
fremantlepress.com.au

Copyright © Julia Lawrinson, 2024

The moral rights of the author have been asserted.

This book is copyright. Apart from any fair dealing for the purpose of private study, research, criticism or review, as permitted under the *Copyright Act*, no part may be reproduced by any process without written permission. Every reasonable effort has been made to seek permission for quotations contained herein. Please address any enquiries to the publisher.

Cover image by wpclipart.com
Designed by Design by Committee, designbycommittee.com.au

A catalogue record for this book is available from the National Library of Australia

ISBN 9781760993474 (paperback)
ISBN 9781760993481 (ebook)

Fremantle Press is supported by the Western Australian State Government through the Department of Cultural Industries, Tourism and Sport.

Fremantle Press respectfully acknowledges the Whadjuk people of the Noongar nation as the Traditional Owners and Custodians of the land where we work in Walyalup.

HOW TO AVOID A HAPPY LIFE

A MEMOIR

JULIA LAWRINSON

Julia Lawrinson has published more than fifteen books for children and young people, many of them award winning. She works as a consultant on legislation and policy when she is not writing and presenting to young people, and is an enthusiastic adult learner of Indonesian, yoga and the cello. Her favourite place on earth is the dog park.

To Nige and Annie

Every life is a piece of art, put together with all means available.
– Pierre Janet

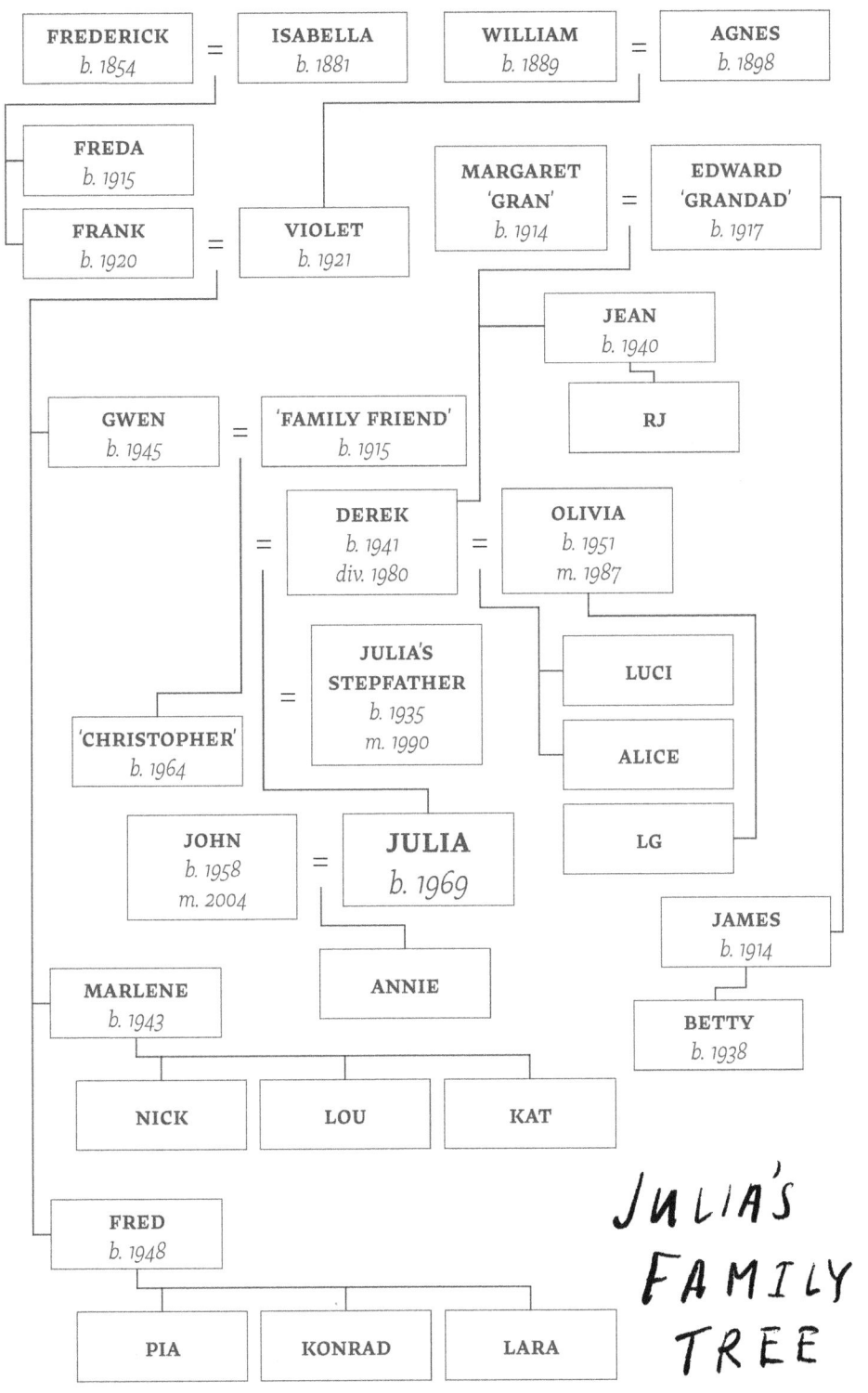

Contents

Prologue: The Party Coffin 11

Get Yourself Born into Intergenerational Misery 13

Experience Vicarious Trauma through Your Friend Being Raped and
    Murdered by a Japanese Serial Killer....................................... 87

Marry Your Ex-Girlfriend's Brother 133

Surprise! Find Yourself Living with a Street Angel, Home Devil............. 161

Find Out Why Your Husband is Urinating in the Kitchen of an Evening 227

Find Yourself and Your New Partner Being Chased Down the Street by
    a Phalanx of Reporters 271

Born to Be Alive 333

A Note on Memory, Accuracy, and Completeness........................... 344

PROLOGUE: THE PARTY COFFIN

There is a photo of my mother in a coffin.

Her eyes are closed but her glasses are still on, indicating that she is, in fact, alive. She's clutching a bouquet of fake red roses and is surrounded by bunches of fake flowers in real (although empty) beer bottles. She's managing not to smile.

The coffin belonged to one of my mother's ex-boyfriends. I think his name was John, but it might have been Allan, or Steve, or Mike. It was a great prop to bring to a Halloween party in 1990, and much hilarity no doubt ensued as people climbed in and out of it, pretending to be dead.

My mother, Gwen, no longer has to pretend to be dead. Just before she reached that inevitable state, we were discussing funeral arrangements.

'Hey Mum,' I said. 'Do you remember that boyfriend of yours – the undertaker?'

'John?' she said (or Allan/Steve/Mike).

'Yeah,' I said. 'Could he do your funeral?'

'No, he's dead,' she said.

And then we laughed and laughed, until the cancer in her kidney gave her a pain in the stomach and she was reduced to wincing and giggling.

It was a moment of levity, taking place for her in the midst of three weeks of surprise suffering, belated and incomplete taking stock, and indignities; and for me, in the midst of surprise anguish, attempted and ineffectual resolution-finding, followed by a years-long eruption of feelings of abandonment hitherto under- if not unfelt.

My mother had been threatening to die since I was seventeen. Then, she'd been diagnosed with emphysema but continued smoking and living until a series of strokes at the age of fifty-six put paid completely to the former, and curtailed the style in which she'd been doing the latter. For eighteen years she'd been a hemiplegic, sustained primarily by a diet of ham sandwiches and pies, increasingly confined to her loungeroom chair, her legs and feet distended with retained fluid. She criticised everyone and everything from this vantage point, softened only by offerings of stuffed or porcelain meerkats, or by beating her husband in the daily cryptic crossword.

Every time someone famous or heroic died, she'd say, 'Here I am sitting on my fat arse, useless as tits on a bull.'

She was regularly taken by ambulance to hospital after falls, unexplained drops in iron levels, twisted bowels, or cysts. After each phone call, on my way to the hospital, I'd wonder if this really was the beginning of the very drawn-out end.

'They reckon there's nothing wrong with me,' she'd say, sounding irritated. 'But what would they know.'

She hated her doctor but would not go to a different one. Her husband was constantly going to specialists and doctors. When I inquired why, she said, 'How would I bloody know? He doesn't tell me anything.' When I pointed out she could, as a concerned wife, ask him, she looked at me as if it was a stupid comment, requiring no response.

After Gwen's actual funeral, I found language to be inadequate to explain to colleagues how I was feeling, or the nature of my relationship with my mother. Instead, I propped the picture of Gwen-in-a-party-coffin on my desk to indicate that I was having a hard day.

When I was crying next to her bedside, close to the end, she said, 'Remember the good times.'

You can't remember the good times unless you've reconciled with The Rest Of It. The Rest Of It is never simple, linear, or confined to one's own experiences. Grief, if you had a childhood resembling mine in any way, dumps The Rest Of It unceremoniously on you. First, you've got to dig your way out of it. Then you've got to sort it – this lump here, that lump there – until you've got piles you can Marie Kondo, and only then, beneath all the rubble, can you find the things that give you joy. Or, if not joy, a sense of satisfaction that The Rest Of It is in the past, and you, by some combination of luck, love, and sheer bloody-mindedness, are here.

GET YOURSELF BORN
INTO INTERGENERATIONAL
MISERY

I

I was born into the hushed suburbs of Perth, Western Australia, not long after the first televised moon landing. In the late 1960s and the 70s, Perth suburbs were hushed because there was no need, yet, for two cars per household in the sprawled public-transport-deficient city whose centre was still called a town by its inhabitants. The United Kingdom, from which the majority of Perth's settler population still hailed, fitted into Western Australia ten times over. Perth was known as the most isolated capital city in the world; whether this was true or not, even blue-collar families like ours had houses set on quarter-acre blocks of sandy soil. You might not have had much by way of furniture or education, but you had a sky that was blue all through the long summer months, and either a river to swim in or an ocean's edge within driving distance to cool you. The smell of eucalyptus leaves was so constant you only noticed it after being at the beach, as the scent rushed in with the air warm from the black bitumen on which you were driven home, arriving hotter than when you'd left.

According to Gwen's family, I was an overly sensitive, fussy, and/or whingeing child. I was compared to my boisterous, fearless male cousin in the first instance, and my sweet-natured younger girl cousins in the second, and found wanting. Although I was told my family loved me, my predominant memories of adult relatives are coloured by their mild impatience with me, their shared frowns and headshaking, which occasionally erupted into outright irritation.

A range of behaviours was produced in evidence of the ways in which I was difficult. To wit:

I was fussy with food. I did not like eating vegetables, eggs, or meat. I choked on sausage skin and was taken to hospital to check for a swallowing disorder; I vomited eggs; the smell of cooking mince made me feel faint. I would only eat the icing off cake after smooshing the un-icing part into a wodge in my hand. If I was not able to eat toast and Vegemite at someone's house, I was liable to collapse into an inconsolable heap and require taking home.

I had a series of anxieties and phobias. Each night I packed a small bag my mother had made me with my favourite teddy and nightie and slept with it at the foot of my bed, in case there was a fire. I went through a long phase in which I refused to wear anything other than pyjamas, and a longer phase where I would not go anywhere without my mini dictionary, yellow covered with a blue L on its front. If anybody gave me a present I didn't like, the object would induce a terror in me to the extent that the giver needed to remove it from the house. I was convinced there was a redback under every toilet seat, like the song, and would not sit on a toilet unless I'd checked.

I did not much like other children, unless they were my cousins, and I found adults even more alien, expecting behaviours of me that I did not understand. I clung to my mother, who pushed me away, which made me cling more. Gwen had an extended family who lived in the south-west corner of the state, and we often visited their houses or farms. I liked dairies and cats but hated being in the strange-smelling houses of great-aunties and uncles. I went to kindergarten for a few days, was horrified by the boisterousness of the other children, and refused to go back. My mother tried peeling my fingers from where I gripped them, as I hid behind the white vinyl armchair, but as soon as she peeled one hand off, I'd reattach the other.

My unfitness to be a regular child was deemed to be chiefly my mother's fault for not using corporal punishment, or, in the alternative, for failing to produce additional offspring so that I would not have been An Only Child. In the 70s everybody knew that Only Children were bossy, selfish, strange, barely human, pitiable creatures who, if their numbers increased, could well be responsible for the downfall of society. The other fault was mine, for being born shy, sensitive, and anxious, when I was not being bossy and selfish etc.

When compulsory schooling began, I wept every morning before school until I was in Year Three. The terror began building as we approached the school and I saw children milling outside; the prospect of getting out and walking among them caused me to panic. Gwen would sometimes comfort me, sometimes snap at me, and other times try to reason with me to stop snivelling and go to class. One time, she was so frustrated she opened the car door, placed her 70s wedge heel against my hip and booted me out. This was witnessed by my classmate April, who was indignant at the maltreatment I'd endured and marched me up to her older sister saying, 'You won't *believe* what Julie's mum just did!'

All I wanted to do was to be with my mother, to play in my paddling pool, or to lie in the back yard on a blanket, clutching my teddy bear, watching the clouds drift along. 'You'd do it for hours,' Gwen would later tell me with mild disapproval. 'I used to wonder what you were thinking.'

One day I cried at school, in Year Three, not because Gwen had booted me out of the car but because I was mortified to discover that I'd left on my summer pyjama bloomers instead of putting on knickers. I was so distressed I couldn't stop crying and had to go sit outside. My teacher, Mrs James, squatted down before me and told me it didn't matter one bit, and nobody would know. As she squatted, I got sight of her white cottontails in the small gap between her substantial thighs, perhaps proving that even sight of a knicker need not cause a person to dissemble. Gwen was not called; I survived the day in pyjama pants and never forgot my proper knickers again.

Mrs James was a fearsome woman, terrifying even the toughest of the boys. But not long after the knicker incident, I was having another fit of paralysing shyness and weeping before school: my best friend Nobbly wasn't there, and I was inconsolable. Gwen, in a state of irritation and despair, delivered me to the classroom and muttered something to Mrs James.

Mrs James had noticed that the one time I openly showed enthusiasm in class was during reading of any variety. I loved silent reading, the fifteen minutes after lunchtime where everyone had to read material of their choice to themselves. I loved going to the library and choosing new books – I cared little for their topic or genre; I only wanted new words to read, as I had so few books at home, I was forced to read the same titles over and over again. And when we had to take turns reading aloud, I shot my hand up to be picked, hoping I would get the longest paragraph with the most difficult words. I cringed at the slowness with which some of my classmates stumbled over sentences, how blankly they intoned the syllables which swung and sang when I read them to myself. The pleasing rhythm of 'The Tale of the Custard

Dragon' was enough to create waves of wonder, paroxysms of pleasure: how did mere humans write such marvels? Surely God (the nice God of Sunday school, as opposed to the fierce God of church) must be helping them.

'I have something special for you, Julie,' Mrs James said.

I thought this might be a ruse to get me into my seat, but not long after the day began, Mrs James handed out a play to a select group of students, which included me. I don't recall what the play was about, or anything about my role, but before recess the players assembled at the front of the classroom to perform our piece. It was all the fun of reading aloud, the delight of reading to and with others, and of adding little flourishes as I went. I remember appreciative laughter, surprise applause, and the happy flush that came over me as I returned to my seat.

'Julie was a star,' Mrs James reported to Gwen later that afternoon.

I understood that I had, inadvertently, been taught a trick. You did not have to show your raw self to others; you could coat it with a veneer of confidence, and nobody would know the difference. I could feel terrified, sure, but I didn't have to show it. I could play a version of myself as a role, and my real self could remain tucked away, observing, hidden.

It was excellent preparation for any life, and most particularly, the life that was to come.

2

As well as being born an introverted singleton, I was born into a family of secrets.

In response to my longing for a younger sister, Gwen told me that she was trying to give me one. While I wasn't entirely sure what this entailed, I soon began to associate it with her being rushed to the hospital from time to time, suddenly and alarmingly. However, she never returned with a baby. When she got home she would sadly tell me that there was something wrong with it, so it was God's way of making sure only healthy babies were born. To my aunties and grandmother, I heard her talk about 'miscarriages' (which I thought had something to do with baby carriages) and 'D and Cs' (which I thought at first might be some kind of chocolate, like Smarties, but the serious response from the relatives suggested it was not).

It was after one of these hospital visits that she told me that actually, I did have a brother. His name was Christopher, and he was five years older than me.

'Can he come and live with us?' I said. The idea of an older brother seemed much more interesting than a baby. Obviously I would have preferred a sister, but I had fun with my cousin Nicholas, so I was prepared to settle.

Gwen explained to me why he could not come to live with us, and why we couldn't even meet him. One, he lived with other people, aka his adoptive parents. Two, he might not know he was adopted, because telling children the truth about themselves or anything much was not considered desirable, or even considered. Three, he might be ashamed of Gwen and not want to know her.

'But why?'

The reasons for the fault and the shame as explained to me over time were thus:

Gwen had been a student at nursing school, going out with the son of a friend of the family. Despite having an older sister, Marlene, and despite my policeman grandfather's suspicions about her moral turpitude, Gwen was almost entirely ignorant of the facts of life. I say 'almost' because when the son of a friend of the family proceeded to do certain things, Gwen had enough wit to ask, 'I can't get pregnant doing this, can I?'

'Of course not,' son of family friend replied.

Next minute, Gwen found her period was late. She would have confided in Marlene, except Marlene was in Melbourne, having made good her escape from the family home early. She told the friend of the family about it, whose response was, 'Is it mine?'

With marriage out of the question, Gwen contemplated her options. She could have got an illegal, expensive, and possibly lethal backyard abortion, but she already knew she wanted the baby. She did not want to relinquish it for adoption, and she knew her father, being such an upstanding pillar of the community, would not countenance having his unwed daughter living with him with a bastard child. Her hope was that her parents would take on the baby as their own, with the baby growing up believing its mother was its sister and that the child itself was a late-life surprise to the older parents.

Had Gwen been born into a different family, this may have happened. The child might have been shocked, confused and infuriated upon discovering the truth of its parentage, but that would be small fry in terms of the wide range of traumatic events that might befall a child sent from the arms of its biological dysfunction and into the dysfunction of families unrelated by blood.

Instead, Gwen sat her parents, Frank and Violet, down at the red formica kitchen table and informed them of her predicament.

She did not get the chance to propose the alternative parent scenario. Upon Gwen offering up her news, Frank stood up. In spite of all he had done to suppress the moral failings he'd seen in the females in his bloodline, Gwen had disgraced herself and him. So he took off his belt without saying a word and brought it down on her: once, twice, and again for good measure.

When he was finished, Frank ordered her to pack her suitcase and get out. She was in her room, crying and packing, when her fifteen-year-old brother came in and said, 'I'll never forgive you.'

I am not sure if my uncle later recalled saying that, but Gwen never forgot it.

Violet drove Gwen to the house of Emily, Violet's cousin, near the railway line. I am not sure what Emily made of Gwen turning up like that, or what explanation Violet made, but everybody knew Frank and what he was like, and women knew to accept what they were dealt. As soon as she could get a ticket, Gwen caught the train to Melbourne.

In Melbourne, sister Marlene helped Gwen find a job as a live-in housekeeper for a Jewish doctor's family, taking care of two little boys as well as doing the required domestics. With the possibility of her parents supporting her removed, her only option now was to give the baby up for adoption, so she worked and waited, hating Melbourne as much as she hated her predicament. She worked six days a week; on her day off she went out with Marlene and Marlene's future husband. If the doctor's family was out, they would stay in and listen to Gwen's treasured LP of *A Hard Day's Night* on the record player far superior to anything her parents had ever possessed. She was photographed at Frank's sister's house in Sorrento on a swing, patting Aunty Freda's dog, leaning forward to hide her pregnant stomach, sporting black-rimmed glasses and a white cowl-necked jumper, smiling because what else was there to do?

The bright spot in this reservoir of generalised misery occurred when she was seven months pregnant. The doctor's wife asked if Gwen might take the boys to see some band that was coming to town: it was sure to be loud and crowded and would she mind?

'What band is it?' Gwen asked.

'Oh, what are they called – The Beatles?'

So Gwen found herself in the second row at the Beatles concert at Festival Hall, Melbourne, on 17 June 1964, exactly two months to the day before she gave birth. She'd never been to a concert; she mistook the rumbling of thousands of teenagers stomping their feet as an earthquake and could barely hear the mop tops over the screaming, but for the thirty minutes the show lasted, she was young and not In Trouble. She was young, dancing and screaming to The Beatles, along with twenty thousand other dancing, screaming teenagers.

When she went into labour in August, she was dropped off at the hospital with the same suitcase she'd brought from Perth and was delivered of her baby, a boy she named Christopher. Gwen told me she was allowed to bottle-feed her baby and change his nappy, which she did because she wanted to communicate to him, somehow, that she was not giving him up because she didn't love him. In this she was lucky, as normally relinquishing mothers of the time were not allowed to see or touch their babies. They often only knew their gender because they were asked to provide them with a temporary name until their forever parents replaced it with something different.

What did not distinguish Gwen from other disgraced girls was the way she was treated. As she was saying goodbye to Christopher when she was leaving hospital, crying as he lay there under the corrective light in the jaundice cot, the nurse said to her, 'That'll teach you to think twice next time.' And when she returned to Perth, after her second and final attempt at completing nursing training at The Alfred, everybody agreed to pretend that nothing had happened. She had returned from a working holiday in Melbourne, and she was moving back in with her parents. That's what everybody was told. No big deal: plenty of girls went to Melbourne before they got married. Privately, you understood what was expected. You'd made a mistake and keeping it secret was supposed to help you forget that anything had ever happened.

A trouble shared was not a trouble halved if the trouble involved bringing shame on your family.

So I remained an only child, and wondered about this sibling I had but did not know, knew about but could not talk about. His absence created its own presence. And it made me cast a curious eye on the family patriarch, Frank, whose name was his nature, and who was rock and fissure both.

3

I learned piece by piece that, as well as secrets, my chief inheritances from my miserable bloodlines were dysfunctional behaviours that impeded the ability to experience life as a gift rather than a trial.

As a child I loved stories about my family, my ancestors, as if they might give me a guide to existing in the collection of people I found myself among. Perhaps it was to secure a sense of belonging from the past that I didn't feel in the present (with the joyful exception of my aunty Marlene and her three children). My elders and betters, however, were mostly reluctant to share the kind of information I increasingly sought. Gwen was fond of anecdotes, but when I asked relatives what various people were like, I received vague and unsatisfying responses.

If I ever asked Frank about his family, he would say, 'What the bloody hell do you want to know that for?' When I replied, 'Because I want to know', he'd say, 'No you don't.'

Frank had a few stock phrases about his father: that his father Frederick stood two piss-pots high, that his father sired him when he was sixty, and that he and I shared the same misfortune, that of having an English bastard as a father.

Frank was the youngest child in a family of six produced by two marriages. The products of the first considered the products of the second inferior: they were certainly the more impoverished. Frederick's second wife, Isabella, was also on her second marriage. Frederick was twenty-eight years Isabella's senior, and all he owned was a small patch of poor farmland in a one-street town called Roelands in an unremarkable part of the south-west of Western Australia. The town was best known for its railway siding and its mission for Aboriginal children, who were sent around the countryside as domestic servants and farmhands once they were finished with getting an education rudimentary but sufficient to be able, in later years, to calculate the extent of the wages they'd never received.

Many people writing memoirs often mention their female forebears' beauty. To this I can make no claim. The *Truth* newspaper article reporting Isabella's divorce from her first husband in November 1917 describes her as being 'a big woman, with florid complexion, and puts her heels down when she walks, as if she meant it'. The ground for divorce was desertion. In support of her claim, she described his inability to perform his 'marshal rites', sending him into a fury in which he attempted to strangle her. Six years previously he had tried to divorce her for adultery, after she'd fled from him in fear of her life. The judge was sympathetic to the 'very unhappy marriage' and granted her the divorce, after which she was free to marry my great-grandfather.

In her wedding photo she is tall and stately, dwarfing my great-grandfather, who looks like a trimmed-down Mark Twain. The one thing Frank relished telling about his parents was that Frederick, after the wedding ceremony, carried the taller and stouter Isabella down the main street of Roelands. However, it would appear that Isabella's second marriage was scarcely happier than the first.

Spouse-carrying levity was crushed under the weight of hard work and poverty. Isabella took in washing that she walked over the hills of Roelands to collect, in the days where washing required the fortitude to build a fire, boil clothes in the copper, stir them, scrub them, wring them, rinse them, wring them again, and hang them.

A photograph from later in her life shows a woman with a careworn face, large in the way women became from hard work and eating bread and dripping. She is sitting outside, dandling a baby on her lap. When I first saw this picture, I thought the corrugated-iron structure behind her was the shed.

'Oh no,' my great-aunt Freda told me, 'that was our house.'

'Five of you lived in that?' I asked.

'It was shameful, being that poor,' she said. Then she looked at the photograph again and shook her head. 'She had a hard life, my mum.'

The only thing Frank volunteered about his mother was offered when I was introducing Boyfriend to the family for the first time. Boyfriend was a medical student – a status so far above ours it made most of the family become rigidly polite – and of Sicilian parentage. Frank walked up behind him as Boyfriend was sitting at the table, put his meaty copper's hands on Boyfriend's shoulders, and said, 'I came home from school one day and found my mother rooting a bloke who looked like you.'

'Pop,' I hissed.

'Sicilian railway worker, the bloke was. They were going at it so hard they didn't even notice I was there,' he said, and went on to serve his Weber chicken and pigs in a blanket while Boyfriend raised his substantial Sicilian eyebrows, and I considered fleeing the scene.

Perhaps it was the desire to avoid a hard life and a miserable marriage that drove Frank to leave the eternal poverty of farming for policing, and having only one set of children among whom friction could be created. However, for his wife, Violet, life could scarcely have delivered a set of circumstances more perfectly poised for almost continuous dissatisfaction.

4

My grandmother Violet was born into the only branch of my forebears whose sufferings were not caused primarily by their own temperaments, failings, and/or addictions, although they too shared in the generalised poverty that limited opportunity and made hardship unavoidable. Hailing from a convict named William Parmenter, who sailed in the mid 1800s and settled in Bunbury, Western Australia after getting his ticket of leave, William's descendants eked out their livings as farmers, timber workers and mechanics in the isolated south-west town of Mullalyup. They were musical Methodists who were prohibited by their religion to dance, but they played church organs and drummed their cutlery on the Sunday plates and sang. Violet and her six siblings were gentle-hearted souls to a person, the men no less than the women.

Violet's mother had rheumatoid arthritis. She was in a wheelchair by the time she was thirty-five and needed to have a fork woven through her knotted fingers to be able to feed herself. My mother told me that when she was a child, she loved having her back tickled by her grandmother's immobile fingers: her grandmother, being otherwise unable to move far, would tickle Gwen's back for extended, languorous periods. This same circumscribed movement had required Violet to leave school at fourteen, to be able to cook, clean, and scrub the men's overalls, filthy from each week's work sawing down majestic karri and jarrah trees, and later with engine grease from the garage they worked in once the trees were gone.

Violet was engaged at the time Frank began courting her: she picked Frank, apparently, because he was charming and handsome and worked hard to win her over, a fact she mentioned ruefully from time to time. To me Violet passed her small hands, the gene for rheumatoid arthritis, anxiety, and insomnia, which may have been why she was so impatient with the traits I possessed that mirrored her own.

'There's always someone worse off than you,' was one of her most common statements if I complained about anything, and which sent me into a paralysis of frustration.

They were both living examples of how deeply you could despise the person you married without actually going so far as doing them physical harm (very often), or taking any responsibility for your own choices, or alleviating the derision by taking yourself in a direction more fitting. Violet and Frank were of the view that if you decided to do a thing, you bloody well did it, no matter how miserable you made yourself and those around you in the process.

'It's bin day tomorrow, Violet,' Frank would regularly say at Sunday lunches. 'Which way do you want to go in – head first or feet first?'

Or, if he was having a bad day, he'd say, 'Other people's wives cark it, but not you, you just go on, and on, and on.'

Violet would produce a crooked smile at these terms of endearment and say to me, or whoever else was listening, 'Oh, he doesn't mean it,' to which Frank would reply, 'Pig's ear I don't!'

. . .

In 1983, Frank and Violet had spent the year travelling around Australia while Gwen, Gwen's depressed boyfriend Steve, and I lived in their Sussex Street house in then working-class East Victoria Park. It was the year I'd developed visible signs of my disturbed mental state and, perhaps to rid Gwen of the sight of her parental failure, Violet invited me to Broome while she and Frank stayed there on their anticlockwise swing around the continent. I spent the week in Broome blissfully boogie-boarding during the day and at other times anxiously pacing the unfurnished house Frank and Violet were camped at because I was unable to sit still, and it was too hot to go outside. Frank made offhand comments about wanting me to go home while Violet told me he didn't mean it. I smiled, as Violet expected me to, and continued pacing.

Late that year they returned to Perth, staying in the caravan outside their own house until our rental was ready, Steve having recently decamped to another more depression-tolerant household. Just after New Year, Frank sat himself at the table on the back patio, which featured a pool table, dart board, stand-up bar, and the print of dogs playing pool found in every 80s games room. Behind the patio was the shed with its home brew and the maze of garden beds he'd tended for thirty years. It was the place where gatherings were held, lunch was eaten, and Scrabble played. It was the place where Frank sat daily at 4pm to crack his first home brew.

In sanguine moods, after his first slug of ale, Frank would browse the crack-spined *Macquarie Dictionary* that was always on the table next to his astringent snacks of home-made pickled onions, olives, or raw garlic. He would read an entry, such as *defenestrate* or *perspicacious* or *ferriferous*, and say, 'What do you reckon that means?', shaking his head in grim admiration at the summary of knowledge furled in each word. 'That word's from Latin.'

But on this day he began drinking home brew earlier than usual. He started off terse and then became irritable, taking draughts in gulps, snapping at Violet, Gwen, or me whenever we appeared. By dinner time, his anger had turned sour. We all tiptoed around him, but at six o'clock food was ready to be served, so the women brought out the plates and the bowls of salad and platters of whatever it was we were eating that night, probably sausages. I sat at the end of the table, opposite Frank. Gwen and Violet started attempting small talk, but Frank's gaze fixed on me.

'You ruined our trip,' he said. 'I told your grandmother I didn't want you to come, but no, she had to ask you anyway. You're her bloody grandchild, bugger what I think about it.'

'Don't listen to him,' Violet said. 'It's not true.'

'You know what your problem is?' he went on, eying me over the sausages.

My limbs turned cold. A lump of something stuck in my throat. Nobody looked at me, except Frank.

'No, Pop,' I said.

'You're a burden on your mother,' he said. 'She'd be better off without you.'

Violet protested. If Gwen did too, I don't remember.

I'd read about people running off in a huff. Ours was not a family you were allowed to huff in, so up until this point it was an attractively dramatic action I'd had no cause to try out. But now I stood up, pushed back my chair, and ran.

I took off up Sussex Street, weeping with outrage as much as hurt, but it soon occurred to me I had nowhere to run to. I ran up the hill, down the hill, and over to a bench near the shopping centre. I had no money and so was contemplating walking into the city when Violet pulled up next to me.

'He's just drunk,' she said. 'We'll sneak you in and tomorrow he'll be all right. Things always look better in the morning.'

Violet parked on the verge outside, rather than alerting Frank to our presence by entering the driveway. But the only way in was through the patio, the front of the house comprised of two sleepouts divided by an always-locked wrought-iron door. Gwen's car was gone: she must have been out looking for me as well. Violet and I eased open the gate, crept up the driveway and edged onto the patio. The patio door was illuminated by the fluorescent lights, which crackled with kamikaze mosquitoes in the silence. We tiptoed closer and peeked around the corner of the outside laundry, hoping that Frank would have passed out in his chair.

When he saw us, Frank reared up from the table and began swearing and yelling.

'How dare you worry your grandmother, you selfish little bitch!' he bellowed, heading in our direction.

'Get inside,' Violet hissed. 'Run down to the sleepout and lock the door.'

I pushed the door open and ran through the passageway, the kitchen, and the lounge room before arriving at the sleepout.

From behind the door I heard heavy footsteps, then yelling: 'No, leave her alone! Frank, don't!'

There was a roar, then a smack, then a thud.

And, for a long moment, silence.

'You bastard!' I heard Violet wail.

I swung open the door. Frank was standing over Violet, his fist still clenched. Violet was on the floor, her hands over her head.

I hung back, waiting to see if he was going to keep coming for me, but he stomped out the back, muttering, 'Fucken women, stay away from the fucken cunts.'

I helped Violet up. She told me he'd never done that before. The next day her cheek was purple and her eye swollen to a squint.

Not long after that, Violet decided she'd had enough of Frank. She told her daughters that she was going to take a leaf out of Gwen's book: she was going to leave him. About time, they agreed. Everyone had tried to talk Frank out of his permanently soured temper. He wasn't coping with being retired, they said. He'd had all that authority, being a superintendent, and he didn't know what to do as a retired man. But Frank, in response, put away more home brew that did nothing to even his mood.

She had just finalised her getaway plans in September 1986 when she felt a headache start. It persisted all day, and it was so bad she had to cancel her regular game of golf. When Frank found her, vomiting in the shower, unable to move or speak, he feared she was going to die.

Violet was rushed into hospital, and after the brain surgery to repair the aneurism, her face was swollen a deeper purple than it had been after Frank hit her. When Gwen and I visited her, neither of us could recognise her. Her ever-capable, pumpkin-scone-making hands were limp, her shape unfamiliar beneath the sheets so stiff with starch even she would have approved of them.

I would have blamed Frank, but he was busy blaming himself. For a time, he became a changed man: he devoted himself to Violet for their remaining nine years while she became as recovered as she was going to get, wheelchair bound, and bound to Frank. He told her he loved her, and it wasn't for years that she was well enough for him to start saying, 'It's bin day tomorrow, Violet ...'

As for Violet, she spent the nine years sitting, trying to smile with the working half of her face, but more often ending up crying instead. Frank's new leaf shrivelled: he became angry at taking care of Violet but wouldn't let anyone else in the house. She became more unhappy than she'd ever been, which was a challengingly low bar.

When she was in hospital for the final time, I asked her what she wished had been different about her life.

She fixed me with her good eye and said, 'I wish I'd died when I'd had the stroke.'

I considered this response. She could have wished that she'd married the first fiancé. She could have wished that my two cousins hadn't died, or that Frank had been born with a different personality, or that she'd been born a man. She could have wished not to have been born into a generation between two world wars, or to have grown up in a poor family during the Depression, or not to have suffered from anxiety and insomnia from birth to death.

There's always someone worse off than you. Sometimes that worse-off person is the self you are to become, living the life you'd avoid, if only you knew how.

5

The weight of intergenerational misery might not have felt so pronounced to me had I not been the product of parents messed up in mutually incompatible ways.

One of the things that drove me crazy about my mother was her refusal to look the past in the eye. It was only recently that I remembered Gwen had been an athlete, and a runner. I remember that she taught me, before my complete lack of sporting ability was evident, never to turn around when you were running. If you turned around, you'd lose for sure.

My mother's hands always shook, a permanent tremor that worsened when she was upset or angry. The only time they didn't shake was when her fingers were dancing around the keys and buttons of the piano accordion she played at Christmas, at parties, and at the end of term at school, where my classmates loved her playing 'Skippy the Bush Kangaroo'.

Gwen's hands shook most noticeably when she rolled cigarettes. She'd won a rollie machine from a radio quiz in the early 60s. It was a square, silver object with a canvas tongue of material inside. You tucked a finger of tobacco in the bottom of the canvas, licked a paper – carefully, not too much spit – and placed it flat against the back of the canvas, closed the machine, and voila, a perfectly rolled cigarette emerged, unless you had mis-licked or mis-positioned the paper, or not tucked enough tobacco in the pouch. I was trained and proficient in the art of rollie-making, because some days Gwen's hands shook too much to place the paper in the right position, or to extract the right amount of tobacco from the bag.

Everyone noticed Gwen's hands: my friends, teachers, doctors, strangers in the supermarket.

'Why are her hands like that?' people asked. 'Has she got Parkinson's?'

'It's because of her dad,' I'd learned to say seriously. 'He used to hit her when she was a kid, and it made her shaky.'

People would frown doubtfully but pry no further. Everyone, after all, had received a disciplinary clip around the earhole for misdemeanours from a parent in those days. Everyone also knew that if the disciplinary clip was something more, you politely ignored it. How parents raised their kids was their business, after all.

As a child, my mother was musical, smart, sporty and lively. In a different family, she might have been welcomed and nurtured, her energies and spirit directed into her studies, encouraged to flourish, her creative enthusiasms cultivated. But that was not the family she was born into.

All of Frank's children, upon the display of any misdemeanour, received applications of the strap, the belt or a grapevine switch. For particularly heinous behaviour, Frank brought out his homemade truncheon, a thick chain wrapped in a black rubber hose, which also doubled as a weapon used in his police work to break up fights between grown men.

Gwen copped Frank's wrath more than her older sister, Marlene, or younger brother, Fred, for reasons she couldn't understand. While Marlene learned to appeal to and appease Frank, and her brother to emulate his uncompromising moral stance, Gwen could not suppress herself sufficiently to get away with so much as a wayward thought. The older she got, the more Frank suspected her of misdeeds that she hadn't committed, and he punished her according to the scale of her perceived sins. When she wailed, 'But Dad, what have I done?', he'd say, 'You bloody well know, now keep still or I'll give you ten more!'

Although child beating was a firmly accepted method of child rearing in the 40s and 50s, Frank didn't stop hitting his kids when they learned to be quiet at the dinner table or not run on the road.

When I was a teenager, my younger cousin Konrad, my uncle Fred's son, developed a brain tumour with a name I couldn't pronounce. My grandmother blamed herself.

'Fred almost died when he was a baby in a bassinet, when Frank was building the front room,' Violet said one day when Gwen and I were visiting, not long after the news that the tumour had failed to stop growing, despite surgery and chemotherapy. 'A beam came down and just' – she showed with her fingers – 'missed him. Maybe he wasn't supposed to be.'

'It's a bit late for that,' Gwen said.

'My mother was epileptic,' Violet went on. 'Maybe that's where it comes from.'

'Was she?' I asked. 'I thought she was just crippled.'

'She was crippled too,' Gwen said. 'Poor Grandma.'

'And then there were your turns, Gwen,' Violet went on. 'Maybe it runs through the family.'

'What turns?' I asked.

'Oh, she grew out of them,' Violet said.

'They weren't bloody turns, Mum,' Gwen said. 'They were from shock.'

There was an uncomfortable pause, and Violet continued, 'It's just not right. About Konrad.'

Gwen rolled, lit, and sucked deeply on her rollie.

On the way home I asked Gwen about the turns, or the shock, or whatever it was that left the heavy feeling in the air after Violet had mentioned it.

'That was after Dad gave me a really bad belting once, when I was sixteen,' she said. 'I kept blacking out for months afterward.'

Of course, I knew about the last hiding he'd given her. But I hadn't known about this one, and I never knew what it was that drove him to it.

Gwen did everything she could to escape having to live with the father who had bashed and then banished her, and the mother who had stood by, mute, while it happened. On her return from Melbourne she took a job on a station in Carnarvon, a day's drive north of Perth, to pay off surgery she'd needed for a bowel obstruction; she lost a stone in weight in the first week from hard work and perspiration. When the job proved too much, she married the first man who came along, who happened to be my father, Derek.

6

If my maternal forebears were marked by misfortunes of various stripe that transmuted into tensions still detectable as I grew up, the misery that inhered in my father's family had more obvious markers, even if its causes were more obscured.

When my parents met, Derek had not long decanted from the north of England, arriving by boat as a ten-pound Pom. Upon being unable to find a regular job, he became a regular in the army and promptly got shipped off first to Malaya and then to Vietnam. At the time he met my mother, he was handsome, drily funny, and escaping from the misery of having been brought up in an orphanage in postwar Lancashire, where he was roundly ignored, then spending years as a teenager in a group home, where the house mother took a vicious dislike to him.

As well as finding Derek handsome, and as gentle as her father was harsh, Gwen felt sorry for the deprivation he had endured, the hunger he'd lived with, and the neglect in the orphanage that he preferred to the abuse meted out by the house mother. Gwen might have been beaten to the point of brain injury, but at least she had parents.

Derek had parents too, though, or at least one that I knew of, growing up. He brought Gran and his sister, Jean, over from Warrington in the UK. Gwen thought Gran was peculiar because once she arrived in Australia at the age of forty-four, she never made a single friend. She was a tiny, bird-boned woman who rarely spoke at family gatherings. She kept the television on at all hours and only left her flat when Dad and I took her shopping on Saturday morning, or when she visited her daughter's house. Everything in her flat was covered in plastic: the chairs, the settee, the spare bed. Every single item in the cupboard, fridge or bathroom found itself wrapped in several layers of plastic bags or even cling wrap if it were particularly prized. Her two recliner rockers remained forever in the protective covering they were delivered in.

Gran hailed from an Irish Catholic family from County Mayo, the county hardest hit by the Great Famine of the 1840s. The family escaped to poverty of a different kind in the Irish-thick county of Lancashire.

Gran and Aunty Jean had conversational grooves that, once set upon, played out in a Beckett-like manner:

Jean: Mum's family came from Ireland, you know.

Gran: County Mayo. We had a house.

Jean: A house with no roof.

Gran: Aye. No roof at all.

I found this sentence charmingly whimsical. I imagined my gingerbread house birthday cake after my cousins had been at it. It was only later when I met an elderly Irishman that I discovered this was a reference to the crimes of the English. During the famine and the subsequent economic collapse, English landlords set fire to the thatched roofs of their tenant farmers if they were unable to pay rent.

Jean: Mum's brothers were all handsome fellas, weren't they, Mum?

Gran: Street angels, home devils.

Jean: But lookers.

Gran: Oh, yes. Easy on the eye, they were.

My father's lifelong hatred of idlers, bludgers, and wastrels rested with his mother's feckless brothers, William and Thomas Cunningham, whom he blamed for his childhood spent in the cold halls of the Padgate orphanage. Thomas was a gambler, while William was a drinker. Gran was fonder of one than the other. In the brief period of his life when he had initiative, Thomas headed to London, anticipating its streets to be paved with gold, instead finding himself destitute in a city that hated northerners almost as much as it did foreigners. Thomas lumped up to the Catholic Church, hoping to find succour from the institution that sent around collection plates to its poorest parishioners and expected them to ply the priest with tea, biscuits, and brandy on his rounds. But Thomas had found Catholic charity was as cold as a bucket of Thames water in winter. He returned home to Warrington, and when the priest next turned up expecting tea, Gran delivered a pithy piece of her sixteen-year-old mind to him and stopped going to church. This was an act that I understood, even as a young person, to have been outrageous, the

1970s equivalent of being female and not wanting to get married. I used to look at my tiny, timid grandmother and wonder what had happened to that feisty defiance.

I had never known why my grandmother had left her husband. As a child, it took a while for the effects of the Commonwealth's *Family Law Act 1975*, which introduced fault-free divorces, to trickle down; my parents' 1979 separation was at the beginning of a very large tide-turning. It didn't occur to me to wonder that perhaps she had required all that feisty defiance to be a woman leaving a husband in postwar England, let alone in the family-celebrating north.

Derek's anecdotes of childhood were few, mostly involving food or the lack of it once he was in the orphanage. Once, for example, when he was sent to work on a pig farm as a teenager, he scarfed the marshmallows from the marshmallow factory deemed suitable only for the pigs and, it turned out, youths semi-starved from years of institutional care.

...

When I was eleven, my aunty gave me a blue envelope stuffed with a blue-paged letter, and suddenly I had a full complement of grandparents.

It transpired that Aunty Jean had on a whim written to her father, care of 142 Slater Street, Latchford, in Warrington – a place the Lawrinson family had lived for hundreds of years, aside from occasional stints in the poorhouse. To Jean's surprise, he'd written back. Now, he wrote to me and my paternal cousin RJ, and we excitedly lined up at the post office to have our return letters weighed and stamped and sent to the other side of the world. When he retired from his job on the Latchford Locks of the Manchester Shipping Canal, he sent my father a worn pair of overalls.

Granddad wrote in strange sentences, half lowercase, half capitals, enclosing clippings of the latest news from Australia that made the British tabloids, usually concerning SHARK attacks, deadly SPIDERS, and other VENOMOUS fauna. I thought perhaps he was semi-literate or mildly deranged. I read these missives excitedly to Derek, who only huffed in response, and I giggled with RJ over Granddad's strange spelling and exaggerated dread of the continent in which we lived.

The only photograph we had of my grandfather showed a handsome young man in an army uniform, looking to the side of the photographer's lens. I wondered what he looked like now, and whether he would be as kind as Frank was ornery. I asked him questions about his life, but he never answered them. I wondered whether he was as forgetful as he was fearful of SHARKS.

. . .

Even before finding Granddad, I had long hankered after England. My hankering grew as my feelings of displacement and criticism from my mother's side of the family increased. As an older child I was less shy and weird, but still Different. I wondered if it was my Englishness that was the cause of this difference, and if, once I went to England, my jagged edges would finally smooth themselves, and I could be at one with myself.

The England of my imagination and the England in which I arrived on 1 February 1991 at the age of twenty-one bore no resemblance to each other. I pitched up in Brixton, London, with a backpack and five hundred pounds during the city's coldest winter since 1963. My friend Claire was there for the first five days, then I was on my own. My first stop on arrival had been a youth hostel, where I arrived dazed with jet lag, my clothes reeking of the cigarettes others had smoked on the flight over. I then secured a 'room' in a 'house' that had been advertised at the hostel. My idea of what the word 'house' referred to turned out to be wildly antipodean: rather than a brick-and-tile establishment with a yard, it was a jammed-in terrace, one among a long row of identical terraces, which themselves were luxurious compared to the council towers nearby. The space I rented was a room to the extent that it was space enclosed by four walls: in all other respects it was better named a laundry, complete with concrete sink and dripping tap. A mattress strewn with dirty linen took up most of the floor space; in vain I dabbed it with Body Shop elderberry perfume to try to disguise the odour of the last several dozen people who had slept on it. The occupants of the lower floors were white South Africans, a black Frenchman, and a student from Liverpool.

On my first trip to the supermarket, I witnessed a group of teenage boys mug an old lady for her shopping. The staff were kind to the old lady, but there was none of the attendant horror that would have ensued had this taken place in Perth. Soon after I got home, my South African housemate came home, flustered. Another teenage boy had ripped her necklace off her neck on the bus. When my housemate asked the other passengers who had studiously ignored her as she wrestled with the boy, 'Why didn't you do anything?', they shrugged or said, 'What do you want us to do?'

As well as not expecting casual robbery to be a tolerated inconvenience, I had not expected to be a racial minority in England. In Australia, I had had the privilege of ignoring race and its significance for most of my life: even though I grew up in working-class suburbia with Aboriginal people around me, I was almost completely ignorant of the history of their dispossession until I got to university at nearly twenty years of age. In Brixton I was often one of a few white faces on the bus. In the job interviews I had, I was shocked at the nonchalance with which employers said: 'Thank God they sent you, all we've had are darkies applying.' In the temporary jobs I had, scrubbing conveyer belts or serving sandwiches in canteens, white managers called black staff monkeys to their faces, and nobody – me included – said anything.

Surely this mean, pinched attitude was not England. Dad and his mostly Liverpudlian friends were jovial and laughing when together. I decided the problem was that I was a northerner in the south: whenever I told managers my family was from the north, I noticed an odd cooling, which I finally realised was an expression of the British class system. So I made plans to head to Liverpool to indulge my Beatles obsession, and to Warrington, to really go home. Surely this would be the England I had been homesick for?

From London I had written to my grandfather and cousins, telling them I would visit one weekend, but I had no phone numbers for them and besides, I wanted the visit to be a surprise. Aunty Jean talked incessantly about the warmth of family life in Warrington, of how aunties and uncles and cousins came and went from each other's houses. She talked of how shocked she was when she'd come to Australia: family lived miles away from each other. Gran's Irish family disapproved of the lack of family life in England; they'd have been even more horrified by Australia, where vast spaces were taken advantage of and placed in between brother and sister, parents and their offspring. In Warrington, things were different.

So, I arrived at 142 Slater Street one Saturday in March 1991, having deposited my belongings in a hostel in Liverpool, thirty minutes away by train. A small, old man peered at me beakily.

'What do y'want?'

'Hi Granddad, it's Julie. Derek's daughter,' I added, in case Granddad always had Australian grandchildren turning up unannounced.

'Oh,' he said. 'Oh. Well. Come in.'

I shuffled into a dusty downstairs room and stood awkwardly while my long-lost grandfather moved things from a spot on the settee so I could sit. I extracted from my backpack the photographs I'd brought of Dad with my stepmother, Olivia, whom he had married with my enthusiastic approval in 1987, and my lovely new baby sister, Aunty Jean, and RJ, but Granddad glanced at them without looking and beckoned me to the kitchen.

'I haven't got milk,' he said. 'But look, come here.'

I tucked the photographs away and followed him into the small kitchen. He opened the fridge, in which there was an end of cheese and some bread, and an open tin of something.

'I do all right,' he said. 'See? I just haven't got any milk.'

I felt a heave of sadness. Gran, living alone and friendless, often made me feel a sense of loneliness on her behalf, but this was something different. I wanted to sit down in the grimy corner of the kitchen and weep.

'Let's go visit Stan, me nephew,' he said. 'There's a phone box at the corner.'

As we were about to leave, Granddad stopped me and said, 'Eh Julie. I didn't know nothing about that business before, you hear me?'

I wanted to ask what that business before was, but he was suddenly vehement.

'I didn't know nothing,' he repeated.

'Okay, Granddad,' I said. 'It's okay.'

He relaxed after that. We walked up to the corner phone box, where Stan did not answer Granddad's call, and then we waited for a bus to go visit my cousins. My cousins lived in an estate charmingly called Sankey Green, although no greenery was evident, and we drank tea and smoked cigarettes, and Granddad became voluble about topics ranging from the ownership of factories to the ridiculous cost of designer sneakers. He was full of bluster, inviting us to laugh at his anecdotes, agree with his observations. He did not once refer to my father or his daughter, nor did he ask after Gran.

In the kitchen, I asked my cousin what he did at Christmas. I thought of him living alone, carless and phoneless.

'He's with Stan or with us,' she said. 'Don't worry.'

But later, as I left him at the bus station, waving, as I headed for Liverpool in the cold and colourless afternoon, I was racked by a feeling I could not understand. When I returned to the hostel, the feeling prevented me from sleeping and drove me out into the Liverpool night in the early hours of the morning, marching furiously in the silent streets, passing closed pubs and bakeries advertising Eccles cakes, my face freezing from the streaming tears that would not stop. I wandered down to the docks, where the day before I had crossed on the Mersey ferry while Gerry and the Pacemakers sang their eponymous song. I hoped the frigid wind would ease the burn under my sternum. The weeping seemed to erupt from a grief that was sudden, terrible, and without cause. I tried to connect it to something – homesickness, existential angst, anything – but no explanation sufficed.

When a man approached me on the docks, I moved under a streetlamp. If I was to be murdered near where my father's life began, I felt it was best not to be murdered in the dark.

'Oi, Miss,' the man said, brandishing a torch. 'You shouldn't be down here. It's not safe.'

I was brought back to where I was – wandering alone through the Liverpool docks at night – and hightailed it back to the hostel, rattled but unmolested.

The unnameable feeling persisted until the bus headed south the next day; I had never thought I would be so relieved to see the grey streets of London and then pull up in Brixton, comforted by the now familiar, chaotic chatter and crush of those washed up on England's indifferent shore. I was even relieved, if not overjoyed, to be back on my smelly mattress in the laundry room.

I concluded, reasonably enough, that I'd experienced a fit of madness. Fits of madness were not unknown to me at that time of my life, prone as I was to extreme untrammelled emotion without understanding the swelling of unrecognised and undealt-with past events that precipitated them, so a fit was as fitting an explanation as any.

Back in Australia, I omitted the fit of madness when I answered Aunty Jean's questions about the house, what Granddad looked like, who I'd met. Gran and Derek listened but asked nothing. Derek's face held the strained expression I only ever saw when Granddad was mentioned. The film in the cheap camera I'd taken to Warrington had jammed, so I had no photographs of Granddad or my cousins, producing only a single shot of the outside of 142 Slater Street. Everything else became superimposed, one image indistinguishable from the next. Warrington would remain in imagination, and Granddad in sepia tones, young, handsome, looking away.

...

It was only later in life, at my grandmother's wake, when I was chatting to newly met cousins from Warrington, that I learned the reason Gran had left my grandfather.

'The Lawrinson men were all brawlers,' Derek's cousin Betty told me. 'They fought each other, and they all beat their wives. It was just the way it was.'

'Even my granddad?' I tried to imagine the harmless man I'd met in 1991 as a wife-beater.

'Your gran was brave,' Betty said. 'All the other women, they just put up with it, but not your gran.'

I thought of the bird-like woman, mostly silent at family lunches; her plastic-wrapped flat; her Northern vowels; her friendlessness. One year, she'd met up with Warrington folk at our cousin's, including an older woman who'd gone to Gran's school. The older woman regaled Gran with the fate of her classmates. On the way home Gran chuckled to herself, occasionally saying aloud with pride-filled wonder, 'Dead, they are. They're all dead.' I thought of the story of sixteen-year-old Gran, refusing the priest tea and biscuits.

I said to Derek, 'So, Betty tells me your dad was a violent alcoholic.'

'They were his good points,' Derek remarked.

'But,' I said, 'why didn't you tell me?'

Derek shrugged. 'Don't know.'

'You should have told me before I went to meet him,' I said.

He shrugged again. 'Oh well.'

After much pressing and more Guinness, Derek told me that he remembered sitting in the back of a police car in the Northern English rain. He was next to his sister, and together they watched the windscreen wipers scrape back and forth as the police were inside the house, trying to restrain my grandfather from inflicting further injury on my grandmother. He remembered this primarily because it was raining, and the windscreen wipers were hinged at the top of the windscreen instead of the bottom. It was not the only time the police visited, but it was the one time that stood for many in his recollection. There were few phones in houses, so how the police came to be summoned at that time or others is unknown. The other reason Derek remembered this is because not long afterward, he and his sister were deposited at the local orphanage.

Aunty Jean told me that she and Derek had always been inseparable. They were born a year apart and had gone everywhere together. When they were driven to the orphanage at Padgate, they sat in the back and held hands, the way they had always done. They were told to get out of the car. One woman took Jean's arm, another woman Derek's, and they were marched to their respective wings. They looked back at each other, crying. For the next seven years, they barely saw each other.

'Nobody cared about how children felt in those days,' she added, unnecessarily.

7

Because I searched for meaning everywhere, I was keen to be supplied with answers by God. I enthusiastically attended services of various denominations our family favoured – Uniting and Lutheran – and was taken by friends to Church of England, Seventh Day Adventist, and evangelical services. Gwen explained their puzzling differences as being insignificant because they were united by Jesus. But there were other kinds of churches too, about which I learned from my aunty Jean and my cousin RJ.

RJ was eighteen months older than me, and I adored her. She had Irish black hair that she insisted on calling dark brown, and was always shorter than me despite her seniority. She was skinny and sporty and enjoyed instructing me on all the things about which she was expert, which was everything. She showed me how to write on a chalkboard. She demonstrated the art of colouring within the lines. I pretended not to know my letters so she could teach me. She even corrected my singing, although it later transpired she was tone-deaf. When, after an afternoon visit to her place, I was not allowed to sleep over, I knelt on the back seat and waved tragically through the back window as she chased our car down the street until her legs, sporting though they were, were bested by our white Valiant's six-cylinder engine, and she disappeared from view. I cried until my face swelled and Gwen told me not to be ridiculous, I'd see her next weekend.

I was, as intended, suitably impressed by RJ's superior skills in everything from knucklebones to rollerskating, and I was jealous that she was allowed to catch the green Metropolitan Transport Trust buses by herself from Thornlie to Perth city from when she was eight. The buses smelled headily of diesel in my favourite seats at the back, but whenever I caught a bus with Gwen we always sat close to the front, where it smelled merely of bodily heat trapped in nylon, Johnson & Johnson baby powder, and leather hard with age and use.

But the thing that most inspired my jealousy was the collection of cards RJ had from L. Ron Hubbard. Each year she received a birthday card especially from him, which showed how special she was: I had no such collection with which to compare. L. Ron Hubbard was the leader of their church, which was just like our church except it had headquarters in town in a large building on St Georges Terrace and was called The Org. That meant RJ was getting mail from the Scientologists' equivalent of Jesus. RJ and I waited at the building sometimes while adults went to their sermons. We drew pictures on the free literature waiting to be distributed to the public after the sermons. I used to look at the board with the list of top donors that was prominently displayed, plus the amount they had given alongside. When the adults came out of the sermons, their faces held an identical serene glow, their eyes glassy. They glided from the rooms and smiled vacantly at RJ and me.

RJ wasn't a Scientologist because you couldn't be until you were a teenager, but Jean was, and her new husband was. On his ute he had a sticker that said *PSYCHIATWIST* in twirly letters. When I asked what it meant, my uncle said there were doctors who wanted to change your head and they should be avoided at all costs. My uncle was the kind of man everybody liked, and, unlike my religious family on Gwen's side, he did not try to press his beliefs, whatever they were, onto the children in their midst. So I liked him too.

My uncle was liked by everybody except RJ. Everybody who liked him said her dislike was because she was jealous. RJ had had her mother to herself for so long, and now her mother was married, instead of living with Gran and getting Gran to help raise RJ. She was so rude to him it made me embarrassed. She yelled at him and called him names. He acted as though he didn't care, and Jean would sometimes say, 'Now, now, dear,' and RJ would ignore her and keep being rude.

After my parents separated when I was nearly ten years old, I spent a lot of time at my cousin's house. One day I wanted RJ to go swimming in their above-ground pool, but she was in a bad mood. She was often in a bad mood, so I was preparing to swim by myself when my uncle said he'd swim too.

I loved swimming underwater. I loved the swoosh of water in my ears, the way the world blurred prettily. I would gather my legs and push hard against the vinyl lining and launched myself from one side to another. I wasn't sporty like RJ, but the water was where I felt weightless and playful.

My uncle would catch me at the side I was rocketing toward, lift me up, and throw me back. This was always the game he played when he swam with us. I squealed, splashed, and returned to my launch site. On this day, my launch site faced the house; the other side, where my uncle waited, was facing the asbestos fence and the scrubby trees that were there to conceal it.

Then my uncle stopped catching me. With blurry underwater vision, I could see he was squatting at the pool's edge. Maybe he was resting. Then I saw he'd pulled his bather bottoms down and had his hand in his lap.

I pretended that I had not noticed that he was being a rudie, and I kept coiling myself up, launching myself, and now running, slow in the water that was up to my chest, back to the other side.

He stopped me the next time I arrived next to him. He took hold of my hands and pulled them toward his lap. I'd only seen boys' doodles, which were like wilting worms. My uncle's doodle was more like an overcooked sausage. I did not know why he was moving my hands up and down it, but I was relieved when he stopped.

'You won't tell anyone, will you?' he said anxiously as I was climbing up the pool ladder.

I smiled. 'Of course not.'

Because I had been reading the Secret Seven and the Famous Five, I knew how important it was to keep secrets. It meant you were a jolly good sort. And I knew, if I kept this secret, my uncle would keep liking me more than RJ. This seemed important.

Six years later, when I was fifteen and RJ was sixteen, a flurry took place in and around my uncle. I can't remember the order of things, or how close or distant they happened, but they involved my uncle punching RJ in the nose, my father – who had never hit anyone in his life – taking a swing at my uncle and my uncle lying on the ground outside my father's house, being kicked by RJ in her shiny black Bata school shoes. And somewhere in there, me breaking a promise.

I had more important promises to keep now.

8

As a child I was fascinated by tales of life-altering illness. In the books I read, such illness was accompanied by the development of moral courage and heroism, and most importantly, it attracted the admiration of others for one's staunch attitude in the face of suffering.

Gwen had kept a volume of medical encyclopedias from the early 60s she'd acquired during one of her aborted attempts at becoming a nurse. I pored over its descriptions of illnesses, injuries, and abnormalities. There were colour illustrations showing organs, bones and blood, as well as engrossing pictures of suppurating sores and skin diseases. A whole section was dedicated to preparing for and surviving a nuclear attack. I felt mildly envious of the pictures of children practising their responses to an H-bomb: hiding under desks, their hands covering their necks, or with their neatly attired families in their bomb shelters, the mother in her immaculate dress preparing meals from their tinned supplies. I understood little of world affairs, but I understood enough to know that the suburbs we lived in were so quiet and boring that I would never have reason to participate in such a drill.

I was particularly affected by the illustrations of the onset and development of polio, beginning with a girl having a sore throat and a fever, being taken away by an ambulance, and emerging with callipers. As a child growing up in a household of smokers, I was always getting sore throats and wondered, each time, if this were the day the ambulance would come for me. I pictured my parents standing worried over my hospital bed, hoped I wouldn't need physiotherapy like Alan Marshall in *I Can Jump Puddles*, but was sure I would emerge with wisdom and patience like Katy in *What Katy Did*.

If that weren't enough, I was introduced to the consequences of child blindness caused by disease – first in Scholastic books on Helen Keller and her fascinating teacher, Annie Sullivan, and then by Laura Ingalls Wilder in her Little House series. In the latter, the scarlet fever that had beset the Ingalls family when Laura was thirteen resulted in her annoyingly perfect older sister, Mary, first having to have her long blonde hair shorn off, and then becoming blind as a result of the fever 'settling' in her eyes. This tragedy galvanises the family, makes them close. It forces Laura to work hard in school so she can become a teacher and contribute money to send Mary to the Iowa School for the Blind. And (it is implied), it causes Laura to become a writer, as she is suddenly required to be Mary's eyes, narrating everything for her benefit.

How I longed for, and feared, a similar tragedy! I tried (and failed) to teach myself braille, or even the raised alphabet, from the back of my Helen Keller book. I wandered around supermarkets behind Gwen, eyes squeezed shut, pretending to be blind, just in case. I constantly narrated my life to myself in case I was called upon to be someone's eyes.

When I was seven, my youngest cousin, Lara, was born. She was a chubby, healthy-looking child, at first, with a halo of bright red hair, but she had a bronchial wheeze and developed a hacking cough. After being told she was a neurotic mother by a raft of GPs, my aunt happened to have two-year-old Lara with her at the children's hospital while getting her son Konrad seen to after a playground accident.

'I'm not worried about him,' the treating doctor said, 'but does the baby always breathe like that?'

Later that evening, my aunt and uncle were told that the suspected asthma was in fact cystic fibrosis, a genetic disease which then had few effective treatments and a high fatality rate.

I understood from the grave tones in which Lara's condition was discussed that her health was poor and her prognosis serious, but to me she seemed mostly normal for a long time. She had a sunny and sweet temperament and didn't seem particularly interested in the excessive attentions she was given by adults, nor the indulgence allowed her if she wanted extra lollies or ice cream, denied to the rest of us not suffering from a life-limiting illness. She didn't want to go on the below-ground trampoline that was my greatest envy. The trampoline had been bought in the hopes it might loosen the mucus in her lungs better than the physiotherapy with which her tiny ribs were hammered morning and evening, and which developed admirable arm muscles in my aunty. So my cousins and I took advantage instead, while Lara waited around inside, wanting us to play more sedentary games which, I am ashamed to say, I often avoided.

As a teenager, I sometimes resented that Lara was tolerated for things I had been criticised for: that is, she wasn't smacked, or told no (very often), and if she complained, she was not informed she was a whingeing child who needed something to really whinge about. Her food fussiness wasn't a sign of moral degeneracy. I thought she was being spoiled, the way everyone treated her. She didn't even seem that sick.

Until she did.

When she was seven, Lara started getting sicker. She was skinnier than I had been in my most extreme anorexic phase, and the kids at her school teased her about her knobbly knees so relentlessly she was taken out of school altogether. She became lethargic, watching her older brother and sister squabble and laugh and play without the longing she used to have; now she was too tired. She found drinking the powders and taking the pills to help her digest harder to stomach.

And then, in January 1985, just after her eighth birthday, she died.

Gwen and I drove to my aunty and uncle's house. I was scared of seeing my cousin's dead body, but she seemed less dead than very, very still, neat in her bed. Her forehead was cooling as we kissed her goodbye. At her funeral, the coffin she was placed in was tiny, and it was not the effort of the weight of it that made the funeral directors lower it slowly down into the waiting earth. Her brother and sister were considered too young to attend: only my cousin and I, both being fifteen, were allowed. There were prayers, and the prayers did not comfort me.

I expected, based on all the books I'd read, that this type of tragedy would galvanise the family. As it was a time in my life when everything else seemed to be disintegrating, not least of which was a reliable sense of self, I was keen for our family to unite over this terrible and unfair event. It seemed particularly galling to me, as someone taken to fervent bouts of Christian belief from time to time, that this disaster was visited on the most religious of my mother's family. The sufferings of Job were not incomparable. After losing Lara, my aunt and uncle's son, Konrad, developed the epilepsy that was the symptom of a to-be-fatal brain tumour.

But the loss of Lara rent the family, and the increasing illness of Konrad was a further demonstration of the unrelenting unfairness that had befallen us. My grandparents raised the pitch of their mutual ire; my mother retreated into beer, cigarettes, and misery; and my aunty and uncle doubled down on the religiosity that promised that Lara wasn't gone, just waiting for them in heaven.

Against their incomparable suffering, my own, which was chiefly mental, was not of a scale deserving of attention from my family. The primary events that had caused the mental suffering – such as my parents' sudden separation, incidental molestation, and Gwen's conga line of men streaming through our various rented houses – were not recognised by my family as being any cause for comment. Indeed, I felt their criticism of me increased. My alternative dress now included dyed and spiky hair and men's clothes worn with wide belts and winklepicker shoes. I painted my Year One school case with a blue-and-red psychedelic swirl, with *DON'T STARE* in yellow capitals over the top, arranging my expression into a punk sneer ready for those who did. Taking Gwen's lead, I regularly drank myself into oblivion and took up indulging in more or less consensual sex with neighbourhood boys. I found a new outlet for my unnameable angst through epic episodes of bingeing and purging, which left me with detailed knowledge of the least smelly public toilets adjacent to food courts in the metro area.

When I did finally land in an adolescent mental hospital later on in the year Lara died, this was not mentioned at the Sunday lunches I was allowed to attend on weekend leave; instead, the usual teasing or mocking I received from certain relatives morphed into a watchful silence. A person was meant to deal with unpleasant feeling through acceptable methods such as imbibing quantities of home brew or flaying oneself into martyrdom. A person was, above all, meant to keep it to oneself instead of putting on a show, or making a spectacle of yourself, or in any other way making the invisible visible to all.

One happy result of my multiple mental hospitalisations was that I finally stopped thinking there was something wrong with me and started thinking there was something wrong with the family I'd grown up in.

. . .

In January 1993, I had my own first close encounter with bodily ills, which, in bringing me uncomfortably close to mortality, provided a new lens through which I saw the world.

I was working in a ski lodge in Dinner Plains in the high country of Victoria. During one of my free days, I had been placed on an ex-racehorse to take up the rear of a trail ride. I had blusteringly said to the owner of the trail ride company that oh yes, I had ridden horses before, not revealing that the horses involved were tough-mouthed nags on trail rides in the sandy plains of Perth, horses that would no more rise to a trot than they would begin discussing world affairs over the feedlot.

The ex-racehorse, realising it had an inexperienced rider lacking the moral force required for control of a large animal, took advantage by racing up the inside of the plodding trail horses the minute he was able, before bolting across an open plain and heading for the trees, most of which featured branches the exact height required for scraping off unwanted passengers.

'Sit back!' yelled the trail leader.

'I can't!' I wailed back.

'Jump off!'

I tried to un-wedge my Doc Martens from the stirrups without success.

'Agh!' I responded.

In order to get to the scraping-off branches, the horse first had to navigate a series of fallen logs. I'd always wanted to try horse jumping, preferably in a sandy ring with nicely painted Koppers logs, rather than involuntarily, in the middle of the Victorian highlands, three hours away from the nearest hospital.

The horse jumped. I did a backward somersault, which might have been okay if a) it hadn't been over the top of fallen logs, and b) my foot hadn't been jammed in the stirrup. Going by the resulting bruising and injuries, I landed first on my lumbar spine on one log, then pivoted onto a second with my thoracic, my ankle sustaining a clean break as it wrenched from the stirrup.

When I realised I was on the ground, rather than being decapitated by a branch or dragged along the ground like a papist during the reign of Henry VIII, I was, for a moment, relieved. Then the combination of being unable to breathe and pain of a magnitude I had never experienced combined to make me wonder if I was dying or, if I wasn't, whether death would be preferable.

The trail riders caught up with me. As soon as I was able to breathe, I began to moan.

'Stand by,' said one of the trail riders. 'I'm a doctor.'

The doctor proceeded to prod and poke various bodily parts, including my back and my legs, prompting me to moan more loudly.

'Be quiet,' he said. 'I've been in Vietnam, and I've seen men in real pain.'

I used all of my Kelmscott words to describe exactly what I thought of him and his opinion.

'Her back's not broken but her leg is,' he pronounced to the assembled.

'The ambulance can't get in this far,' the trail leader said. 'We'll have to get the ute to get to the road.'

Being lifted into the tray of the utility and being transported on a bumpy bush track to the ambulance took the pain to yet a new, piercing level. The ambulance then took some hours to wend down the mountain to what was less a hospital than a nursing outpost, which did not possess X-ray equipment equal to the task, so I was bundled back into the ambulance and transported a further hour to the mainland hospital, by which time I was retching with pain unrelieved by a Panadol lozenge. The pain constricted my ribs as if I were encased with barbed wire, and my foot and ankle bloated and throbbed.

The pain around my ribs was caused by compressed thoracic fractures, apparently to the surprise of Dr I've-Been-In-Vietnam, and the ankle was a Pott's fracture that was pushed back into place by the orthopaedic surgeon after filling me full of pethidine.

Gwen flew over to Victoria, with a mixture of concern and annoyance, to return me home, an echo of the trip she had made in 1964, except this time returning with an injured adult child. It was the first time she'd set foot in Melbourne since relinquishing her son nearly thirty years before, and she hated it no less on this occasion. She wheeled me around the city, which was not especially wheelchair-friendly in 1993, all the while complaining about the cost of everything and how stressful it was and how she missed her husband. We arrived back in Perth, to my dismay and her delight: my wheelchair didn't fit in the house, and neither did I.

I was admitted to hospital for a couple of weeks, in the hope that my pain levels would subside long enough for me to use crutches. As I had been hospitalised interstate, I had a single room until they were sure I wasn't harbouring golden staph. The room was abutted by a shower cubicle that had a partition under which one could see. Although it was supposed to be for disabled folk, it was not quite big enough to accommodate a wheelchair, nor did it have a working lock. Gwen got her GP in attendance, an ever-smiling man whose eyes kept dipping below my neckline as he spoke to me. One day I was showering – my cast foot wrapped in plastic while I sat on a plastic chair, having hopped over to it – when the doctor came and said he wanted to see me.

'I'm in the shower,' I told him, redundantly, as I could see his shoes under the door.

'I just want to see how you're moving,' he said.

I turned the shower off and hopped toward the towel. 'Just wait,' I said.

He pushed the door open; I leaned back on it, hoping my wet, good foot wouldn't slip.

'I'll be out in a minute,' I said.

'I don't have time,' he said angrily, and started shoving against the door while I, with my newly fractured back, held the door as fast as I could.

Eventually he gave up, and I shakily retreated to my bed. When they moved me to the women's ward later that day, I was relieved, even though I was kept awake by my fellow residents, old women with dementia wailing, or snoring, or else trying to get into bed with each other. It was better than having my mother's GP get into bed with me.

Sometimes I do not feel I have been well served by the books that I read as a child. They did not correctly inform me of the effects of the tragedies, or mere misfortunes, born of bodily ills. You might find yourself getting wisdom through being forced to re-examine your life from the unusual prism provided by pain, illness, and life-limiting diseases in your close kin. However, you are much more likely, in my experience, to find your family fracturing in imitation of a crushed bone, or to find yourself preyed upon by those attracted by your vulnerability.

9

It was a school day in August 1979 when my parents separated.

I was nine years old and in Year Five. It was the International Year of the Child. There was a public service song that played all year long about how important it was to care for kids. One of Gwen's friends burst into tears every time the song came on the radio, haunted by parental guilt about the way she had treated her daughters, pretty girls slightly younger than me who gazed suspiciously at the world through their round, solemn eyes. Gwen thought this was ridiculous sentimentality she was in no danger of sharing.

The separation was sudden in that it occurred on a school morning without warning. I'd got up to find Gwen sniffling as she conveyed the news to her sister over the telephone; I sat stiffly at the kitchen table until she was composed enough to impart the same information to me. When I asked where we would live, she told me we'd be staying with her friends Ray and Jeannie at their house on the other side of the railway line until we found a place of our own to rent. She was apologetic and I cried at her distress. She explained that Derek had gone to work but I could speak to him later. She said that they still loved me, but they no longer loved each other.

As we drove to Ray and Jeannie's house, Gwen asked if I felt confused.

But I was not confused, because the signs of marital disharmony had been multiplying for some time. First, Gwen had disappeared for some weeks to accompany her father, Frank, on his superintendent policeman visits to remote Kimberley towns during the wet season. I vaguely understood that the reason for this was to relieve Gwen of whatever it was that had been making her swing wildly between fury and rue. Then the three of us – Gwen, Derek, and I – had driven to Broome during the May holidays. The unsealed roads of the last stretch and the consequent lurching, dusty bumpiness would have forced silence between the adults in the front seat even if it had not already been firmly established as soon as the car was rolling north over horizons of bitumen. And finally, I'd returned home from school one day to find that Gwen was now in the spare room next to mine, as far distant from Derek as she could get without resorting to moving into the redback-filled shed.

'Are you going to separate, like Anna and Björn?' I'd asked.

Earlier on in the year, Agnetha (known as Anna) and Björn from the Swedish band ABBA, with which my best friend Nobbly and I were obsessed, had announced their split. The depth of my devastation was profound. I could not conceive of a world without ABBA and was not reassured by their assurances that they would persist. The world of adults, which I had believed to be composed of constellations of permanent relationships, now proved to be as fickle as week-to-week playground alliances.

'No, Jules, I promise,' Gwen said. 'We just need some time to sort things out.'

But in the intervening months, Gwen and Derek had continued to display more or less consistent signs of unhappiness. Gwen attended all of her tasks with an air of frustration and listened to Anne Murray's ballads so often I once hid the record to prevent the mournfulness from pervading the house. Derek, never voluble, receded into detached silence. One winter's day I had been home with a sore throat and fever, and Gwen drove to a tavern for lunch with her squash ladies while I lay in the car, dipping in and out of prickly skinned sleep. After some time I became anxious about Gwen's persistent absence and shuffled into the tavern in my slippers. I was alerted to where the squash ladies were by the loud squeals of mirth they were producing and found them sitting in a circle in low-slung chairs in the ladies' lounge. The cause of their mirth was immediately apparent: there was Gwen in the centre of their circle, on her hands and knees on the carpet sticky with spilled beer, in imitation of what or who I could not tell, only that it caused the loud amusement that my appearance did not temper.

When she'd righted herself and the laughter had subsided, I informed Gwen I didn't feel well and wanted to go home. When Gwen didn't immediately respond, I began to cry.

'This is why I don't have kids,' Gwen's friend Brenda declared. 'They ruin everything.'

'Come back to our place!' Gwen had said. 'Derek won't care!'

The rest of the afternoon and evening is a series of fragments. Watching the electricity poles whoosh by as Gwen said that no matter what Brenda said, I was her number one. Derek's cautious face as Gwen announced that we were having a party. The patio door open; Gwen singing to Rock Follies. Gwen calling 'Dance with me, Derek!' and 'I still love you, you bastard.' Lying in Gwen's bed, calling for water like Mary in *Little House on the Prairie* when the whole family is stricken with a malaria-type disease. Derek bringing dissolved Disprin to my bedside, his black eyebrows drawn together with concern, even though I had been calling for Gwen. The texture of the pillow hardening into sleep-preventing concrete, overloud sounds like sticks being rubbed near my eardrum, observing myself from the corner of the ceiling, an unmoving outline under the bedspread. The party going on and on; waking to the creepy, quiet dark with a feeling of dread that did not recede with the fever.

So I was not confused that my parents were separating. As we drove to Ray and Jeannie's in our old blue Toyota – Derek would have his work van – Gwen reassured me that she would be happier, that she would not be as snappy as she had been. It would be for the best. She promised.

...

Gwen, having endured the strictures of an upbringing with Frank and then a marriage to escape him, took advantage of being free of both. We moved to a duplex on the other side of the railway line, and from there Gwen embarked upon late-70s single life. We didn't have a television but we did have a radio, which was now always on, playing disco hits like 'Born to Be Alive', to which she sang along with particular gusto. She and her other recently separated friends would host gatherings where we children ate salt-and-vinegar chips and, after wine had been squeezed out of casks and beer emptied from bottles, joined in the dancing that went well past anyone's bedtime. The heaviness that had sat over Gwen before was gone; she played the piano accordion and belted out dirty ditties like 'Roll Me Over in the Clover' to the delight of her friends; she sewed new clothes to go out in, sometimes with matching outfits for me; her olive skin was warm with energy. Nobody could keep up with her.

Because nobody could keep up with her, she began going out by herself. One night RJ came to stay in the new duplex; Gwen fed us and departed, wearing the new gold mesh sandals I soon understood as being the marker of a big evening in the making. We watched out of the window as Gwen strode off toward the tavern; we were woken later in the evening as Gwen, unable to insert the key into the lock, was accompanied by a man who could.

RJ was never allowed to stay over again. The parents of the few other friends who'd allowed their offspring to have a sleepover on the already slightly dubious side of the suburb with the new phenomenon of a single parent reached the same conclusion for similar reasons.

Gwen might have been oblivious to or uncaring of the parental standards others expected, but she was nevertheless careful to limit Derek's awareness of her new social life.

One time, early on, Derek returned me from my fortnightly stay with him, only to find an empty house. We waited under the carport until Gwen arrived in an unfamiliar car, out of which piled several men only mildly more sober than she was. Gwen was jovial until she spotted Derek; Derek had words to her I couldn't hear and returned me to his house until Gwen assured him she was alone and with a blood alcohol content low enough to understand she had come close to making a big mistake.

'If you want to go and live with your dad, you can,' she said in a trembling voice after Derek had deposited me at the duplex for the second time. 'If you really want to.'

'I love you, Mum,' I said, understanding the answer that she expected was the only one I could give. 'I want to stay with you.'

Thus commenced a cycle of shame and regret expressed by her and proportionate reassurance from me. When I heard adults murmuring – which they now did, regularly – about how hard the separation must have been on me, and how mature I had become as a result, I enjoyed feigning deafness and holding myself proudly, but I knew the truth. Gwen might be charging through her life now with a bluster and boldness that brought upon her as much judgement as the separation, but underneath it all, all she wanted was me, the child she didn't have to give up but who she could come close to losing, if she wasn't careful. I was the reason for Gwen's existence, she'd told me. She'd promised me. Her feelings were stronger and mattered more. She was a different mother from the one she'd been at Derek's, angry and impatient. Before, she'd pushed me away. Now, she needed me. It was a surprising but welcome turn of events.

The other thing I knew not to say is that compared to what life was like when my parents were together, life was now definitely much more fun. We might have kept up a vestige of regular routines – Gwen had to drive me to school every day now, seeing as we were now relatively distant – but now, you never knew what was going to happen. One of Gwen's friends – Brenda, Glenda, or Jeannie – might be popping in, and dinner might end up being a Vegemite sandwich, which suited me fine. Sometimes Brenda or Glenda arrived with tales of woe about some bloke who'd run off with some floozie, to which Gwen would say, 'Bugger them! Tell them to get stuffed!'

At weekend barbecues, the assembled kids – which included Shane and Brett, Ray and Jeannie's boys who were slightly younger than me – were able to wander at will, playing cricket in cul-de-sacs, smashing pig melons on the roads with satisfying thwacks, and, once it grew dark, gathering in front of televisions turned up to drown out drunken adult conversations, watching whatever we liked until we fell asleep and were carried into cars. One time, our telly-watching was interrupted by females yelling, and then screams. We leapt up and ran to the screen door. Jeannie was being pinned back by her arms but wouldn't stop lunging, kicking her heel against the shins of the guy struggling to keep her in place. The woman to whom her fury was directed had ribbons of blood across her cheek.

'You bloody bitch!' Jeannie was screaming. 'You were supposed to be my fucking friend!'

I had been to plenty of adults' parties, but none of them were like these ones, where you never knew what was going to happen. There was a newly released song warning – or celebrating, it was hard to tell – that there was going to be heartache and heartbreak tonight. I marvelled at how this type of party, containing partygoers so different from, say, my grandparents' friends, had already been translated so accurately into a lyric. You could feel in the air when something was going to happen, and I began to look forward to it.

I didn't take part in the parties, being a kid, but I was an eager and attentive witness.

I remember thinking that if someone had asked me if I wanted my parents to stay together, I would have said: no way. The unexpectedness that life suddenly contained was too interesting. I felt closer to being grown up, being so close to grown-ups who paid scant attention to who was watching. At the time I couldn't imagine wanting things to be any different.

...

I first saw Daniel Boone through the dusty net curtains at Glenda's house in Gosnells. I'd had to stay there one night with Glenda's younger daughter while Glenda and Gwen went out. I didn't want to be left in the strange house and was relieved to hear car doors slamming. Gwen had left with Glenda but returned arm in arm with a man. I stomped to the car, irritable when I realised this man was coming home with us, but then he turned around from the passenger seat.

'Good evening, I am Daniel Boone,' he said to me politely, except he said 'Daniel' like 'Dannel'.

The man seemed nice and not as drunk as some of Gwen's other male friends were, plus he had an accent I'd only ever heard on television.

'Say hello, Julie,' Gwen said. 'Daniel's a sailor.' She giggled. 'I mean, Dannel.'

'Is that your real name?' I said.

He started singing the song I knew from the television re-runs, except he sang different words to it.

'My momma thought she was real funny,' he said.

From then on, I was a fan of Daniel, who later showed us his passport proving his name. Daniel was from the Midwest of the US and attached to the USS *Midway*. He was a keen photographer, and he showed Gwen and me pictures of places I had not even known existed, such as Kenya. Glenda had brought home her own sailor, Daniel's friend, so over the next days we drove all around Perth, showing the sailors the sights and enjoying how they relished what we thought of as ordinary. We drove to the Cohunu wildlife sanctuary in the bush at the back of Gosnells and showed them how to feed the kangaroos: their velvety lips scooped up the pellets and tickled the sailors' palms. We took Daniel to the Kelmscott pool, and he took photographs of the pool, of me and my friend April dunking each other at its shallow end.

The night before Daniel was due to sail away, he told Gwen that he was going to leave the navy when he returned to the US. He was going to move to California and he was going to go to college, and she could come. She could go to college too. They could both make a better life. I could be their daughter. It would be great.

'Do you want to move to California?' Gwen asked.

'Yes,' I said, seeing from her eager face that this was the answer she wanted. I would get an American accent, instead of merely pretending to have one, as I was wont to do. Then I said, 'I'll miss Dad, though.'

'Don't tell your dad yet,' Gwen said.

Daniel left. Gwen and I cried. I wrote to the captain of the USS *Midway* to beg them to return but received no reply. Daniel sent a toy robot from Japan that spat red plastic bullets from its hands. He sent the photographs he'd taken of me and Gwen, of me and April in the swimming pool, and then new photos, of him in new places, without us.

In time I figured that we weren't moving to California, because a) the furthest we moved was to another rental unit, back on the other side of the railway line, closer to school, and b) Gwen commenced bringing new blokes to our new rental, including her friend Jeannie's now former husband, Ray.

...

Ray was six foot two, ginger-haired, and always had a packet of Winfield Reds tucked under the sleeve of his t-shirt. He was never still. Even when he sat in an armchair, reading the wild west pulp fiction he was fond of, his leg would jiggle. He'd been briefly jailed in his late teen years for, he said, breaking into postboxes, before the early production of children set him on the relatively straight and narrow. Now he worked for the water board and had a house in the state housing area at the far reaches of Kelmscott. He taught me how to siphon petrol from his work vehicle by sucking periodically on a hose inserted for the purpose, and listening between inhales to the gurgling fuel as it was coaxed up the hose and then poured, thanks to gravity, into the waiting bucket. He had a battered Landcruiser with purple curtains Gwen sewed for it, and in the Landcruiser was a CB radio for communicating with his friends and listening to the police channel.

Ray and his mates – Mick D, Mick F, and John – began regularly showing up at our unit at irregular times. One school night, we were woken by banging on the front door. When Gwen opened it, Mick D fell inside and onto the lino, followed by Ray. Gwen made black coffee in the hopes that this would assist Ray in depositing Mick home in a state less likely to precipitate divorce. Mick proceeded to roll around on the floor, money spilling out of his pockets. I was allowed to keep the coins but had to reinsert the notes into his jeans.

There were barbecues in the bush, where we kids would roam, extracting bardi grubs out of the hollow trunks of knocked-over grass trees and pretending we enjoyed the taste of them. The men formed convoys and we drove half an hour to go prawning at dusk. The adults would wade their sheet-sized nets through the shallows of the freshwater Swan River in old sandshoes to protect them from the poison of a cobbler spike, while we kids would throw translucent brown, frilled jellyfish at each other and spoil our appetites with thick white bread slick with margarine. Armed with a long rifle, we drove through the bushland of the Serpentine hills after dark in Ray's Landcruiser. Once out of town, one of the men would climb on the roof rack with the rifle while one of us kids balanced on the bull bar, sweeping a spotlight through the night until it caught the glint of a kangaroo eye. If their shot was good, we kids would ride home in the back, legs drawn up against the still-warm animal that Ray would butcher into steaks and Gwen cook into kangaroo tail soup. I helped Ray skin a roo, once, in the hope that I would be able to make a skirt like Leela from *Doctor Who*, but it stiffened after I salted it to deter maggots and remained impervious to my sewing attempts.

The arrival of drunken men and their going out to murder marsupials weren't the only sleep-interrupting nocturnal activities this time heralded. One night after a party, I was woken by percussive calling which, when I got up to investigate, was being produced by Gwen, lying legs akimbo on the living room floor, even though it was Ray atop her who seemed to be exerting the most effort. Even when I later begged her to, she would never close a door or reduce her volume. I was never sure if she was incapable, being so lost in her own obliterating pleasure, or whether it was something she thought I would just have to learn to put up with. She never explained, and I didn't know how to ask.

...

When the lease on the unit near school was not renewed, no doubt due to the complaints of neighbours who were less pleased than Gwen about the Landcruiser rumbling down the driveway at all hours, Gwen and I moved in with Ray, into the house we'd first stayed in when my parents separated. It was far away from my primary school but close to the high school that Gwen was now attending as a thirty-five-year-old mature-age student. Daniel Boone had left Gwen with the conviction that she should go back to school and make something of herself. The indignity of having to repeat the final two years of high school with teenagers in order to go to university might have dissuaded her from this path if Frank had not been so scathing.

His 'What the bloody hell do you want to do that for?' was enough of a catalyst to keep her going even when the parties, the de facto parenting and the hangovers gave her doubts. She set her sights firmly ahead, turned Ray's spare room into a study, and studied. To help out and stay out of her way when assignments were due, Shane, Brett, and I learned how to wash Ray's coffee-coloured Pyrex cups and plates until no grease from our preferred dinners of sausages, mashed potatoes, and peas remained; we took Fang, Ray's red heeler bull terrier cross, for lunging walks around the unpaved streets; or spray-painted Ray's collection of car husks that sat out the side of the house. When the weather warmed up, Ray installed an above-ground pool, with corrugated tin on the outside and a blue sweet-smelling lining, for us to cool off in. Although I got recurrent doses of pharyngitis, thanks to living with two indoor smokers, our time with Ray and having sort-of stepbrothers and a sort-of regular family life was good. When Gwen graduated from Year Twelve with top percentile grades and was accepted into university to study accounting, we all celebrated with her. I started high school the same week she started at university.

We hadn't been at Ray's a year when I returned from school one afternoon to find Gwen weeping and throwing our belongings into boxes.

'He's been screwing around,' she said. 'We're moving out.'

. . .

We were in our new rental, another duplex in the same street our first had been, not long before my thirteenth birthday. Unlike her separation from Derek, which had been her own decision, and which propelled her into frivolity, Gwen suffered the unsought split with Ray profoundly. She had ignored her friendships with women during her twelve-month coupledom, so now the only person present to hear her recounting grievances and plumbing the depths of her feelings of rejection and sorrow was me.

Gwen took to buying and consuming flagons of moselle. She drank angrily out of cordial glasses and instructed me never to trust a man. When she had consumed enough moselle she would begin weeping and, after the weeping, take off in the car to tell Ray what she thought of him. I would pace around the unit, checking the front window from time to time, the radio loud for company, wondering what I would do if she did not return, or if, like one of Ray's friends, she drove drunkenly into a power pole and had to go to jail. When she progressed to exorcising her feelings through picking up blokes from the local tavern, I began pouring the remaining flagon contents down the sink, knowing that the gap between last week's single-parent pension and the next would reduce the frequency of the angry drinking and noisy copulation that kept me awake as surely as anxiety about her absence did.

I had fortnightly relief from excessive displays of feeling on my weekends with Derek, who remained as mild mannered as ever. He was going out with a person as different from Gwen as he could have found, a potter called Wendy who had a southern English burr. With Wendy we went to the art gallery, to the gallery openings of her friends, and to her house in Mahogany Creek, where I brushed her two rough-coat collies endlessly and learned the challenge of centring a lump of clay on a spinning wheel. Wendy's son Colin and I would wander with the dogs as far as we could on the Bibbulmun Track across the road, pretending we were the only people alive on the gravelly trail between the towering jarrah and honky-nut-producing marri trees, with banksias, grass trees and she-oaks nestled between, stomping loudly to ensure snakes would remain out of sight. Derek drove us to the tip, where Colin would identify and collect what was needed to build go-karts, then busy himself in the shed, only requiring Derek's assistance in the wheel-adding stage. We would haul them to the top of Wendy's steep driveway, jump aboard and yank on the rope steering apparatus to curl the hurtling vehicles around the house to a patch of kart-slowing grass, brakes being beyond Colin's engineering prowess. Derek would go to the tavern on a Saturday afternoon, sipping his Guinness while I played the new game of Space Invaders.

When Gwen settled down again after a month or so, there was a new bloke, Steve, and new younger stepsiblings, Dianne and Michael, who were adopted. Gwen always had a soft spot for adopted children and the men kind enough to take them in, but Steve was quieter than Ray and lacking Ray's edgy charisma, and I found it hard to take to him. Frank and Violet were embarking on a year-long trip around Australia, and offered for Gwen to move into their house in East Victoria Park at a discounted rental rate. Steve moved with us, to my annoyance, and I had to change schools.

I moved from the large high school – from whose roughness I had been insulated by my group of friends and primary-school familiarity with the prime troublemakers – to one in which violence, actual or threatened, was ever-present and, to my shock, not infrequently aimed at me. Having malevolence aimed at me for reasons I could not determine underscored my increasing sense of being adrift from my own life, the conviction that something was not right, that I was not in the right place with the right people. And it increased my attempts to try to find ways to correct the unexpected and aimless course I'd found myself on after primary school, to narrow my exertions to those things I could control, or to scrabble about for some meaning to attach to the things I could not.

10

After Gwen and Derek split up, as I was entering upper primary school, I had begun placing a new value on doing things well. At school I'd received good marks due to aptitude rather than effort. My handwriting changed from week to week depending on my mood. I was much more interested in finishing first than the quality I was producing, and was too impatient to check my work before I handed it in. Often I fell into friendships with kids who were keen to enjoin me to take part in their mildly illicit activities, and my enthusiasm for schoolwork sat in inverse proportion to my interest in the activities, such as making fake vomit mixture to aid in being sent home, plotting to 'borrow' a tenor recorder from the music room unnoticed, and sneaking out to cross the river at lunchtime.

Now, I wanted to improve myself. I joined the school choir in Years Six and Seven, which meant that I arrived at school early for rehearsal every day, no matter what interruptions I might have experienced the night before. Being trained to produce crisp consonants and well-formed vowels in our renditions of English folk songs from 'Sumer Is Icumen In' to 'Bobby Shafto' gave a direction to my sudden, generalised desire to focus. I stretched my fingers on the bass recorder in the consort that rehearsed at lunchtime and learned to take care through the careful calibrations required to assemble, adjust, and play the clarinet. I learned to iron through smoothing out the long blue pinafore dress and white blouse I wore for performances and to carefully part my hair and tie it with even blue ribbons. My best friend Nobbly and I were chosen to be part of a select group of the choir who got to dress up in period costume and be filmed singing for a Christmas segment on the ABC. The uncertainty in daily life at home was allayed by my determination to achieve something.

And I began carving myself a place away from the vagaries of adult relationships through creating my own worlds. Even before the separation, I had begun writing 'books' whose stories featured the creek, cousinly tensions, and dramatic turns of events sorely lacking in daily life, such as magical implements and portals to other worlds. I was always more interested in depicting the world from which the escape was made than what came next, so endings were far less frequent than beginnings. Now I embarked on creating guidebooks to a new solar system and the planets Nobbly and I had allocated to ourselves and our friends; song parodies and lyrics; tales of the kidnappings of Nobbly and my cats, occurring while on a tour of the solar system with our pop group, which bore a striking similarity to ABBA; and stories about the adventures my cousins and I would get up to in our dusty, spider-infested, and occasionally snake-harbouring cubby house in Mukinbudin. The worlds I imagined, and the ones Nobbly and I, or my cousins and I, imagined together existed as a feeling akin to excitement, close but not quite in reach, something that with enough faithful imagining might become tangible.

My confidence in my self-improvement skills had been dealt several blows in my final year of primary school. I had channelled furious energies into producing several volumes of a year-long social studies project about travelling around Australia. Alongside my desire to improve myself was a desire for recognition from particular adults, about which I had previously been indifferent.

I spent hours at Wendy's house and at Ray's on our social studies project, which was supposed to be learning about Australia by researching particular towns and writing up the results, a long project stretching over two of the three school terms. I transformed this into 'My Adventures Around Australia', and wrote it as a diary, including imagined exchanges with my cousins who I included in the project. I plotted our chart around the country, cut out photos from tourist brochures, and tried to make my handwriting as neat and consistent as possible. Everyone else handed in a single volume; my three, fat with glued pages, had to be tied together when I triumphantly handed them to Mr Sandshoe. I received the top mark in the class, which must have made me expand visibly with pride, because Mr Sandshoe kept me after class.

'Julie,' he said, smiling. 'In the valley of blind men, the man with one eye is king.'

I had been expecting to be praised; instead, I stood, smile still fixed.

'You understand what I mean, don't you?' he said.

'Thank you, Mr Sandshoe,' I said, and left the classroom, pleasure in my achievement transformed into a shameful burning in my chest.

Mr Sandshoe wasn't done with me yet. The local high school was commencing an academically gifted program, which would enable participants to complete school in four years rather than five, which was appealing enough, and I was keen to sit the exam. However, when the names were called out to sit the exam, mine was the only one among my friends not to be called. I waited for Mr Sandshoe to correct his mistake, but he merely added, 'And if your parents would like you to sit the exam anyway, tell them to come and see me.'

I discussed the matter with Gwen, pretending I was not in the least injured by the slight against my intelligence, and she conferred with the English teacher she knew at the local high school, who said the program would put too much pressure on me. When all the children deemed brighter than me had been taken by bus to the exam, my Year Six teacher came across me with surprise, and I took some small comfort from the way she shook her head when I told her I had not been selected for the test. I took more comfort when only one girl and two boys – none of them my friends – were accepted into the program. Besides, I didn't want to go to the local high school. I wanted to go to Perth Modern, the specialist music school.

The entry tests for this school were held all the way on the other side of the city, in a large auditorium of a university. Gwen, who was never late to anything, left the house late, meaning we arrived late. I entered an auditorium already full of students who had received the instructions on how to complete the first test. Someone gave me individual instructions before we started, but I was flustered. That test involved determining whether one tone was higher or lower than another and marking dots on a grid.

Next, there was an IQ test, and one other I don't recall the details of. Possibly to ensure fairness for those who had not been in the state music program for Years Six and Seven, there were no instrument auditions. I ate lunch happily at the park across the road with Nobbly and all my other friends. I was confident that if one of us got in, we would all get in. We all seemed to be musical to more or less the same degree, apart from one girl who'd started composing songs in Year Four and another who had an angelic singing voice.

A tingling dread began to overtake me when, one by one, Nobbly and my friends celebrated their letters of acceptance, while our mailbox remained empty. Finally, after a few more days during which I alternated between hope that the letter had been mislaid and fear at the result that was more likely coming, the more likely result was confirmed.

I declared that I didn't care; I hated practising clarinet anyway, and who wanted to catch the train an hour each way to school? My music teacher was so perplexed by this outcome that she contacted the examination board, and discovered that had I answered the questions to the tone-distinguishing test in the reverse to how I had in fact answered them, I would have got in. Her sympathy deepened my shame. It was unclear whether I had misunderstood the instructions but, as I experienced it, my fate had suddenly taken a turn that I had lacked the imagination to contemplate. I would be going to a high school where, by my reckoning, there was no point in succeeding academically because the teachers were only focused on the intellectually talented program I could never be promoted to. I would learn clarinet but would find myself dropping behind my friends in the specialist program. My expectations of myself had been dashed – not good enough at the things I had been led to believe were my strengths. Without the comfort of striving, I feared what the striving enabled me to look away from, a murk-filled chasm that I could edge past while I clung to the idea of something better that was to come, fashioned from my own efforts. I had relegated all of the tricky feelings of the previous two years there. Now, as I headed toward my teens, with nothing better to focus on, I could no longer look away.

II

At the beginning of Year Nine, at thirteen, I found myself newly enrolled at the high school Gwen had gone to. Gwen remembered the high school fondly: the glory days of sporting achievements, performing in *The Mikado*, and grades which had been stellar until she lost concentration, possibly due to the paternally inflicted brain injury she'd received.

I managed to secure two friends in the first weeks. One was a fiercely Christian Dutch girl and the other an Aboriginal girl whose adoptive mother introduced us on the first day. This relieved me of having lunch alone or sitting solo in class. Then the Aboriginal girl was co-opted by the other Aboriginal girls, the Dutch girl enrolled in a Christian school, and I was on my own.

My arrival at the school had coincided with the arrival of several hundred students from a closed-down school consisting mainly of teenagers from Brownlie Towers, Perth's version of the Bronx.

One day I was eating my lunch alone. I had found a vacant tree, sat myself at its base, and leaned back, my lunch on my lap, my knees up. Despite my best attempts at trying to take on tree-like qualities that would render me invisible, a group of Brownlie Towers girls happened along. When they saw me, they stopped and stared, whispering and pointing. They seemed to be pointing at my sandals, known as 'squeakies' due to the sound the woven leather made on perambulation, popular at Kelmscott but unknown at this new school. I kept chewing on my sandwich, pretending I hadn't noticed them.

It was not my sandals that had caught their attention, however. One of them pointed and yelled, 'You're on your rags! Look! We can all see!'

'No I'm not,' I said, a statement which had been true the last time I had checked.

'Yeah ya are! Don't you even know what ya period is? Don't ya fucken know anything?'

I feigned nonchalance until they ceased pointing and yelling; as soon as they were out of sight I rushed to the toilet to find that I had, indeed, started bleeding. I stuffed toilet paper in my knickers, and for the rest of the day moved cautiously, convinced that a bloody wodge would fall out, or that I would stain the back of my uniform. I had become accustomed to the idea that my skills and abilities might fail me when I least expected it, but now, it seemed, my body was joining in.

That weekend we visited Steve's mother in hospital, where she was having the new-fangled procedure of stomach stapling. I had become horrified at the way adults seemed unable to curb their own appetites of various descriptions, but when we went to the hospital, I was shot through with longing to stay there. The atmosphere was hushed, with purposeful people striding about and, above all, it felt safe.

Not long after that, Steve, whose depression did not dampen his enthusiasm for making mocking commentary about my appearance, interrupted my consumption of milk laden with several tablespoons of crunchy, chocolatey Milo by informing me that I'd better watch it, or else I'd get fat.

I had already commenced obsessively reading and re-reading Deborah Hautzig's *Second Star to the Right*. I found a sympathetic echo in the mournful misfit of its main character, alienated at her new school and defined by her family's history, different as a Jewish home in the Upper West Side of New York might have been from a broken home in suburban East Victoria Park, Perth. Now I paid particular attention to when the protagonist became ill enough through starvation to be hospitalised. Going to hospital, I felt, would surely cocoon me from the injuries of human interaction that I felt unprotected against. I imagined Gwen standing by my bedside, realising that she had done wrong in endowing Steve with all the attention and regard I craved. I imagined being saved from having to go to school and being bailed up in the change rooms by the Brownlie Towers girls. I imagined reclining on the clean white sheets, not having to express my feelings with words because I had done so with my shrinking body.

I was galvanised into action. I bought a calorie counter and was appalled at how fattening most food was. My main food source became the carrots we grew in the garden, metallic-tasting knotted growths that I wrapped in foil to take to school. I scraped cottage cheese with chives onto crispbread. If I consumed anything else, I compensated by running around the oval or by doing gymnastics in the lounge room. I fed my dinner meat to the dog, Patch, under the table, and made a show of eating the boiled potatoes and beans or carrots or whatever else was on my plate. I felt strong and determined. I wrote poems to myself about the desirability of thinness and recorded my daily weight and food consumption in my diary, alongside complaints about Gwen, exhortations to continue my restrictive eating, and moods varying between euphoria and blanketing misery. I stopped wearing jumpers to encourage peak caloric burn.

I had lost nearly ten kilos before I was called into the nurse's office. The nurse – a short, round, cheerful woman – declared that I weighed what she should, and that I should not weigh what I did, and called Gwen. Gwen was shocked to take in my bony hands and gaunt face, even though I lived with her. It appeared my attempts to shrink myself from the present I was reluctant to inhabit had been more effective than I'd imagined. She explained to the nurse that she had been distracted.

Until then, she relied on my normality as an endorsement of the style of parenting that caused other adults, even if they weren't aware of the finer details, to look askance. So when the nurse suggested I begin consultations with a psychiatrist – in Victoria Park, not far away – Gwen took the number but didn't call it. She took me to her GP, whose advice that I needed to eat more was welcomed. As someone who was trying to eat less as her girth expanded, Gwen found my stubborn refusal to eat – including the sausages and lamb chops curled around with glistening fats, and calorie-laden bread-and-butter puddings, apple pie, and cheesecake that had formerly been my favourites – perplexing.

She didn't have to be perplexed for too much longer. One morning, when I was staying at Derek's, I woke up feeling perfectly fine until I stood up. The room yo-yoed around. The dread of imminent vomiting made me ignore the unstable floor and run to the bathroom, where I collapsed on the August-cold tiles, limbs shaking. I retched but produced nothing, because there was nothing to vomit, having managed to eat nothing more than a piece of toast and an apple the previous day. I thought about Karen Carpenter, who had died earlier in the year from anorexia, and understood that while I might have wanted to go to hospital, I was less keen on the idea of actually dying.

I crawled to the kitchen, finding it necessary to resume a horizontal position from time to time en route, glad that Derek was not yet up. In stages I put bread in the toaster, poured milk in Milo, spread honey on the toast, and sat on the kitchen floor eating and drinking until the blackness receded from the edge of my vision and I could stand without nausea. When Derek emerged, I told him I was unwell; when he drove me back to Victoria Park, I announced to Gwen that I was going to resume eating normally. Gwen made me several rounds of toast and vegemite in relief, and promptly forgot about this disturbing intermission.

I might have frightened myself out of starvation, but the appetite I had successfully suppressed returned, determined never to let itself be ignored or reined in again.

...

I had switched back to my original high school in second term, electing to stay more at Derek's and less with Gwen to avoid both travel and Steve. While I'd been away there seemed to have been a Brownlie Towers–equivalent influx of girls from the tough towns of northern England, whose edges required the existing cohort to change shape. These girls took over the most convenient toilets in the school in which to smoke and bail up unsuspecting interlopers; they scowled through classes and mocked those who appeared studious or responsive; they threatened girls who were too pretty or too mouthy or too smart. They occasionally turned on their own kind: once I saw them trip up one of their former friends and kick her down the stairs in the maths block because she'd been rumoured to sleep with some other girl's boy.

In no small part to escape the possibility of coming onto the radar of these girls, my friends and I auditioned for and joined Kelmscott High School's one artistic activity of note, the school musical.

Rehearsals took place in the gymnasium, which until that point had been the site of sporting humiliations and interminable school assemblies. Now the gym was overtaken by the shy and the theatrical, able to take advantage of the gym toilets, which were as free of danger as they were of toilet paper. The musical that year was *Dracula Spectacula*, and I was an Idiot. Our directors were strict, and I was transported back to the heady days of primary school choir, where things were expected of you. I was never late for a rehearsal, revelled in the noise and chaos of blocking out scenes, never needed to be reminded of where to stand or how to move or the words to songs.

And then I became aware of Karen.

Karen had been cast as Dracula. The extent of her thespian skills was evidenced by her securing the lead role in the musical despite being unable to hold a note. Instead, she performed songs recitative-style with an assuredness that she carried, in my mind at least, into her everyday life. Karen had recently arrived from a working-class town not far from where Derek was from, but to me her rounded vowels and articulated consonant endings contrasted pleasantly with our dulled antipodean ones. She wore her dark hair in a sleek New Wave bob with a blonde streak at the front; she carried a basket rather than a schoolbag, and wore court shoes instead of the Dunlops, desert boots, or squeakies the rest of us scuffed around in. She drew and painted. She listened to Big Country, China Crisis, and early Bowie, and was already going to clubs with her other English friends at weekends to dance and socialise. When I inveigled myself into her home, I saw how she offered guests, self-invited or otherwise, hospitality in the form of refreshments, instead of the you-know-where-the-kitchen-is style I was more accustomed to.

Her presence electrified me. I was desperate for her approval and attention, which I sought through asking her opinion on the draft of a novel I'd written called *A Space to Fill*, not letting my limited insight into the causes of my brief foray into anorexia nervosa get in the way of attempting to fictionalise it. Her encouragement of my writing provoked me to press upon her volumes of my diaries, which contained the details of my angst-filled adoration of her interspersed with lines from Shakespeare's 'Sonnet 116'. If she understood that I was determined to push my feelings for her to the edge of doom, she was too kind to mention it; her attempts to suggest that I might, for reasons of self-preservation, want to alter my fixation fell upon my determinedly deaf ears.

The following year, when I was in Year Ten and she in her final year of high school, I took to showing up on her doorstep at all hours in various states of self-pitying intoxication and begging for admission. When Gwen, post-Steve, recommenced loud encounters with blokes she'd picked up from the pub or Parents Without Partners, I marched in the dark to Karen's house, where she would, without asking questions, make me a hot chocolate. I cradled the mug until I calculated the noisy event would have reached its conclusion and wandered home again later in the night. I got my first job at Hungry Jack's, Gosnells, because Karen briefly worked there. When I secured the lead role in the next year's musical, *Bye Bye Birdie*, I was delighted because it demonstrated that becoming like Karen, if not actually Karen, was indeed achievable.

What I could not properly imitate was Karen's contentedness with what life presented to her. She quite liked the idea of working in a bank, she told me as we waited in the queue for a teller one day. I was immediately floored: how could anyone want to spend their days in such a stultifying environment? Any idea I had of my future involved something interesting, which precluded the idea of any regular employment that my limited experience had exposed me to. 'You always want things to be more exciting than they are,' Karen said, in what was her kind approximation of constructive criticism. 'Life just isn't meant to be exciting all the time.'

But I was determined that I was going to make my existence more interesting than what I saw with most of the adults around me, dulled by their jobs, limited in their ambitions, made docile by habit. I didn't know what I was going to do or how I was going to do it, only that I had to try.

...

All the authorities I surreptitiously consulted on the subject – a child health encyclopedia at the library, the Dolly Doctor section of *Dolly* magazine, Deborah Hautzig's second novel *Hey, Dollface* – suggested that my fervent feelings of love toward Karen were a passing phase. To test whether this was indeed the case, I embarked on the project of having, if not a boyfriend, encounters with boys that would give me something normal to compare my other feelings to.

The first candidate for this was a fellow employee at Hungry Jack's, who was seventeen to my fourteen and had his driver's licence. His face might have been studded with acne, but he was friendly and flirted with me consistently over the broiler steamer, which were qualifications enough in my view. When he invited me to the drive-in, I said yes. Mr Broiler Steamer turned up at my house in his grandmother's Hillman Hunter, the back seat of which was covered in his grandmother's crocheted rugs. I hid beneath them as we went through the gate because he didn't want to pay for two tickets to a movie neither of us were going to see. I can't recall whether we'd mutually agreed that this would be the occasion of my deflowering, but I for one was determined to rid myself of the virginity that was no prize in working-class Kelmscott in the mid 80s. The actual event was uncomfortable in a non-specific way, and I was only sure it had taken place when Mr Broiler Steamer emitted a groan and said, 'Oh God, what if you get pregnant?' He clothed himself and urged me to join him kneeling on the crocheted rugs to pray to God to look kindly upon his, not to mention my, sin, the sin of contraception being unavailable to him as a Catholic.

The encounter did nothing to shift my preference from the chaste adoration I aimed at Karen, but it did encourage me to begin taking the Pill to ensure I did not again have the dread-filled contemplation of teenage pregnancy that might dissuade me from further experiments with heterosexuality.

My imitation of Karen's mod-girl cool succeeded in landing me the attention of the boy most wanted by the tough girls at school, AJ. AJ was good-looking, with a carefully gelled flat-top favoured by English migrant boys, and prone to violence. When the call went up at lunchtime that there was a fight on the oval, causing spectators to hurry toward it, AJ was often the chief protagonist. His older brother was on the run because he had killed someone in a pub fight; that and AJ's own reputation made lesser males at school avoid him while making the tough girls swoon. So when a friend of a friend passed on a message that AJ thought I was a top chick and what did I reckon about going out with him, I disguised my surprise and immediately accepted.

There was about as much romance involved with AJ as there had been with Mr Broiler Steamer. Our first date comprised AJ, one of my friends, and a few of AJ's friends drinking goon down at the local park, then wandering around the suburbs looking for unfinished houses to ransack for the rubber seals we used as bracelets. AJ was a surprisingly tender kisser, and I adored the scent of his hair gel, but the subsequent sex on a school oval, with me looking up at the stars while he went about his business, could not match the swooning that being proximate to Karen invoked.

One day AJ turned up at my house dripping with blood. The blood mostly wasn't his: he'd got into a fight, which had descended from punching to grappling. He'd hooked his thumb in the other guy's nostril and loosened it from his face. Even AJ, experienced fighter though he was, found the spray of blood impressive. I enjoyed tending to his wounded knuckles and cleaning the blood off his face and soaking his formerly white t-shirt in cold water. I felt properly adult, tending to the wounds of my injured boyfriend. In later years, when I heard that AJ had done a stretch in prison, I thought about him turning up that day, his gruff gratitude at my ministrations, the tender side of him in the aftermath of violence or passion.

As soon as I had been introduced to alcohol by Gwen's friends, the mystery of adult behaviour under its influence became explicable. But with sex, its chief appeal was gaining access to sides of boys like AJ otherwise not evident. Being with AJ did not make me regard my infatuation with Karen as a passing phase, although it did provide some buffering from the accusation of being a lezzo. Nobody would dare say that to AJ's chick, or, as soon would be the case, his former chick. I was publicly devastated and privately relieved when he decided that whatever had attracted him to me had been spent. He still came to the parties I started hosting during summer at my house when Gwen was out, and I still retained the social benefit of our association in the last days of Year Ten. My preoccupation with what sexual identity might best fit me went into abeyance for a time, because I found a new activity into which I could direct excesses of feeling.

12

One Saturday in 1984, early in Year Ten, my friends and I caught the two trains necessary to go to Fremantle. We chatted and laughed on the long journey on the rattling orange diesel trains with carriage doors that opened manually and generally stayed open during the journey. Kids swung themselves in and out of the door, daring themselves to face oncoming trains and pulling themselves in at the last possible second, until the ticket conductors told them off.

Once in Fremantle, we traipsed over the liquorice-black floors of the markets, a maze of stalls selling everything from soap and incense and flowing Indian fabrics to crepes and cheese and vegetables. I wanted to buy the type of wicker basket Karen had introduced to our school, and I also wanted to buy black nail polish, unavailable in regular chemists and supermarkets. I'd been doing the closing shift at Hungry Jack's on Friday and Saturday nights – which not irregularly entailed mopping up food thrown and blood spattered during fights between the Gosnells boys and the Armadale boys in the restaurant in the early hours of the morning – so I had money to spend. I purchased a basket, then we all went into the busy stall selling beauty products. The owner looked suspiciously at us, our outer suburban origins apparently evident in our manner; I took umbrage at the way she'd asked me not to pick anything up unless I was going to buy it, and I decided I didn't want the nail polish after all.

When we emerged into the sea-smelling air, one of my friends stopped. She drew various items from her sleeve, including the black nail polish.

'How'd you do that?' we pressed her, astonished. We were right next to her, and didn't notice.

She'd learned from a cousin, she explained. It was part observation, part nerve, part sleight of hand. You have to know if shopkeepers are looking. The woman was so focused on me that my friend knew she was safe. You only take what you can comfortably fit up a sleeve; if you put things in a bag, it could be searched. You pick up and put down what you are not taking with the same unhurried air as the things you are taking. You make sure you keep your face calm, your eyes steady.

On the way back home I walked into the local deli. My pulse had already quickened; the coloured cellophane of the confectionary aisle seemed especially bright. I bought a packet of Chesterfield cigarettes – although still fourteen, I looked enough like a legal adult for shopkeepers and liquor store owners to turn a blind eye – and on the way out, I lingered by the chocolate bars until the man behind the counter was serving the next person. It was all I could do not to run to the exit once I'd manoeuvred the bar into place, casually hooking the same arm under my basket and wandering outside. I waited for the chase, heart accelerating in case this was needed, cheeks hot, but I walked on, unmolested. A wave of glee rushed through me, an aliveness I had been missing. It was like being on stage, but I did not have to wait for a performance now.

In the same way I could no longer control my appetite once I'd resumed eating, I soon found I possessed the same restless craving if I went too long without shoplifting something. Although I did compensate for being brought up wearing second-hand, home-made or hand-me-down clothing by now stealing the latest white jackets, mostly what I wanted was not the items I stole but the adrenaline that accompanied the stealing. I stole make-up palettes, nail polish, shoes, laxatives, books, underwear, tights; once I stole a rainbow-coloured clown wig. I never took anyone with me. I felt safer being by myself, and drew less attention. I dressed neatly and was polite to shopkeepers and sales assistants. If I felt I was being watched, I did not proceed. I never had to run and I never got caught.

Two things eventually caused me to stop pilfering. One of the tough girls at school got wind that I had stolen the much-coveted white jacket I wore. She instructed me to shoplift more of them: she said she would sell them and we would split the proceeds. When I protested, she said she'd tell if I didn't, and so I did. I stole a number of the jackets, one at a time, from a shop in Perth, and my blackmailer sold them and did indeed split the profits.

Gwen might not have noticed my radical weight loss the year before, but now she was alerted to the fact that I was working less and buying more. She phoned my bank and learned that my savings were growing; she opened the top cupboard of my wardrobe and was rained on by an assortment of items I neither wanted nor needed, including the multicoloured wig.

My early adoption of drinking, sex, and parties did not concern Gwen, or if they did, she must have felt she was hardly in a position to chastise me over these activities. We had never discussed the eating disorder that was beginning to morph into bulimia. But she was a daughter of a policeman, and stealing was the one thing she could neither understand nor tolerate.

So, after I promised her I wouldn't do it again, she finally made the call to the child and adolescent psychiatrist whose number she'd been given the previous year, and made an appointment. The psychiatrist's name was Dr Ian McAlpine.

...

Not long after I won the lead in the musical, early in Year Ten, I was chosen to be one of a handful of Kelmscott students to audition for the Western Australian Youth Theatre Company. Youth Theatre was a vehicle for encouraging performers from public schools across the metropolitan area to develop their skills, and Youth Theatre productions were well known and attended by established theatre people. Neither Karen nor anyone from Kelmscott the previous year had been successful, so I did not rate my chances, mindful of the last time I'd got my hopes up about an audition. I prepared the required soliloquy from *The Diary of Anne Frank*, where Anne is imagining herself out of where she is (Look, Peter, the sky!) and performed it in front of an expressionless panel. I was given a script to sightread, and a topic to improvise, and then caught the train back to Kelmscott with my fellow auditionees.

This time I was the one receiving the letter of acceptance, and an invitation to a fortnight of acting workshops during the August school holidays in far distant Subiaco, along with my friend Esti. At the workshops, we were electrified; at school our theatrical demeanours made us different, approved of by some teachers and regarded with impatience by others. Here, we were encouraged to harness our excessive energies and at the same time hone the raw talents we had. We had voice coaches, dance lessons, and movement training, and at the end of the fortnight we were selected for productions to be held at the beginning of the next school year.

Esti and I were cast in the Yukio Mishima play *Kantan*, about a dream pillow revealing to its angsty main character the futility of existence. I relished the strange story of its author, a closeted gay man who committed ritual suicide after a failed right-wing coup, a story conveyed to us with glinting eyes by our director, ST. ST was a member of a cult stationed in Fremantle, had extravagantly long red hair and swore casually in front of parents and patrons alike. ST believed that an actor needed to have full awareness of their bodies, and how best to convey emotion through them. To this end, we spent a lot of time running around the rehearsal space embodying particular states, or devising how one would represent a particular feeling without words. One such exercise led to the mostly female cast surrounding the male lead as he lay prostrate on the floor, proceeding to give him lovebites over the exposed parts of his torso.

My dreams of being an actor, perhaps already flimsy, were dashed when ST, in some frustration at how hard we were to corral after all the lovebites and excesses of emotion, chastised us by saying, 'None of you have any *technique*!' I had no idea how one got technique in acting – possibly by following ST's instructions – but, ever sensitive to criticism, I decided that this must mean I had limited acting talent, despite being in the Youth Theatre Company, and my desire to perform was relegated to the same dark recess as my desire to be a musician.

We were rehearsing in the week that my cousin Lara died. Unlike the just-put-up-with-it response I got from my family, and the just-drink-yourself-numb response I witnessed in Gwen, ST encouraged me to let it out. I flung myself about the rehearsal room, screamed, collapsed into ST's arms, wept in a way that I wished connected to my actual feelings, but which felt merely performative. Nevertheless, even if it didn't provide comfort immediately, it was instructive to be shown a different way of responding to things, to regard emotions with interest instead of fear and avoidance.

During the weeks of rehearsals for *Kantan* and in the weeks following Lara's death, an unsoothable disquiet disrupted my sleep and played on my nerves. Now that I was deprived of the adrenaline surge of shoplifting, and with the physical exertions of rehearsal taking the merest edge off, I felt that the agitation was akin to hunger, and so I ate. At lunchtime I ate KFC; when I got home from rehearsals I made thick pancakes and soaked them with butter and honey. The eating dulled the sensations for a time, only to return once I became sensible of the calories I had consumed in my attempts to swallow my feelings along with the food. Gwen was concerned. When I emerged from the bathroom at the end of January 1985 with the realisation I had put on six kilos in three weeks, she said, 'You'd better watch it, love.'

If my ballooning weight was obvious even to Gwen, I thought, I was really in trouble.

Despite exhorting myself each morning before rehearsal to eat modestly, by lunchtime I found myself walking back to KFC. I remember thinking that if only they let me behind the counter, I could have eaten everything in sight and still not been sated.

I reasoned that if I could not contain my appetite, then I needed to reduce its collateral. I began visiting the toilet after each meal and inserting my fingers down my throat, choking until I heaved the half-masticated food into the bowl then flushing over and over again until the last residue was gone. I was spent, numbed with effort, both disgusted and relieved. My weight did not reduce, but at least it stopped going upward.

The beginning of Year Eleven coincided with the three-week season of *Kantan*. We performed each night until nearly 11pm, then Gwen picked me up and we drove nearly an hour back to Kelmscott. I had always been under the impression that attendance in upper school was more or less voluntary, so when teachers chastised me for my lateness, I growled that I was tired, and also, didn't they know that I was representing the school in this production? I was told that there were no special circumstances and no excuses.

Even without being set against what I perceived to be the unreasonable exercise of authority, now that Karen wasn't at school anymore, I was less inclined to attend than I had been. In the last term of Year Ten, once Karen's compulsory classes had ended, my aunty, newly separated and living with Derek, was so willing to write notes excusing my attendance at school that the education department sent a truancy officer to quiz us about the nature of my attendance-preventing maladies. It wasn't that I didn't enjoy learning.

Most of my truanting days were spent with my cousin watching various trials in the District Court. I was still writing short stories and parodies and poems, and reading everything I could lay my hands on, except for anything that was on the school curriculum. I'd had interest from *Dolly* magazine when I'd sent them my melodramatic anorexia-inspired novella, but when they'd suggested I write teen romance, I sniffed to myself that I wanted to write real books, and didn't bother to reply. Whatever it was I wanted to do, I knew that school played no part in it.

The final showdown occurred one Monday morning, just after Easter, when I turned up to school sporting a new haircut. An apprentice hairdresser friend, displaying more enthusiasm than competency, had unleashed his developing cutting and bleaching skills on my bob, turning it into something reminiscent of an alarmed orange echidna. In spite of the regular displays of violence witnessed and experienced by students and occasionally teachers, the high school had a strict uniform policy, which forbade hair dye.

After a brief visit to the deputy headmaster, I was given a two-week suspension and sent home. I was outraged at the school's continuing persecution on such spurious grounds and enjoyed sharing the story of my persecution with all and sundry, even convincing a television crew to do a story on the pettiness of hair-based offences. Gwen and I went to visit the school's guidance counsellor, who told me that she could not dissuade the deputy from his determination to make an example of me, but that if I wanted to go to university to study journalism – the only writing-related course I knew about – then I could always go and work for two years and do Year Twelve at a senior college later on. I officially withdrew from school the same day. My English teacher gave me a glowing statement of recommendation, tactfully omitting the cause of my truncated secondary education, and I went out to find work.

In 1985 the chief line of work open to a fifteen-year-old high school dropout was in food outlets, which would have been fine had the fifteen-year-old not been in the midst of attempting to wrest control over her life through bingeing and purging. In the six months after I left school, I worked at Hungry Jack's, Chicken Treat, the deli section of a supermarket, and a bakery. I briefly managed to get a job as a checkout chick in a supermarket, but my inaccuracy with the push-button till saw me return to fast food and faster access to bingeable items.

Gwen had recently started work as an accountant, having finished her degree the previous year. It was hard for her to get a job as a forty-year-old graduate, but even when she did, she found the work she'd fought so hard to secure was stultifying, even for someone as enamoured with the ordering of numbers as she was. To add to this, she was refusing to get the hysterectomy her doctor recommended due to a growing number of growths in her uterus that caused her to bleed heavily for increasing weeks of any given month. I couldn't understand her reluctance, and when I asked, she said, 'It means I can't have any more babies.'

'But Mum,' I said. 'You haven't been able to have a baby for – how old am I? – fifteen years.'

'Still,' she shrugged.

I later realised this desire to cling to her long-faulty reproductive organs was an expression of a connection with the son she had given away, but at the time it seemed an unfathomable stubbornness. Later, I also realised her reluctance to deal with her ill health was an expression of a disconnection from her body generally. Unless it demanded particular types of gratification, or protested in ways requiring hospitalisation, she proceeded through life by ignoring it and any symptoms it displayed.

While her exhaustion gave me a welcome respite from the noisy visits from Mikes, Allans, and Steves, it also meant that she was asleep by 7pm most weeknights, leaving me in peace to binge and purge on whatever I'd brought home from work that day.

Even though it later transpired that most of my friends were going through various iterations of disordered eating, we did not, or could not, speak about it to each other. This left me only one place I could be honest about what I was doing and, more to the point, how it was leaving me feeling out of control and desperate. As 1985 wore on and I came loose from the things that had tethered me to any helpful sense of myself, this place was where I told the one person who listened that I was unsure if I could bear the thought of going on at all.

When Gwen first made the appointment to see Dr Mac, in November 1984, I was full of anticipation. In the Australia of the 1970s and 80s, the general sense one got, growing up, was that if you had a problem, you kept it to yourself and got on with it. In its blokey, laconic culture you no more expressed a feeling than communicated your achievements. You took the piss out of yourself and others, and if you couldn't take a joke, well, tough titties. Any tall poppies were cut down to the level playing field more appropriate to the convicts who'd set the tone for the future white settlers. Nor were you supposed to complain, which deafened the white invaders to hearing the consequences of their actions on the Aboriginal people who were variously massacred, displaced, or forced into slavery, and if they coped with the violence and genocidal brutality by drinking the rum the colonists brought with them, they were pilloried for that too. With such a background, newfangled American ideas of therapy, or older German ones about talking cures, were viewed with deep suspicion. If you were so fucked in the head you needed to see a professional about it, you were regarded as being already beyond help.

I, however, had a different view of therapy, because I'd read books where girls were saved from their tortured selves by the judicious intervention of sage psychiatric treatment. Sure, Sylvia Plath had killed herself, but that was because of Ted Hughes: I already knew *The Bell Jar* was barely disguised autobiography. I imagined a therapist like Dr Nolan, the female therapist whose sensible wisdom rescues Esther Greenwood / Sylvia Plath from herself. I'd disregarded the first one, the one who had prescribed her electroconvulsive therapy and failed to take notice of anything she was saying, either directly or indirectly.

Dr Mac, as he was known by his patients, was a leading child psychiatrist who headed the state's main adolescent psychiatric hospital, Hillview Terrace Child and Adolescent Psychiatric Hospital, known as Hillview. I did not know this when I turned up with Gwen, wearing one of my customary pencil skirts I'd sewn myself, a men's shirt I'd cut the sleeves out of, and a wide black belt, my hair still spiked and dyed, and pointed court shoes. In the waiting room there were small chairs for children and bigger ones for us adolescents and the parents of both, who wore the pained expressions of those at their wits' end. The windows at reception looked out onto the gardens of Hillview hospital, its thick green lawns regularly shadowed by the pine trees that lined the driveway. As I sat, waiting, I was hopeful that surely, now I was here, somebody would tell me what I was to do with myself, my thoughts, my life.

In our first session, Dr Mac spoke to me first, and then Gwen, and then both of us together, getting background if not consensus on why we were there.

In subsequent sessions, Dr Mac seemed warmer and less formal. He only needed to ask a question and I was off, narrating events and, from time to time, my feelings about them. He did not judge anything I said; at first, he would listen with his eyes half closed, like a cat. The advice I'd been wanting was never forthcoming, but I took his 'hmm-mms' and nods as a kind of support for the things I was proposing. He was less an oracle than an avuncular listening ear. He never took notes, and seemed to be paying me his undivided attention, which was a rare enough event from an adult that I began to crave it.

Over the summer that Lara died, when I was sourcing most of my caloric intake from KFC, Dr Mac first began hugging me in greeting, then moving his chair closer to mine during sessions, and finally running his hand over and underneath my clothing, while sitting with his other arm casually leaning on the back of my chair. He continued to make 'mm-hmm' sounds as I both expounded upon my misery and refrained from remarking on – or even showing that I was noticing – his wandering hand. I wondered if his behaviour, which made my flesh shrink, was part of my therapy. So I did what I had learned, which was to ignore what was happening and channel my feelings of fear and anxiety into self-loathing activities, such as dysfunctional eating, drinking, and sex, which in turn required more therapy.

The self-loathing activities also, around the time of my sixteenth birthday, led me to the conclusion that I was tired of life and would prefer not to be living it. Derek had forgotten my sixteenth birthday until

I reminded him, my peers were off at school celebrating sixteenths with the people they saw every day, rather than people who had drifted out of school and out of consciousness, and I was generally and specifically miserable. This was not the sweet sixteenth that I had, despite my pose of disdain for mainstream culture and regular life, been expecting. The only thing notable about turning sixteen was that the two muscled thirty-year-old doormen at the cinema complex I worked in invited me and my also-just-turned-sixteen friend over to a house in Hilton so they could show us what men, and not boys, could do. If Dragon sang 'Are You Old Enough?', the answer now was 'Apparently'.

Having sampled what I thought was all of life's experiences, I'd now had enough. So I announced this to Dr Mac and was alarmed at the pace at which he completed the admission forms to the adolescent psychiatric hospital next door. Because I was sixteen, he didn't even inform Gwen, except by a standard admission letter outlining the things I was and wasn't allowed to bring to hospital in a week's time. On the front of the admission brochure he gave me, I wrote, '10am Sunday', and underneath, 'Tell Mum.'

I was relieved. I wanted a way out of my life, which I'd seemed to have messed up while trying to take control of it, and if death wasn't it, then going to an adolescent psychiatric hospital was surely a reasonable second.

Although there was no need to do so, I decided that I was leaving the cinema and, in particular, leaving the doormen who'd stopped flirting with me and become superior and sneery. When I went to collect my last payslip and say goodbye to the women behind the candy bar, I found myself, to my considerable and then increasing surprise, making the acquaintance of my replacement.

Her name was Carita.

EXPERIENCE VICARIOUS
TRAUMA THROUGH YOUR FRIEND
BEING RAPED AND MURDERED
 BY A JAPANESE SERIAL KILLER

13

As I walked across the violently striped carpet from the flight of stairs I'd just ascended and up to the candy bar, I found it necessary to tell myself not to stare.

Carita was standing to one side of the freezers in which the teeth-breaking choc bombs were stored after we made them out the back. I'd seen pretty girls before, but Carita was something else: large-eyed, high-cheekboned, perfectly proportioned to my sixteen-year-old eyes, ridiculously graceful in her carriage and gestures. Immediately I understood this girl was from another planet, and there was no way I would have anything in common with her: just the sight of her made me feel awkward in my skin. It wasn't that I was comparing myself to Carita: she was so beautiful that there was no point. She was yet more proof of why the only place I belonged was in the psych hospital I was about to enter, no doubt filled with awkward, depressed misfits like me. Carita symbolised a type of existence, pleasing and easy to navigate, so far from me that merely looking at her evinced a bittersweet longing for the imagined and the impossible.

There were a number of casual candy bar staff employed at the cinema, all from the same public but upmarket school which resembled mine in no way at all. They were to a person lovely but groomed the way my cousin's private school girlfriends were, having opinions about clothing, eye make-up and skincare completely alien to mine, and full of gems of wisdom about topics such as why you should never wear tights darker than your dress, and other information I couldn't believe anyone cared about. Carita was evidently drawn from this group, dressed in the same studied casual way, curls of her beach-girl hair framing her heart-shaped face.

One of the casuals, emerging from the back room, now said, 'Hey, Jules, this is Carita.'

Then Carita smiled, and all the longing that her unreasonably good looks had generated dissolved. Her smile was kind and shy and made me want to protect her from the base impurity of the world.

I was definitely, I concluded, going mad. Just as well I was going to a mental hospital, I joked to myself.

'Carita's from my school,' the casual confirmed. 'She's your replacement.'

One of the doormen sidled up, leaning his beefy forearms on the black countertop. 'Hi Carita,' he said to her. To me he said, 'What a replacement, eh?'

I wanted to punch him right in the middle of his smug, supercilious smile.

'She's way out of your league,' I hissed in his ear.

'Not like you, eh?'

When the casual invited Carita to come to lunch with us, my awkwardness reappeared. I didn't eat and instead blustered on about how I was quitting because I was going to a loony bin for teenagers, and how I hoped I would get better, and how I wanted to go back to school at the new senior college that had opened. Carita offered that she had just left school, even though she was in Year Ten and technically wasn't allowed to, and gave me a look I couldn't decipher. For all the world it seemed that she wanted to say something to me. What could she possibly want to say, I wondered as I walked back down the steps, away from the cinema and my perfect replacement and the reminders of all the bad decisions I'd made. I was relieved to be stepping out of my own life, to no longer have to put up with the exhausting rounds of trying and failing to control my eating, my thoughts, my tedious self. By going into hospital, I was admitting failure. I had defeated myself. The fight, I thought, was over.

Gwen dropped me at the hospital on Sunday morning, before the other residents had returned from weekend leave later in the afternoon. The hospital was an old two-storey building at the end of a long driveway, obscured by pine trees. The stairs creaked as we climbed them to see my single room with its plain old dressing table and view of a shiny tin roof and the home for autistic children behind the hospital. Gwen did her best to look sober and normal, then hightailed it back to Kelmscott in her purple Kingswood, perhaps to reflect on being the parent of a teenager in a psychiatric hospital, or perhaps to drink an extra King Brown to put on hold the feelings that may have attended such reflection.

When I came downstairs I found that an ex-resident had dropped in for a cup of tea.

'Hey Stuart,' she said to the nurse. 'Remember when I made Sue that smashed glass sandwich?'

'You lot were the worst,' Stuart said.

'She didn't eat it, but,' the ex-resident smiled.

I was relieved when the other new resident arrived. She was awkward-looking, overweight, and when we sat at the dining table to have lunch, she started emitting quiet sobs. After a few moments I joined in.

'Oh, come on,' joked Stuart. 'We're not that bad, are we?'

I wondered what the other residents would be like. Would it be *One Flew Over the Cuckoo's Nest*–style mayhem, complete with smashed glass sandwiches? Would it be inhabited with Sylvia Plaths and Virginia Woolfs, tortured geniuses whose suffering produced unsurpassable works that spoke to the souls of people like me? Or would there be merely lots of muted sobbing, as at the lunch table?

I watched as the other residents returned from weekend leave with their parents or parent-substitutes. One girl stomped wordlessly up the stairs, leaving her mother wide-eyed at the bottom. The parents seemed uniformly anxious and unsmiling. Their offspring were a variable lot: a couple of normal-looking girls, a soft-looking boy who hid behind his fringe, a girl who yelled rather than spoke, a boy who ran up and poked the yelling girl and ran off again. Stuart introduced me as people came in, but they didn't seem particularly interested. I sat and shredded a paper napkin into tiny pieces, trying to listen without looking.

Then a quiet voice said, 'Hi.'

It was Carita.

...

'You live here?' I said. 'You're an inpatient?'

'I was trying to tell you at lunch,' she said.

'But,' I said. 'You?'

She shrugged, and told me she'd been there for five months already.

'Why?'

In my sixteen-year-old logic, there was no reason for someone who looked like Carita to be in a place like this. She didn't seem messed up.

She explained that she'd taken an overdose when everyone thought she was at school. She almost died. And then she came here.

I felt inadequate in a new way. Carita had wanted to die, and she had done something direct about it. I had wanted to die, but I'd eaten a cupboard worth of food, vomited, then cried to Dr Mac.

I didn't ask her why she'd wanted to die in the first place.

14

Life in Hillview was like school camp in some ways, while retaining a hint of *One Flew Over the Cuckoo's Nest* in others. An anorexic girl remained upstairs for months, lying on a sheepskin so she didn't get bedsores, not allowed out of bed to go to the toilet unless she'd eaten and put on weight. We were allowed to visit her when she was not engaged in her mealtime battles of wills, during which she cried and reluctantly ate teaspoons of food at a time. A boy who'd tried to set fire to his own house was sent home for hitting another girl. One fleshy boy refused to move or exercise, convinced he'd damage his joints or run out of heartbeats if he did so.

In this company I felt relatively normal.

I only binged one time when I was in hospital, on one of the first nights. I was anxious and pacing, so I snuck down the creaking stairs, opened the glass-fronted industrial fridge, and started shovelling leftover cold apple pie and custard into my mouth. One of the kind psych nurses walked in. She didn't have to ask what I was doing, but I said, 'Oh, I was still hungry,' put the bowl back, and ran back up the stairs. I was too afraid to be caught vomiting, so I lay in bed, anxiously wondering how many kilos I was trapping in my body from doing so, the shame of being caught making me want to claw my own face off. But I survived the night and never raided the fridge again.

This was just as well, as the approach to eating disorders, aside from trapping anorexic girls in bed, was to never allow the person with disordered eating to discuss food, or weight, or the actual conduct that landed one in hospital in the first place. The hospital was based on milieu therapy, which held that if you changed someone's environment, you could allow them to defeat their undesirable behaviours. The other aspect of milieu therapy was that you could learn positive social interactions and experience positive peer pressure. One of the nurses, when I asked, explained to me that the staff, with their various personality characteristics, would allow us to work on our relationship skills. We would be attracted to, or repelled by, staff who reminded us of people in our families of origin; we would learn new ways of relating in a safe environment. It sounded great, in theory.

It certainly was the case that the hospital possessed psychiatric nurses with various psychological dispositions which would not be unfamiliar to anyone with a dysfunctional family. What was also familiar to us, who after all were not in an adolescent psychiatric hospital because we came from families known for their stability or predictability, was the complete lack of what one might call boundaries from the adults charged with our care.

Some of the conduct was benign. One nurse, for example, took a few of us to her church, a modest building in a neighbouring suburb. The minister was not in robes, and his pitch and tone were more strident than what I was used to in the Uniting and Lutheran churches I'd been taken to by my family. His pitch continued to rise through his sermon, his tone more urgent, until members of the congregation one by one stood up, muttering and calling. One woman staggered toward the minister, arms outstretched and eyes half-closed, like an extra in *Poltergeist*. The minister praised the Lord, added something about His power of healing, and touched her forehead, causing her to fall back in what appeared to be some kind of seizure, which did not seem very healthful to me. The other residents and I exchanged looks of bewilderment, not only about what we were witnessing but also that we were the ones considered mentally wanting. But at least the nurse was trying to improve our spiritual wellbeing. Such concern for wellbeing of any kind was not always observed.

There were nurses who mocked the extreme emotion coursing through our adolescent hearts, or our expression of the same. Our behaviour was assessed and criticised, both privately and in front of others. For example, a week after four of us older girls had broken out, bought a flagon of moselle from the bottle shop on the corner, and sat on a kerb drinking it, I developed a sore throat and intermittent fever. A blood test for glandular fever came back negative. As my symptoms worsened and were attended by lethargy mental and physical, I was forced by staff to go on outings, join in softball, and go to the beach, despite my complaints. One nurse accused me of faking illness; another commented that I was doing it for attention and that I needed to be more direct in expressing my feelings. When a second blood test, taken to prove once and for all that I was malingering, showed glandular fever,

I was sent upstairs, all cutlery was sanitised, and my 'illness behaviour' was never again referred to.

The head nurse, Sue, inspired fear and awe in both the residents and the staff. While she wasn't quite Nurse Ratched, neither was she entirely dissimilar. She was forthright and blunt, naming the residents' failings in behaviour and patterns of thought, and challenging those who disagreed with her. I saw her capacity for kindness in the way she treated the soft-fleshed boy, asking him gentle questions, coaxing his reluctant responses. Mostly, however, she would engage in stand-up disagreements with her adolescent charges, maintaining a steady voice and unnerving eye contact while enumerating their failings until they retreated.

I thought Sue was wonderful. I understood that she was in charge, that she was strong, that this represented a way of being a female leader in the world. Her being manipulative and, as it turned out, disturbed did not dent my admiration. Telling the truth, however unpalatable, seemed an admirable goal. Not long after a young, depressed boy entered the hospital, Sue began losing an astonishing amount of weight, the previous excess of which had been the one area in which she showed any sign of lack of control, in turn inspiring in me one last, brief effort at anorexia.

Being in control, I also decided, once Carita started complaining to me, that we should tell Sue about Dr Mac.

...

Being the grandchild of a policeman, I believed in authority. If there was a wrong that should be righted, you appealed to the nearest person or organisation to act on your behalf.

It was shocking to me to discover, when I became an inpatient, that Dr Mac's wandering hands were not just part of my therapy: he did it to everybody, including Carita. I felt mildly betrayed by this. I had believed he had a special relationship with me, but now I understood that I had been mistaken. I also felt my protectiveness over Carita rise up. The fear I felt on her behalf on account of her fragility, her innocence, her ethereal beauty, emboldened me to lead the charge on stopping his hands wandering over Carita, or any of us.

My ears ringing with Sue's exhortations to speak directly about things, and flanked by a small posse of residents, including Carita, I approached Sue.

'Sue,' I said, 'can you ask Dr Mac to stop touching us?'

Sue did not ask for more detail on the unwanted touching. Her opinion and advice was, 'Oh, he's just touchy-feely. If you don't like it, tell him to stop.'

The report and request were not, unlike the references to my glandular fever 'illness behaviour', referred to in my hospital notes. However, following these instructions, I attended my next session with Dr Mac. When he drew our chairs together, I said, 'Dr Mac, I don't want you to touch me anymore.'

Dr Mac seemed hurt by this request, and my feelings of strength and clarity shrank to a guilty wondering if I had done the right thing. He moved his chair back to the psychiatrist-appropriate space he'd used when Gwen attended a session, and he never moved it back again. After this, Dr Mac's attitude toward me chilled. He seemed to favour the other girls, especially Carita, who remained too scared to say anything to him. I was offered fewer and fewer appointments with him. I felt punished.

Carita's appointments with Dr Mac increased at the same time mine became less frequent. When he visited the hospital, she would hide under her bed until he had safely returned to the clinic. One of the psychologists at the clinic later recalled seeing Dr Mac standing close to Carita, who was leaning against the wall, his arm above her head. Both of them were laughing.

Not long after we'd both left the hospital, in 1986, Carita and I moved into a flat together. Gwen had decided she was moving in with her latest boyfriend, a round-gutted, silent man called Brian who exclusively wore tiny Hard Yakka shorts that revealed his testicles when he sat down and who hailed from a suburb even more bogan than Kelmscott. I refused to accompany her. Carita, after nine months in hospital, and like so many of us after a separation from them, did not want to move back with her family, so we found a place in walking distance of the hospital.

Into the flat we brought foam mattresses purchased from camping stores, begged a fridge and a kitchen table off Gwen, and set up Carita's record player in the living room. I had started working from six until nine each morning and studying Year Eleven by correspondence; she was working as a model in the city three nights a week, doing runway shows. The flat was frequented by hospital residents and ex-residents, and what we lacked in cleaning ability we made up for in social liveliness.

We were excited to be living independently. We might have been sixteen but we felt older. So, one windy, rainy night in June, we decided to host a house-warming. Carita had invited some of her high school friends over to the house-warming; I'd invited our former fellow hospital residents. It was going be great. We would celebrate our freedom, the bright future we had now that we were free of school and the hospital, free of our parents and our old lives.

But the first visitor to arrive – early, before the party had started – was Dr Mac.

. . .

Dr Mac arrived with Carita, with whom he'd just had an outpatient session.

Carita raised her eyebrows at me as she carried in the bottle of champagne Dr Mac had brought with him.

'Happy house-warming, girls,' he said.

He came in, and sat down on the floor with us, as we had no furniture aside from the kitchen table, and poured champagne. He put his arm around Carita, who shrank from him, with me on his other side. He rubbed Carita's back and at one point flicked her bra strap. The atmosphere was tense but I kept talking brightly, as I always did when I was uncomfortable, and ripped holes in my tights. Dr Mac put his finger in the holes of one of the tights and traced the hole, smiling the way he always did when he had his hand under my clothing. I did not move away.

When Carita's schoolfriends arrived later, Dr Mac made his exit, taking one of the ex-residents to her calisthenics lesson on his way home. On his way out he said to Carita, 'Don't tell anyone I've been here, will you?' She agreed.

Even though Dr Mac's visit made us feel uncomfortable, it was only slightly more uncomfortable than he made us when he visited the hospital. But it was the way one of Carita's friends responded after their intersection – 'That was your *psychiatrist*?' – that made us pause.

Later, when the house-warming was over and the only people left were Carita, another ex-resident, one of Carita's male friends, and me, we were agitated. Was it wrong for Dr Mac to have come over? He told Carita she was not to say anything. But he hadn't told me not to.

'Do they all know about it?' I said. 'The staff? Do they know he came here?'

Against Carita's wishes, I called the hospital and asked to speak to Peter, one of the nurses I trusted, but he wasn't there. I eventually asked D, the nurse who answered, if Dr Mac had got home all right. He said he would check, sounding puzzled. I asked him to promise not to tell. Then Dr Mac called. He spoke to Carita, and her face was serious.

'You shouldn't have told the staff,' she said to me when she got off the phone. 'You could get Dr Mac in a lot of trouble.'

'I told D not to say anything, and he did,' I snapped. 'It's not my fault.'

'You shouldn't trust them,' Carita said. 'You should know by now you can't trust them.'

We sat around the table, agitated. We took turns scribbling in my diary.

'What's real?' I asked. 'Is this real?'

'Friends are real,' the ex-resident said. 'People. Who you can reach out and touch.'

'We're involved in someone else's mind,' Carita said. 'Mac's mind. That's the problem. We need to free ourselves.'

'The things you care for and love cannot crumble,' the ex-resident said.

'I need to walk,' I said. 'Let's go. Let's ask them what the story is.'

In rain so cold it made us laugh and run, the four of us made our way on the wet footpaths down Albany Highway to the hospital, occasionally sheltered from the weather by the awnings of closed shops. We jumped in puddles, splashing and stomping.

After making our way up the long driveway, the pines *shhhing* above us in the whipping wind, we stood throwing gravel at the hospital's windows.

Eventually the nurse I'd spoken to earlier came out, brought us in, and gave us cups of warm Milo. Face to face I lost my nerve to ask whether Dr Mac's visit was okay. D drove us back to the flat in the hospital van.

Later, unknown to us, the friend from Carita's school mentioned it to his mother, who happened to be a social worker for a sexual assault centre. She wrote letter after letter to health department heads about the inappropriate behaviour her son had witnessed at the flat. When they didn't respond, she wrote again. The one letter she got was brief and dismissive. She followed the letters up until she managed to secure a brief and dismissive meeting with mental health administrators, who assured her that her complaints had been duly noted.

At the time, in 1986, nobody asked us about what had happened, and we wouldn't have expected them to. What had really happened, after all? Dr Mac had visited us at home. He'd brought champagne. He didn't behave any differently from the way he always did. Only the location was different.

The next day the sense of unreality I felt intensified. Carita told me to write down a list of the things that were bothering me. I listed betrayal by D, the nurse; Gwen deserting me; not being able to cope with schoolwork; loneliness because there was no-one to trust; Dr Mac making me feel strange; instability; fear of failure.

Carita talked me through each one, then took my pencil and crossed each of them out. The one most heavily crossed out was the line about Dr Mac.

'There is no failure, Jules,' she said. 'Accept it all, and you're not vulnerable anymore.'

Then we wrote lists of what we wanted to do, where we wanted to be. From life, I said I wanted accomplishment, creativity, individuality. Carita wanted to be special, to feel content, to be loved and to love. We both imagined happiness, even if we weren't sure how we were going to arrive at it.

Surely our determination to achieve it would be enough.

15

Not long after the house-warming, Carita brought home a new friend whom she'd met modelling.

Lynda was tall, tan, and languid, and took to walking around the flat wearing lingerie bought for her by admiring married men. She and Carita were infatuated with each other, and began sleeping, entwined, on the mattress on Carita's bedroom floor. Carita told me that Lynda was one of eight children, and her mother was a drunk, and she'd brought herself up.

'Look at her now,' Carita would say. 'She's so beautiful, you wouldn't know what she's been through.'

'You're more beautiful,' I'd say, but Carita wouldn't hear it.

In my opinion, Lynda urged Carita on to do things she would not have done by herself. They found themselves, at sixteen, invited to hotel rooms with visiting celebrities. They attended parties thrown by policemen, who advised them on how to identify unmarked vehicles and how long particular drugs remained in one's system. Carita told me how Lynda was making extra money on top of modelling: Lynda had started going out with a wealthy, older married man, taken photographs of them together, and then proceeded to extort money from him. When I suggested to Carita this might be a dangerous activity, she said, 'Lynda's not scared of anything.'

In keeping with this observation, Carita and Lynda announced that they were going to hitchhike around Australia in September 1986. I was hurt at Carita's sudden departure but glad to be away from Lynda's unnerving presence, and stayed on in the flat with another ex-resident. When Gwen moved to a suburb even more distant than Kelmscott, into the first house she'd owned since leaving Derek eight years previously, I went with her. I got straight As for Year Eleven, including ninety-eight percent for my final English exam and, the minute I was able, my driver's licence.

I was ready to go somewhere, but without Carita, I felt I had nowhere to go.

...

Carita reappeared in early 1987, alone. She'd dyed her hair black. She was different: she was not the vulnerable, scared girl I'd met at the cinema in 1985. Something in her had grown wary.

I drove to her shared flat in Maylands, where she told me, bit by bit, what she and Lynda had done. They'd hitchhiked across Australia in trucks and cars, taking advantage of every man who thought he was taking advantage of them. Carita told me of one guy whose place they'd stayed at: while he was sleeping, they took everything valuable they could carry and left. She also showed me a series of proofs of herself and Lynda, posing naked, smiling for the camera.

Before she'd gone away, Carita had refused to have pictures taken with a professional photographer her mother had recommended, pronouncing him as sleazy. He'd wanted her to do shots that were too sexual for her liking. Plus, she didn't like the way he looked at her.

I stared at the proofs.

'Oh Jules,' she said. 'I feel like I've lost my innocence.'

Perhaps because I reminded her of other times that didn't involve hitching, robbing, and disrobing, we started seeing more of each other, particularly when she moved in with her mother again, sleeping on a couch in her mother's flat in Fremantle. I hated living with Gwen, seeing what I haughtily perceived as her limited life and narrow horizons; I hated living past the last stop on the train line, so far from everything. Carita and I discovered simultaneously that our lives were better in each other's company, and suddenly I found myself as her new Lynda.

We partied when the America's Cup was on in January 1987; we went to the markets and ate crepes, we drove out to a Christian-run hostel in which one of the former hospital residents was staying, which was filled with recovering addicts and mentally ill young people. All the way back we talked about how we wanted something different for ourselves, how we wanted our lives to be different, how we could make something different, together. She came to my cousin's birthday party in Busselton. She wore a pale-green dress as she played pool, and the guys who normally ignored me in favour of joking boisterously with each other now behaved in a strange, excessively polite way, trying to attract her attention, trying to elicit a smile from her.

When my high school friend Kitty suggested Carita and I move into the house she was sharing not far from the city, we hightailed it from the unsettled discomfort we felt at our respective homes and made ourselves a new unsettled discomfort independently. All of my belongings fitted into the purple Galant Derek had bought me; again, I slept on a mattress on the floor. I started Year Twelve by correspondence as the school year began, studying at a desk I'd borrowed from Kitty, but I quickly found it onerous. I was doing six difficult subjects, having refused all sensible advice to make my study load easier, but which was in keeping with my tendency to attempt impossible goals before quitting them with high drama.

Anyone positing the natural domestic tendencies of females would have had their convictions challenged by the level of filth the house quickly achieved. While none of us cleaned in general, the girl whose father owned the house had a reckless disregard for the environment we shared. She would boil two-minutes noodles and eat them from the pot, leaving the pot in the sink with uneaten noodles which, when tipped out, would clog the plug hole. She once left an open tin of jam on the bench: the next morning the bench was covered in a writhing black mass of ants that had marched in through the back door, through the kitchen, and over the dishes to reach their prize.

Carita and I both proceeded to sink into our own depressions. I worked each night in a pizza shop and was regularly bellowed at by the manager, and the enthusiastic responses of my English teacher, Patricia, to my voluminous writings were not enough to re-enliven my usual pleasure in learning. I procured the books Patricia recommended – Hermann Hesse, Anaïs Nin, Virginia Woolf – but the effort of entering their distant, fictional worlds felt too great. I could only return to the books I already knew. I sought comfort from *The Bell Jar* but instead felt unnerved by Plath's descriptions of being slowly and irrevocably separated from the world she inhabited. The happy ending Plath suggested, involving a baby and the marriage it implied, was confected and unconvincing. I knew the truth, which was that the production of real babies had not prevented Plath from inserting her head into an oven and gassing herself. The detail of her pouring glasses of milk for her children and sealing off their doors to protect them from the toxic fumes, oblivious to the more toxic effect of a voluntarily dead mother, confirmed to me that the production of offspring could not be relied on for future solace.

One morning I decided I could bear it all no longer – the filth, the pointless job, the essays I could no longer concentrate on, the misery that kept returning to me, as if it were tidal and life was fixing me to the shore. I gathered all the pills in the house, including a bunch of diet pills, which seemed sufficient to me to find me purchase into eternal life, and swallowed them while everyone was out.

My heart started racing unpleasantly not long into what I had hoped to be my final hours of futility on this mortal coil, and by the time I heard keys in the door I had chickened out and called out for help.

'What did you do that for?' Carita frowned at me in the back of our housemate's car on the way to hospital. 'I told you how stupid it was. Why didn't you talk to me?'

I was taken to have my stomach pumped. Although I warned the doctor that as I was a practised bulimic with a highly developed gag reflex, the mere act of the tube touching the back of my throat rendered unnecessary both the tube and the bowl intended for the toxic contents of my stomach. The doctor stood there, vomit sprayed over his glasses and coat, looking at me as if he wished my friends had left me to meet my intended end. When I got home, Carita sat me down and said, 'We need to get out of here. Anything is better than killing yourself.'

Within days I'd moved my mattress and books back to Gwen's, and packed Derek's army bag that had toured Malaya and Vietnam first with beloved books and then with everything I could cram around them. I withdrew from Year Twelve at Distance Education, my only regret being that I'd no longer be getting feedback on my writing from Patricia. Carita and I went into the old, red-bricked Distance Education building and returned the collection of high-minded, serious books Patricia had lent me. After a brief meeting over hot chocolate in the staff room, Carita declared Patricia a phony and someone who couldn't stand up to life, while Patricia was disturbed that Carita accepted violence so readily. I was disappointed they hadn't liked each other, but it didn't matter now. Carita and I were together, and we were going to be inseparable.

I announced to everyone we were moving to Queensland and never coming back. I hadn't been outside Western Australia before, but my declaration was sincere. Perth was small and boring and restricted, peopled by the small-minded and scared, and I was going toward freedom from all that.

Before we left the share house, when nobody else was home, Carita went into our housemates' rooms and rummaged through all their clothes. She jammed into a bag a pair of tracksuit pants affixed with a brightly painted design our housemate had created, and a few tops, including one I knew Kitty loved. I felt uncomfortable, but I didn't stop her.

We waved goodbye to Perth, my cousin, and Gwen, who stood waving in the wind tunnel of St Georges Terrace; Carita's mother, sister, and Lynda were nearby. I had a hundred dollars that Derek had given me, and money I'd made from hocking my guitar and Carita's sister's clarinet. Lynda ran after the bus, and when Carita lost sight of her, she turned to me, teary.

'My Lynda-friend made me sad,' she said.

I was glad to be able to comfort her. I was determined that I would protect Carita against further sorrow, further disappointments. We would live a new life, a better life, a life we chose, not the one we were born into. It would be Carita and I against the world, against the Dr Macs and Lyndas, against the things in her past she never spoke of but which I knew haunted her.

We were on our way.

16

From the moment I first spied it as a smoggy stain on the horizon, I loved Melbourne. I loved the bustle of it, the clanging trams, the way it seemed attractively old, with its terraces and asphalt footpaths. Gwen had told me how she'd hated Melbourne. My instant love was yet another way in which we were different. Carita and I had booked three nights at a youth hostel in North Melbourne, the maximum number you could book at a time, and I felt I'd come home.

Our first task, aside from walking until our feet blistered, was trying to get money. We lined up for hours at the Department of Social Security, only to be told that because we had no fixed abode we could not register for unemployment benefits, and we were too young to get emergency payments. We begged to be able to stay on at the youth hostel, full as it was with Danish, Swedish, and English backpackers whose stories of travel and adventure we listened to rapturously. We were allowed to stay another few days, but that was strictly it. We moved to another hostel, but the manager from the first came and told us we couldn't just move from hostel to hostel like that. Youth hostels were designed for travellers, not Australian teenagers without homes.

So Carita called Garry.

Garry had been one of the psych nurses at the hospital. Each of us girls had our special male nurse, and Carita's was Garry. He was good-looking, youngish, and Carita had had a crush on him. When he'd left Western Australia he'd given Carita his number, and they'd met up for coffee while I'd stayed at the hostel talking with one of the English girls we'd made friends with. Carita had been swoonily looking forward to coffee, rhapsodising about Garry's English accent and wondering what she would say to him. When I inquired how coffee had gone, Carita told me that Garry had a live-in girlfriend, which disappointed her, but he still wanted to catch up with her again. She also told me that he had offered for us to stay with him if we got into a tight spot. As we were officially now in a tight spot, I stood by the phone box while Carita dialled his number.

Garry was true to his word, so the next day we hitched a ride in a Kent truck to Garry and his girlfriend's house in Doncaster. I didn't like how far away it was from the city to which I already felt attached, but when we arrived, it was good to have our own rooms, and plenty of hot water in a bathroom that did not smell of the twenty other girls who'd used it before us. Best of all, it had a stereo with big boxy speakers. While Garry and his girlfriend were at work, I played a tape of the cast recording of *Hair* I'd found in a record store in Melbourne. We were finally letting the sunshine in.

I wasn't sure how we were going to find work, living in the middle of the suburbs without transport, but I was glad to have a respite from the bustle of hostel life. Days drifted by, and I was content, reading my way through Garry's library, writing dramatic prose in my notebook, and listening to music. Sure, mealtimes when Garry's girlfriend was home were awkward. I wasn't sure if going out with a psych nurse usually entailed having interstate ex-residents rock up from time to time, and occasionally we heard them having strained conversations in their room. But for me, the benefits outweighed any awkwardness, which I was well practised at ignoring.

Carita, however, grew restive, especially after Garry took her out to dinner one night when his girlfriend was doing a double shift. Carita wanted to head to Sydney, but I protested that we couldn't afford a bus or a hostel there. She was adamant she knew where to hitch from, and what we needed to make sure of in a truck – primarily, it must be loaded, so that the driver had a deadline to meet, and secondarily, there could be only one driver. When we got to Sydney, we would use the rest of Derek's money to pay for a hostel, and then we would both get jobs to save for Queensland.

One morning, Carita called out to me from her room after Garry and his girlfriend had left for work. I found her standing, legs held uncomfortably apart, her yellow tracksuit pants and the sheets covered in a Rorschach pattern of her blood. Thanking goodness that nobody was home, I left Carita to shower and took the bloodied items to the laundry, where I scrubbed them with cold water then put them in the washing machine.

'You've got your period?' I said.

'We have to go,' she said. 'Today.'

This time I put up no argument. Carita composed a note to Garry, stuffed our belongings into our bags, and trammed out to some truck depot Carita knew about from her last trip. We needed to be there in the late afternoon, to catch the trucks driving up to Sydney through the night.

We stood on a grey road beside a trucking terminus, looking neither attractive nor pathetic enough to encourage any eighteen-wheelers to slow down, let alone to pick us up. The sun started dropping along with the temperature, and just as I was having images of Carita and me dying of hypothermia before I'd even eyeballed the Harbour Bridge, a truck wheezed to a halt.

'Sydney?' The driver was a man with a belly as big as a full-term pregnancy, but his eyes didn't wander, and he had all his teeth. Besides, what else were we going to do?

We climbed up and left Melbourne behind.

. . .

Carita had told me the rules of hitching, which we'd been practising in Melbourne. Always keep them talking. Tell them about yourself, even if it's a lie, so they think of you as a person – it makes them less likely to want to murder you. Never disagree with anything they say. Never show fear.

The last instruction was difficult. At first the driver merrily recounted the amount of speed drivers took to get them through the long days and nights, about trucks drag-racing, side by side, on the two-lane highway we were on, about the derisive terms the truckies had for regular vehicles and their occupants.

Perhaps sensing our disbelief, the truckie felt the need to show and not tell.

'Here,' he said. 'This is how fast she can go.'

In my opinion we were going fast enough already, but the engine rose a fifth higher as he pushed harder on the accelerator. A small suburban car appeared in front of us, keeping to the speed limit that we were now far exceeding. The driver blew the horn as he steered into the oncoming lane.

Into which another small suburban car appeared.

I closed my eyes, so all I heard was swearing and a car horn. When I opened my eyes next we were safe-ish, with the only thing ahead being a reflective sign informing us the turn-off to Gundagai was approaching.

'Hey,' I said. 'Are we going near the Dog on the Tuckerbox?'

'It's a bit out of the way,' the truckie said. 'But yeah, why not.'

Away from home, I'd become nostalgic for the songs Gwen used to sing. There was one which was a rollicking tune about being on the road to Gundagai, and another about a dog sitting on the tuckerbox, five miles from Gundagai. When I was a child Gwen had told me that the dog was waiting for its master to come home, and I was moved to tears at the pathos of it. Later I discovered the original poem refers to bullock drivers heading for Sydney from Gundagai, but instead of going home they pissed their pay packet up the wall at the pub nearby, which was more apropos to my experiences of childhood and Gwen, but in any case, both the detour and the dog were disappointments. With the truck's massive high beams trained on it, the dog looked small and miserable.

And the truckie, who had hitherto been gentlemanly, decided that he should try to extract payment for the detour.

Carita was sitting in the middle when he said, 'Hey, youse should learn how to drive this rig.'

He snatched at her hand and put it around the gear stick, his hand over hers. Then he grabbed her wrist and pulled her hand toward his lap.

Carita yanked her hand away and made a show of yawning.

'I'm going to crash for a bit,' she said, and leapt over the back seat to the narrow mattress at the back of the cab. She shot me a just-keep-him-away-from-me look. I nodded sagely and looked ahead into the black night and the white beams of the headlights.

The truckie kept driving while I stayed as close to the door as I could, trying not to look as if I was wanting to exit the vehicle as much as I now did. A country-and-western tape was playing. I hoped that the playing of music, such as it was, excused the obligation on me to speak, as the only topic I wanted to discuss, which was how much I did not want to perform sexual acts of any type on the way to Sydney, was likely not on the conversational menu.

As Carita had previously warned, however, not speaking gives drivers the opportunity to think, and to think about their passengers and the uses to which they could be put.

The tape stopped. The truckie looked at me. The look indicated that I was less satisfactory than Carita, but I would do.

'Come on,' he said. 'You need to learn to drive.'

Obediently, keeping in mind the dictum that you should never argue with the person who could murder you as easily as they gave you the lift you're currently enjoying, I leaned to the left and put my hand on the gear stick. I clung onto it as the driver attempted to prise my fingers off it and in the direction he'd tried to take Carita's.

I was rescued by the bright lights of a service station.

'Oh great,' I said, retrieving my hand so I could grab my bag. 'I'm starving.' I called through the curtains. 'Crit, servo!'

Carita and I climbed down one side of the cab, the truckie down the other. He offered to buy us food, but Carita insisted we buy our own hot chips, which resembled hot chips in shape only. We went to the toilet and discussed whether we should get another lift with another cab.

'We've just got to keep him distracted,' Carita said. 'He's not too sleazy, we can handle him.'

As it turned out, we didn't need to handle him. Back in the cab, once the heater was back on, we became aware of the ripe and unmistakable stench of male urine emanating from an indeterminate location. Each of us pretended not to smell it, but it was pervasive, persistent, and, fortunately for Carita and me, sexually off-putting. I wondered whether the truckie had pissed himself or sat on something. He may have wondered if we'd deliberately applied something to discourage his advances, as his previous cheery-if-mildly-sleazy disposition turned sullen and irritable, but luckily for us it stopped there and didn't descend into violent or murderous.

We drove on, and in the early hours of the next morning we arrived in the Sydney suburb of Alexandria. We climbed down from the cab, thanked the truckie, and hitched to Kings Cross, where Carita knew there were plenty of hostels. In the car of the officer worker who took pity on us, I was sure I could still smell urine: maybe it was in my nostrils. I couldn't see the Harbour Bridge or the Opera House. There were just alien suburbs that looked depressingly like the alien suburbs we'd left behind in Perth.

In Kings Cross we were too early for the backpackers to open, so we found a bench and waited. A street sweeper hummed up and back; a woman with smeared make-up staggered in her high heels along the street, not looking in our direction; an old drunk was slumped outside a closed shop, hand still around the bag holding his bottle of booze.

I wanted to go back to Melbourne.

When we made it into the backpackers, which smelled of mould, Carita and I took turns in the shower. When I took off my boot, I noticed a discolouration on the white leather. I took a whiff and retched. I must have stepped in a puddle of truckies' piss at the servo. I scrubbed and scrubbed at the stain with soap and toilet paper, but the smell persisted.

'That's disgusting,' Carita said when I told her. 'How could you?'

'It wasn't my fault,' I said. 'It was their fault for pissing outside!'

But Carita seemed to stay annoyed with me for some time. In Melbourne, we shared our hopes and our troubles. In Sydney, Carita started sealing herself off. I'd seen her do this with other people, but I didn't think she would do it to me.

So I did what I was accustomed to doing when people upset me, or disappointed me, or started behaving in ways I didn't understand. I pretended nothing was happening and that everything was all right, squirrelling away my feelings, hoping the feelings would take their cue from my outward demeanour and conclude that there was no place for them here.

17

In Sydney our money ran perilously low. When we could no longer pay the ten dollars a night at one hostel, we snuck to the sister hostel in Potts Point, sleeping during the day while the occupants worked, or else sleeping on the floor. The Cross was peppered with young people more desperate than we were, more broke and more broken, and I wanted to avoid their fate. One evening Carita and I sat with a group of street kids, drinking goon out of a shared plastic cup, appreciating how readily they welcomed us and asked no questions about our stories, why we were teenagers alone in the seediest place in the nation. I understood how easily we could slide to where they were.

We both undertook to get jobs while we still had properly laundered clothes. I got one first, in a café in the newly renovated QVB in the centre of Sydney. I walked from the Cross to save money. The sight of the harbour and the Harbour Bridge was the high point of my day. I found myself working in food service, just as I had when I'd left school, and I hated it no less because of its location. The sight of the lunchtime queues and impatient hungry office workers filled me with panic. In my break I scribbled in my notebook but found none of what I wrote satisfying; after work I trudged back to the noisy and dirty hostel. The Swedish girls dried their handwashed knickers in the oven and otherwise provided a backdrop of cheery enthusiasm from which I felt increasingly alienated. I paid for beds for Carita and myself as soon as I could afford to and bought all our food, which was mostly cereal for breakfast and hot chips for dinner, although often Carita felt sick after a few chips so I got the whole tub to myself.

One afternoon, when I had a day off, I decided I would walk over the Harbour Bridge while Carita was out looking for work. I'd called Gwen reverse charges from a phone box from Kings Cross, then wandered down the 113 steps from Potts Point into Woolloomooloo and turned left, certain I'd be able to find my way to the Bridge, if only I kept going in the right direction. It was a sunny winter's day and I had a sudden surge of optimism. Sydney was spectacular, sparkling and oversized, and maybe I could keep pace with it. After passing by the brilliant blue water at the wharves, I wandered through a maze of streets with old workers' cottages. And then I noticed the footsteps behind me.

'Don't worry,' a man said, jogging to catch up with me. He was in his twenties, I guessed, and otherwise nondescript, wearing jeans and sneakers.

'I'm not worried,' I said, adopting the even tone I'd learned to use when hitching, keeping my pace brisk.

'Where are you going?' he asked.

'I'm meeting someone,' I lied.

'Oh yeah?' he said. 'I'm going to walk across the Bridge.'

'Nice day for it,' I said.

We walked. He was too close to me, so I kept trying to go slightly faster, to get away from him without him noticing. I did not understand how we could be in the middle of Sydney, so close to the city centre, yet the streets were deserted. I kept my eyes to the front.

'You're from Perth, aren't you?'

That was when I realised that he must have been listening to my conversation with Gwen, back at the phone box at the Cross. I'd told her where I was going; I must have mentioned something about the time difference or asked what the weather was like at home.

It was also when I realised that wherever we were headed, it wasn't going to lead over the bridge, the grey underside of which started to loom overhead. At every cross street, the man corralled me into going away from where I wanted to go.

'I just want to go for a walk,' I said.

'You're a long way from home,' he said.

Then we turned into another street. Several hundred metres away I saw a group of schoolchildren being herded by their teachers. The man tried to grab me as I bolted toward the middle of the street.

'Hey!' he said. 'It's this way!'

'Wait!' I yelled to the teachers. 'Wait for me!'

By the time I reached them the man was gone.

. . .

The uneasiness that had begun to creep in between Carita and me since the fermented-truckie-piss incident sometimes abated, and we forgot ourselves and talked about how we were feeling instead of what we were doing. One day, when I was lamenting leaving Melbourne, she said, 'Jules, I had to.'

Then, finally, she told me what had happened with Garry.

Garry had taken her to a café as planned on their first meeting, but when it became dark, he'd taken her to Fitzroy Gardens, where he'd then taken off her coat, laid it on the ground, and had sex with her. Every meeting they'd had followed the same pattern. When we'd moved in with him and his girlfriend, he'd had sex with Carita on their bed, where his girlfriend slept. Carita didn't want to keep doing it, and he wouldn't stop, so we had to leave. I remembered the blood then, but I didn't ask any more about it.

I was hurt that she hadn't told me at the time and felt like an idiot for not noticing. There I was, thinking how nice he was being to us. I was six months older than Carita and thought I should have known more, but I was hopelessly naïve.

Carita and I composed a letter to Garry, explaining how we never wanted to see him again, and included barbed comments about his age and his sleaziness, and posted it.

For a little while, united against Garry, we had our old closeness back. She was continuing to look for work, heading out each day with a few of the other backpackers, and I kept on at the café. Then one day I was carrying two cups of black coffee and one of my co-workers backed into me, spilling the hot coffee over my hands. I was sent to a doctor, and when I returned with neat white bandaging over my fingers, I told them I needed to have two days off. They informed me that my services were no longer required, opened the till and counted out what I was owed.

I arrived back at the hostel, wondering what I was going to do now. One of the English girls with whom Carita had been going to find work was making lunch.

'Where's Carita?' I inquired. 'Did she get work?'

'Oh no,' she said. 'They all went to Bondi today, but I didn't feel like going.'

The betrayal shocked me. I knew Carita lied to other people, directly and indirectly. I'd seen her steal my friend's clothes and her sister's clarinet. I'd seen her put on a face to Dr Mac and to others when I knew her true feelings. I knew from my own frenzy of kleptomania that stealing is an expression of anger and lying can be a way of protecting yourself from others. But I did not expect her to lie to me, to let me work at a job I hated to earn money for us both. So that neither of us ended up drinking goon on the street because there was no other option.

I fumed. I scribbled in my diary with my pen held awkwardly in my unburnt fingers. When Carita arrived home with a gaggle of other travellers, she was laughing and relaxed.

Until she saw me. But instead of being apologetic or ashamed, as I'd expected, she looked straight at me and shrugged.

I pointed to the tiny courtyard at the back of the hostel, and we sat at the table that was wedged close to the fence.

'What happened to your hands?' She nodded at the bandages.

'What happened to you getting a job?'

'You're not the boss of me,' she said.

'I've got enough to get us to the end of the week,' I said. 'What are we going to do?'

Carita rolled her eyes and drew a hundred dollars out of her sock.

'My dad gave it to me,' she said. 'I wanted to save it until we really needed it. To see how you would go really having no money.'

I was too shocked to reply. I was being treated as someone who needed a lesson. I remembered that when we'd been in hospital, Carita and some of the other girls had made fun of Gwen's house, the bogan area where we lived after they'd visited one day. It was the first time someone had openly mocked me for our lack of means. Now Carita was being critical of me because having no money in a strange city made me anxious.

I did not know how to respond. The hurt burnt my gullet like goon.

We sat there until one of the residents called Carita back in.

I was not sure if I could compose my face in front of the cheerful Swedes, so I walked in, grabbed my purse, and went to the only place I knew that might help me.

. . .

Patricia, my English teacher, had told me about the Wayside Chapel. I'd walked by it plenty of times, it being around the corner from the overcrowded youth hostel. Now, I went into the chapel itself. Almost as soon as I lowered myself to the pew I started crying. Someone ushered me into an office. I asked if there was any place I could get money for rent or help getting another job. He asked me about the situation Carita and I were in and, with a few omissions, I told him.

'Have you got somewhere to stay in Perth?'

I thought of the room I had at Gwen's. Armadale did not seem so far away from everything to me at that moment, lonely as I was on the other side of the country.

'Yes,' I said.

'Could your mother help you get home?'

'No,' I said, without needing to ask. 'She hasn't got any money. But I don't want to go home anyway. I just need some help.'

By the time I left the Wayside Chapel, I had an offer for two bus tickets back to Perth. I had to tell them the next morning what I'd decided.

'We see what happens to girls like you,' the man said.

Back at the hostel Carita was adamant. She didn't want to go back to Western Australia. Western Australia was the past, and she didn't want any part of that past.

'Well,' I said. 'I'm going.'

I wanted her to beg me to stay. I wanted her to tell me I'd got it all wrong, that she'd get a job, that we'd be together like we'd planned.

Like I'd planned.

'Okay,' she shrugged.

She went out with some of the English travellers that night. I stayed in the hostel, writing in my diary. The next morning I told Wayside Chapel my decision, and three days later, early in the morning, I was heading for the bus station as Carita was heading out for a job in a drycleaner's she'd finally got. Our frostiness gave way to a long hug.

'Oh Jules,' she said.

'You could come,' I said.

'I'm never going back,' she said. 'I just want to travel.'

'Well,' I said. 'I'll work and save up. I'll come back.'

Carita looked doubtful. I wondered if I was doing the right thing, leaving her there. She looked so small and alone as I walked away. In Sydney, she was still beautiful, but her beauty was blunted in the bustle of the Cross, its drab streets, hard-eyed men hustling for shows, street kids looking to score, and gaudily attired women angling their hips outside doorways.

I felt diminished, wanting safety, a bed, a room, books. I felt myself wanting, as if I should want something different. But I let the bus driver swing Derek's army bag into the luggage hold, climbed into my seat, and leaned my head against the cool window as I was carried away.

18

On the four-thousand-kilometre bus ride back to Perth, it was strange, at each stop, buying hot chips only for myself. I was used to having Carita there all the time; for six months we had spent every night together and most of our waking moments. I had moulded myself to her. Now, I was a strange shape.

Back in Perth, at Gwen's house, I had a wave of relief at the warm bed, the clean towels, the wider selection of books I'd left behind, the absence of Swedish girls drying their knickers in the oven. I wrote to Carita at the hostel I'd left but didn't hear back.

I started going to university lectures with my primary-school best friend, Nobbly, drifting around the sandstone university campus next to the placid blue river that wound its way to the sea. When Nobbly had told me she was doing an arts degree, I thought she meant she'd taken up painting. I sat in lectures on music, helped with her Latin homework (afternoons with Frank's dictionary turned out to have been well spent), and looked enviously at the novels she was reading. I knew, then, what I wanted to do, but there was a six-month wait to redo Year Twelve and the university entry that would allow.

As well as shadowing Nobbly at uni, I began to hang around Patricia, who was at first encouraging and then alarmed by my neediness. Her calm, bookish house in Fremantle was an age away from the sandy-yarded, smoke-filled one in Armadale, which was coated with migraine-inducing dust from the nearby brickworks. No matter how many books I bought from second-hand shops, I had no idea how one might acquire the middle-class attributes that seemed to render life's edges softer.

I also began visiting Carita's mother. I couldn't explain to her what had happened or why I was back, and she didn't ask. Both of us felt the other provided something of Carita, and that sufficed. For me, Carita's absence was still wounding. Even though I was the one who left, I felt she had abandoned me. Carita's mother got occasional calls: Carita was moving from hostel to hostel, and soon she would be moving into a share house and provide the address. Carita's mother read my horoscope, fed me, and ferried me to a beauty salon, where middle-class ladies experimented with doing manicures on me and each other. I drove to one in the back of a leather-seated Mercedes with one of these ladies, while the woman complained about her husband, who was such a drag.

'Why do you stay with him?' I inquired.

She swept her free hand around the plush interior, as if the answer were obvious.

My sense of myself, left to myself, began disintegrating.

'Are you ever going to stick at anything?' Gwen asked me, Derek asked me, I asked myself.

At Nobbly's eighteenth birthday celebration at the Sail and Anchor in Fremantle, in June 1987, I watched her and her friends laughing and chatting, comfortable in the future they were making for themselves, comfortable in their acceptable trajectory of school and university, part-time jobs, homes in which they could expand, in which they did not have to build their own safety. They had succeeded early in life, getting their scholarships to Mod, which set them up for more successes. In contrast, I was the high school dropout, their shadow lives, the psych patient whose life was already careening out of control, disappointing and disappointed.

I wandered to Patricia's house. Finding my teacher gone but the back door open, I left a knife stuck in her sink plug, as her kitchen table was too hard for the purpose, and scrawled a desperate note. I went into Patricia's shed and stayed there, pacing, until the sun came up and I paced instead around East Fremantle. I phoned the hospital from a phone booth and ranted; I sat on a swing and watched children playing and ate a roast potato purchased with the last of my money. It lodged like a stone in my gullet. When the sun receded, I returned to the shed, where an alarmed Gwen, who had been called by my equally alarmed teacher, was waiting to take me back to Armadale.

Head nurse Sue would not readmit me to the hospital because I was now seventeen, so I was sent to Heathcote, a red-bricked mental institution

I knew from children's taunts. I was the youngest patient first in locked and then unlocked wards. On my first morning, at breakfast, a patient upended a bowl of cornflakes over his head; on my first evening, a man stood by my bed, revealed his rounded stomach, and sang 'The Yellow Rose of Texas' until he was led back to the men's section. There was a woman who was there because she'd told the police about her husband molesting her children, to which he responded by getting her committed. There were thoughtful, serious people suffering the ravages of long-term mental illness uncontrolled or uncontrollable by medication, which made them attempt to chop down powerlines or drive down suburban highways like Ayrton Senna. My snoring roommate responded to my asking for her to turn over by screaming until every nurse in the unit came running.

...

Fresh from that experience and equipped with a new horror of admitting mental instability, I decided I would work, save money, and go back to visit Carita. The only problem with this plan was that a) I didn't have Carita's contact details, and b) after three weeks in any food-service job, I ended up walking out or locking myself in the toilets, weeping. I took a job in a roadhouse, thinking that I would trap myself into continuing to work. Instead, after three weeks that included me trying to throw myself out of a moving car at night, I ended up walking out of the roadhouse and hitchhiking to Albany, a pretty town best known for its former whaling station, with nubbly hills and winds straight off Antarctica. In Albany I slept in a panel van with the guy who'd picked me up. The panel van was parked out the back of a house of former Satanists turned fundamentalist Christians who looked at me with suspicion and told me I should never listen to Peter Gabriel. But I'd saved enough for the bus fare to Sydney.

When I got back to Perth, Carita's mother gave me Carita's new Sydney address. I wrote to her, recounting the events of recent months in an ironic tone, as if none of it had mattered. In early December I got a card back in her spidery writing, acknowledging our last weeks together had been shit, chastising me for ending up in Heathcote, telling me of her new, English beloved called Rob, and inviting me to visit their Darlinghurst share house.

Three days later I was on another bus, imagining the joy of being reunited. We could travel together, just as we'd planned. It would all be fabulous. Harmony would be restored. We would be kinder to each other, we wouldn't be waking to the smell of warming underwear, and it would be summer. We were going into 1988. It was the year of the bicentenary of English colonisation, and the mood of the country was celebratory, if you weren't one of the people for whom colonisation was more appropriately a cause for lamentation.

...

I arrived in Darlinghurst dazed, sleep-deprived and with legs cramping from consecutive nights on the bus. Carita was out. The townhouse was small and damp-smelling, but neat, with rosters tacked to the fridge for the division of various tasks. I was shown to a room whose occupant was elsewhere, and slept fitfully until I heard her voice: 'Jules?'

She seemed smaller than I remembered as we hugged. I had turned eighteen in the intervening months; she was still seventeen but somehow seemed older than me. We went to her and Rob's tiny room, sat on the mattress that abutted the door. The window looked toward the city but was closed against Sydney mosquitoes, trapping in the humid heat and the over-familiar smell of the sheets. On the back of the door hung two kimono dressing gowns, his and hers. She told me she had spent the last months in the room all day while Rob worked. He had been earning money labouring and saving everything they could so they could travel, but it was time for her to get a job now. Tomorrow morning we would go to the employment agency at 5am and line up for casual work, with all the Islanders and blokes in singlets and travellers, and see what we could get.

I imagined Carita, lying in the tiny room over all those months, window closed, watching the changing colours of the Sydney sky. She didn't read; there was no radio. I wondered what she had thought about.

When I met Rob, he was polite but cool. He was from Liverpool, like my father's friends, but was, unlike my father's friends, disinclined to humour, at least where I was concerned. Carita wanted me to like him so I told myself he did seem to really care about her, and at least he had tried to protect her from the world by allowing her to retreat from it.

Carita and I both secured work by 6am. Hers was in a screen-printing factory. The factory owner had taken one look at Carita and hired her. I began work as a kitchenhand in a donga on the Sydney Harbour project, making sandwiches for construction workers far more polite than their suited-up counterparts in the QVB had ever been.

'Oh Jules,' she said, when we both returned to the Darlinghurst house that first evening. 'I knew I'd hate it, and I do.'

For a moment we shared her disconsolateness, but when Rob returned home she was able to contain herself. It wasn't so bad, she said. I noticed he didn't know her enough to be able to tell that she was lying.

I found the ease with which Carita changed into a regular, domesticated girlfriend alienating, as if discovering that she spoke a second language or could recite pi to a value of a hundred decimal places. In our flat, the kitchen was where cockroaches bred, and goon could be refrigerated. Always delicate of digestion, she never indicated a capacity to cook any more than she was inclined to eat. Now she was in possession of fruit and vegetables from the markets. She made wholegrain sandwiches crammed with salad. On weekends she cooked Rob breakfast, wearing her kimono, and sat by him while he ate it. When we went out to a pub, she danced to one song then retreated to Rob's lap. One night, headed to the toilet, I heard the grunt of her outbreaths as they had sex. I remembered Carita telling me how much she hated the smell of sex. I wondered if that had changed too.

January crept on. Carita and I applied for new jobs at the Sydney Cricket Ground for the bicentennial celebrations after being told we could make heaps of money, walking through the stands and selling souvenirs. The guy whose bed I'd been sleeping in returned, and I was relegated to the couch next to the door the residents came in and out of at all hours.

One night the guy and I wandered down to the Cross and, beckoned by a hard-eyed guy in a leather jacket, we got a three-for-one ticket to strip joints. I'd never seen anything more devoid of sex. If the audience were turned on by the dead-eyed girls simulating coitus with the terrified men they pulled from the front row, it wasn't obvious. One woman marched up and down the club, whip cracking down unexpectedly here and there. At my flinch, she leaned in and said, 'I wouldn't hit you, darling.' Afterward we sat down with a busker and sang gospel songs.

After a few weeks one of the housemates handed me a bill, calculating the amount of money I owed for my position on the couch. I protested to Carita, but by her reaction I could tell it was pre-discussed and decided. Stung, I announced, once again, that I was going back to Perth. Once again, Carita seemed relieved. I would be back in time to enrol in Year Twelve. As I packed my bag, I pretended I did not realise the cassette of INXS's *Kick* was in my Walkman.

'It's weird,' she said to me at the bus station. 'Seeing people from back then.'

And with that, we were relegated to each other's pasts.

I listened to 'Never Tear Us Apart' all the way back to Perth.

In a fit of guilt, I posted the INXS tape back to Darlinghurst, apologising for taking it with me. I told Carita I had enrolled in Year Twelve at Canning College, a senior campus designed for overseas students, kids who had failed their exams, and people like me who'd never finished high school. I tried not to sound apologetic for wanting to go to university, for not wanting to travel the way she did.

I never heard back from her.

19

Once I was doing something purposeful, I never fell to the pits of despair that had formerly led me to stints in psychiatric facilities. This is not to say I did not have fits of extreme feeling, only that these were contained by a mostly pleasing structure of daily living, sometimes deliberately, sometimes by happy accident. I veered off in various directions, unable to quite fully follow what I actually wanted, always prone to taking other people's well-meaning but ill-fitting advice.

When I finally got to university I was surprised to see Carita's mother, who was studying psychology. When I first saw her, she told me Carita was travelling, in the States perhaps. When I asked again, the following year, she looked at me, unsmiling.

'I haven't heard from her,' she said, as if I had offended her to ask, or as if she thought I might know something she didn't. Although I saw her regularly after that and we talked about other things, I did not have the courage to ask her about Carita again.

I had always imagined I would see Carita, later on. When I lived in England, I kept expecting to bump into her, and in Liverpool I kept a particular eye out. I did not see her in Sydney, where I was sent on student guild conferences, but I walked past our old temporary abodes, still filled with travellers, which I finally understood were her people. And I had finally found my own.

In the second half of 1992 I was in a tutorial with Carita's mother for a history unit called Witchcraft and Crime. Again we spoke only about the events about which we were studying: how women accused of witchery were bound and tied in a lake, and if they drowned they were innocent, but if they floated up they were hauled out of the water and hanged in their wet clothes. Again and again I almost asked about Carita. Again and again courage failed me.

After our final tutorial for the semester we went to the university's social club for drinks, sitting in a circle in the warm November air, which smelled sweetly of the eucalyptus trees we sat beneath. I was determined to ask for Carita's contact details. I was ready for a new reckoning with Carita, to meet her again without blame or angst, to see how experiences had changed her. To see how we had changed to each other.

I got up to change seats, but Carita's mother had gone.

'Oh,' I said to my classmate. 'I was hoping to speak to her.'

'You know her?' my classmate said.

'I used to,' I said.

'She's so brave, isn't she?' my classmate went on. 'Especially after her daughter dying like that.'

I heard my heartbeat fast in my ears. I knew. I already knew. But I asked anyway.

'She's got two daughters,' I said. 'Which one?'

'The youngest one,' she said. 'So tragic.' Then, 'Are you all right?'

...

My first thought was *She must have committed suicide*. It all must have got too much, and she'd completed what she'd tried at fifteen.

My second thought was *It's all Dr Mac's fault*. I had not thought about Dr Mac for years, but now, I was certain that what had happened was connected to him, his failure to keep her safe, his wandering hands.

But when I spoke to Carita's mother on the phone that night, weeping – 'Is it true?' – she told me that Carita had been working in Japan, living with her older sister, saving money to travel again while Rob studied in Sydney. She had died of liver failure in the Tokyo Women's Hospital. It was a tragic accident. Carita's mother and father had flown to her bedside. They were all with her when she died in February 1992, a week before her twenty-second birthday.

Carita's mother hadn't mentioned it to me because she thought I already knew, and that I was keeping quiet out of respect or fear. Her high school friends knew. Her hospital friends didn't.

I remembered Carita telling me, one night in a pub in Melbourne, that she would die young. She had said it with an eerie certainty. At the time I'd rushed in, 'Oh, me too.' Because all young, sad, desperate people think that.

I asked a few times for details, but the answers were vague, unsatisfying, and I didn't want to further upset Carita's mother. We cried some more, and then I hung up.

Two weeks later I flew to Queensland, stayed with friends on a permaculture farm in the hinterland, where snakes curled in fireplaces and spiders the size of plates spread themselves over my mosquito netting at night, and the sea was a humid smudge on the horizon. One afternoon there was a thunderstorm, and I lay on the bed, listening to the deluge hosing the earth. When the lightning cracked onto the tin roof, the electricity tingled in my limbs for the rest of the afternoon. How close it had come.

. . .

Five years later, in 1997, I was in the witness stand in a courtroom. Dr Mac sat on the other side. I glanced at him only once. He seemed so old. Also, he wasn't smiling. He always used to smile when he saw any of us.

I was not there because I had got the wherewithal to complain about Dr Mac's conduct, back in the day. Well, I hadn't complained of my own volition. I was there because in 1995 there had been a ministerial inquiry into the hospital conducted by a law firm, and I had been contacted by a former nurse who asked if I would tell them what I knew.

I took the lift to the highest levels of a skyscraper that swayed with the wind and, in response to their careful questions, recounted what had happened. As I described it all, from the wandering hands during consultations to Dr Mac's visit to the flat, the expressions of the two lawyers conveyed their opinion of what Dr Mac had done. I had never quite been able to express his offence, not really. I mean, he hadn't raped me. The lawyers, however, were men alien to me, suited and serious, and their reaction made me reconsider what had happened, cast it in a light not available to me as a fifteen- and sixteen-year-old. I'd known it was wrong later, when I had started thinking about it again after Carita died. The wandering hands, the smile that never wavered. But somehow having someone outside of us think it was wrong stopped me from adding 'but it wasn't that bad' when I described what had happened.

Then a police officer from the child abuse unit turned up at my flat, and soon afterward a prosecutor talked to me about a trial. It would be hard to convict him, they told me. Juries don't often believe women, and they less often believe women who were girls in adolescent psychiatric hospitals. But he'd been struck off the medical register for a time after admitting to an inappropriate relationship with a private patient, and now he was trying to get re-registered. To go back to being a child psychiatrist again.

I thought about Carita, and said yes, I would do it.

. . .

By the time the trial came around I had a four-month-old baby, rheumatoid arthritis, and a partner who thought me giving evidence was such a bad idea that he refused to help me, either psychologically, in the lead-up, or practically, on the two days my evidence extended. A child abuse detective picked me up on the first day, Gwen on the second day, driving my car so my daughter could be accommodated in her baby seat. From time to time proceedings were interrupted so I could breastfeed her – almost as often as the jury were asked to retire as the defence and prosecution argued over points of procedure through the nearly two days I was in the stand. At one point, as I was leaving the courtroom, I heard the judge ruling that evidence about Carita being sexually abused as a child could not be presented. It was not information that I'd known. I wondered where that information had come from.

The prosecuting Queen's Counsel led me through my legally truncated version of what had happened, why I was here, what I remembered. How I got to be a teenage psychiatric patient in the first place. How I wasn't there because I'd complained myself. How the charges had been brought about some other way.

The Queen's Counsel defending Dr Mac began his cross-examination, languorous and condescending. I had received my notes from the hospital through a freedom of information request two years before (they'd lost all of our notes in the meantime, including Carita's), so I'd had to produce them during the defence's discovery process, along with choice excerpts from my journals. This provided a rich line of questioning, aimed at suggesting I was either fabricating, disturbed, or faulty of memory.

In support of the first line of questioning, he asked details of what had happened when. He asked me to describe the exact location of Dr Mac's hands, when these alleged offences had taken place, what I was wearing. How did I know he wasn't just trying to comfort me? After all, I was unstable and often upset, as my notes no less than my journals attested.

In support of the second, he required me to confirm details of my disturbed thinking and conduct leading up to me being admitted to hospital, including information about having sex with the bodybuilder doormen at the cinema, bulimia, and compulsive shoplifting.

'You would agree that you were psychologically disturbed?' he asked.

'Emotionally disturbed, not psychologically,' I said, repeating what Dr Mac had written in my diagnosis.

And in support of the third, he peppered his cross-examination with questions he may or may not have known the answer to, such as the name of the school nurse at my high school. I answered each question, which had the effect of deepening the furrow that had appeared on his brow.

The languor with which he began questioning turned into a pinched frustration. He asked me to say whether my treatment with Dr Mac had been good or bad for me. I said I couldn't say it was one or the other. Some aspects were positive.

'In your opinion, on the whole, was your treatment by Dr McAlpine beneficial to you – yes or no?' he said.

'It wasn't that simple,' I said.

'I instruct you to answer the question!'

'Then ask me a question I can answer,' I responded.

The barrister changed tack. He asked about my anger, expressed so eloquently in my sixteen-year-old diary. Then he drew himself to his full enrobed height and said, 'I put it to you that you blame my client because your friend Carita Ridgway committed suicide!'

I blinked at him. 'She didn't commit suicide.'

His eyes were fixed. 'Then how did she die?'

'She died of liver failure.'

I wanted to look over to Dr Mac then. I wondered if he would feel less guilty, knowing that.

'Who told you that?' the barrister said.

'Her mother,' I answered.

His ruffled black robes drew in like a deflated piano accordion as he muttered, 'No further questions,' and lowered himself into his chair.

I was dismissed, and walked out of the courtroom, trying to hide the stiffness the rheumatoid arthritis created in my joints.

One witness was former head nurse Sue Butcher. A couple of years previously, Sue had pleaded guilty to unlawful and indecent dealing with a minor, which arose from her 'relationship' with a boy who was thirteen when he entered Hillview in 1986, and who, after his discharge, had gone on to live with Sue and her daughter, who was the same age as the boy. Sue was thirty-eight at the time. When I later thanked her for giving evidence at the trial she said, 'It was the least I could do.'

When Dr Mac was found guilty and fined $4,000, I was too exhausted to feel more than a flicker of satisfaction that he wouldn't be practising again. I had, I hoped, saved other young women like me, like Carita. Even if I couldn't save Carita herself.

...

I was thirty-one and halfway through writing my second novel, *Skating the Edge*, based on my friendship with Carita as well as our hospital experiences, when I sat down to have a break in front of the Saturday newspaper. An article at the bottom of a page was entitled 'Charge laid over Aussie barmaid death'. It stated that alleged serial rapist Joji Obara had been charged the previous day with causing the death of an unnamed twenty-one-year-old Australian woman in February 1992. The report noted that Obara was the prime suspect in the murder and dismembering of British air hostess Lucie Blackman, also twenty-one, who had disappeared in Tokyo after going on a date with a man.

I knew, as I searched the news with a shaking coldness at my core, that the unnamed woman was Carita. Later that day a brief clip on the evening news confirmed it.

I thought, numbly, of how annoyed she would be, having worked so hard to leave the place behind, to be described as coming from Perth.

Piece by piece, I learned of how they had finally discovered what had really happened to Carita, nine years after I had learned of her death.

In July 2000, Lucie Blackman had disappeared shortly after arriving in Japan, where she had worked as a *gaijin* hostess, as Carita had. Like Carita eight years previously, she had been very well paid to smile at stressed businessmen and pretend they were interesting and sip expensive champagne the businessmen bought by the bottle. She was saving money while deciding what to do with her life, having quit her job as an airline hostess for the more lucrative and less tiring earth-bound version. Hostessing was, by and large, a non-sexual job that drew on the ancient geisha tradition, and clubs approved of their hostesses going on paid dates with clients. It made the clients eager to come back and spend more money at the clubs.

Seven months after Lucie arrived in Tokyo, she went missing. Much later, in no small part due to the incessant media campaign her father led, her body was found in pieces, which had been set in concrete and hidden in a cave at Miura, a fishing village near Tokyo. The remains were too decomposed to determine the cause of her death.

After some lengthy delays the Japanese authorities searched the home of a forty-eight-year-old Japanese-Korean businessman who lived nearby. He had purchased a large vinyl mat, a camping table, and a chainsaw four days after Lucie disappeared, as well as cement. The police discovered hundreds of videotapes of Obara raping apparently drugged young women, mostly Westerners. One of the young women was Carita.

Obara had kept the receipt from the hospital where he had taken Carita, claiming she had food poisoning from shellfish. She had died of liver failure a week later with her family around her, as her mother had described to me. Except her mother had, like everyone else, thought the liver failure had been caused by hepatitis. A piece of her liver, preserved by the hospital, was tested after Obara's arrest in the year 2000. It was riddled with chloroform, the drug Obara used to render his victims unconscious.

...

I had lost touch with all of the residents from the hospital. The way we reminded each other of this strange section of our adolescence was too awkward and uncomfortable. I hadn't spoken to Carita's mother since I'd delivered her photos of Carita back in 1992. Nobody in the life I was now living – a PhD candidate, young-adult novelist, and part-time teacher and tutor, with a four-year-old and a partner and a mortgage – could understand the way this news sledgehammered me.

It came to this: all her life she was preyed on. For all her efforts to outrun the predators – at first by trying to die, then by taking her revenge on them, and then by keeping on travelling and moving – one of them ended her. All the agency in the world, all her efforts to save herself, create a new life: none of it meant anything against the men who could only see her as a way to satisfy their own desires. They fetishised her and robbed her of personhood.

She couldn't save herself. And I couldn't have saved her either.

When I found out she'd died, I realised how I had kept up a dialogue with her, even though we never spoke again after 1988. I had been explaining to her – to the Carita of my imagination – how my life, even though it was different from hers, was okay. I'd always felt as if I had disappointed her somehow, even before I'd abandoned her in Sydney that first time. I didn't measure up to something she wanted, or something I felt she wanted. Being a disappointment to others was a groove I knew well, fell easily into. So I kept explaining to the Carita in my head how things were, expecting that at some point we'd run into each other again and we could have the conversation for real.

Now the dialogue was one-sided. It had always been. And I was the sole custodian of our story.

...

In 2018 I was in court again. This time I was there only to give evidence of what a jury already found Dr Mac guilty of. I was there as evidence that Ian Stuart McAlpine – who had not been a doctor now for over two decades because of my previous testimony – had a propensity toward acting on his sexual interest in teenage girls.

When the Department of Public Prosecutions called me out of the blue, saying they wanted me to give evidence again, I did not need the explanation of what propensity evidence is because I had recently been awarded a law degree with distinction. I had done two stints of legal practice at Legal Aid in criminal appeals. So I also knew that when I was called to the stand, my evidence would have to be brief and confined to only what had already been aired in court.

After two trials and evidence from three of us, McAlpine was sentenced to four years and eight months in prison for raping one of his patients on her eighteenth birthday.

After I gave evidence, a woman outside was agitated. She had been a receptionist at his private practice, and we'd been waiting for hours next to each other but not able to speak to each other about why we were there or even whether we were defence or prosecution witnesses.

'I didn't get to say half of it,' she said.

'We never do,' I answered.

MARRY YOUR
EX-GIRLFRIEND'S BROTHER

20

Along with becoming a writer or a teetotaller, becoming a lesbian was not something easily imagined in the suburb I grew up in.

Any girls holding hands in high school, or walking too close to each other, or showing anything other than brief physical affection, would be met with jeers of 'Lezzos!' from passing boys. These same boys were often the ones who introduced us to the shiny contours and sometimes puzzling close-ups of 1980s pornography, in which girl-on-girl activity was considered in quite a different light. The activity of the women in these videos seemed to involve a lot of manual work, like a housewife trying to remove a stain from a carpet, and a lot of moaning that seemed unconnected to the manual work. Neither of these were as stimulating to me as they were to the boys we were watching with, so I concluded that I probably was not a lesbian.

I should clarify that I did not reach this conclusion because of any shortage of un-heterosexual feelings on my behalf. At fourteen, as outlined earlier, I had fallen deeply into unrequited love (normal) for a sixteen-year-old girl (not normal).

I had never come to an adequate answer to the question of whether I wanted her, in a romantic way, or wanted to be her. By the time I'd landed at university at nineteen I had kissed women in Perth's one gay nightclub, and twice had had sexual encounters with other girls, to see if my Karen crush had been a sign of latent lesbianism, or, as all the guidebooks of the time promised, a passing phase. The kissing was nice – nicer than with the guys – but the sexual encounters were awkward, possibly because there was no expertise to be had on either side. It reinforced my conviction that sex and love were better left separate, and that the latter was ineffably more desirable.

All that changed with Boudicca.

At the beginning of 1990, the year I was to turn twenty-one, Boudicca moved in with me and my housemate, Bridget, in a suburb not far from the university I'd started attending the previous year.

Bridget was an ethereal, Enya-loving young woman who wore a lot of cheesecloth, and I was a recent escapee from a conventional relationship with Boyfriend to which I'd realised I was as ill-suited as I'd been to the nursing degree I'd briefly attempted in order to do Something Useful. Bridget and I had placed an advertisement on a noticeboard at the university, which included the words 'Must like cats' in deference to the two kittens we'd recently acquired, sweet but entirely resistant to being toilet-trained. The notice had not attracted a single applicant, so when Boudicca called to make a time for an interview, the prospect of having another forty dollars a week to ease the pinch on our student allowance was heady.

Boudicca rolled into our driveway one February morning on a loud 750 Kawasaki motorbike, wearing a worn leather jacket, jeans, and motorbike boots. She shook hands hello without smiling. She took in the kittens without smiling. Bridget and I looked down at our prepared list of questions and were too nervous to ask any of them. She explained that her name was the correct form of the Iceni warrior Boadicea and instructed us on its correct pronunciation. She informed us that she had recently been living solo up a tree in Tasmania for some months and was rusty on human interactions.

'Um, wow,' we said. Bridget and I fancied ourselves as lefty greeny sympathisers, but our activism had been limited to affixing *Vote 1 Greens* and *Magic Happens* stickers on the rear windows of Bridget's leaded-fuel-guzzling Hillman Hunter.

'So do you want me to move in?'

Bridget and I glanced at each other.

'Do you like cats?' I asked.

'I'm vegan,' Boudicca said. 'I respect all sentient beings.'

'We're vegetarian,' Bridget smiled.

This information, which caused paroxysms of consternation when announced at family gatherings or social events, did not rate anything but a vague nod from Boudicca that may have been either approving or dismissive.

We showed her around the sparsely furnished house. There was a large, neglected back yard, which was met with approval.

'I do permaculture,' Boudicca informed us.

We nodded, as if we knew what that was. Due to her shaven head and the context for her comment, I figured permaculture had no relationship to perming, a hair affliction I was still suffering from, and which made me resemble Beaker from *The Muppets* rather than Andie MacDowell.

'Right then,' Boudicca said as she left, holding out a firm hand for us to shake.

'Right,' Bridget and I echoed.

And with that, Boudicca moved in.

Before Boudicca moved in, Bridget and I had spent long hours talking in the kitchen, listening on repeat to our limited supply of vinyl on the record player and bemoaning our recent disastrous encounters with males. We danced to Kate Bush, wrote long entries in our diaries that we read out to each other, and hung rainbow scarves over the windows to prettily refract the light. We did not discuss politics or the state of the world except in spiritual terms. We were all for putting flowers in guns and were convinced that feminine energy was the transformative corrective the world needed.

For some time after Boudicca moved in, the house was almost entirely silent. Well-thumbed books appeared in the toilet and on the table: Rachel Carson, ecofeminism, manifestos of various stripe. The kitchen was commandeered for the growing of sprouts, the soaking of soybeans preparatory for the making of soy milk, the storage of brown paper bags containing the various dried legumes and nuts required for a vegan diet. I guiltily hid my cheese at the back of the fridge, behind the miso and Nuttelex and slab-like rye bread that required patience and a good set of teeth to consume.

For weeks, it seemed, we did not see Boudicca smile. I greeted her in the morning and she would respond gruffly, 'Morning.' She would go outside, do yoga, and return to her room to read her books. She looked balefully at the kittens, at which point we realised that respect for sentient beings was a long way from liking them. She smelled of earthy essential oils and the ancient leather jacket that she rarely removed. When she left for university on her bike, Bridget and I sighed with relief.

'She's so cool,' Bridget said.

'She's so ... scary,' I said.

'Do you think she hates us?'

'I think she maybe hates everyone.'

One evening we were all in our various parts of the house, minding our own business, when a strange, repetitive sound started up. It resembled a cross between a braying donkey and a car alarm. Bridget and I rushed into the kitchen, where Boudicca stood, her hands on her stomach, bent over. The melamine phone was on the bench, its receiver lying nearby, indicating that a phone call had been taking place when Boudicca began emitting this unusual sound.

'Are you all right?' I said, peering at her. I'd heard about people having episodes like this as a feature of some kind of epilepsy.

But Boudicca was not in pain, nor in a state of seizure. She was laughing.

She picked up the receiver, gasped, 'I've gotta go,' then sank down onto the kitchen floor.

'She's so funny,' Boudicca said, wiping her eyes.

Bridget and I sat down on the floor too.

'I thought you were having a fit,' I said.

'I thought you were possessed,' said Bridget.

'I got kicked out of Gino's the other day because of my laugh,' Boudicca said. 'They thought I was drunk.'

'Do you drink?'

'I could go a port right now,' Boudicca said. 'What do you reckon?'

Bridget, the possessor of the only passenger vehicle, grabbed her keys and held them aloft.

'To the bottleshop!' she said.

. . .

Boudicca introduced me to a community of strong, intelligent, informed women in and around university. Some of them were straight, most of them were not. They were able to articulate the reasons things were unfair in the world – for women, for Aboriginal people, for queer people, for people who were not white or well educated or part of the 'dominant paradigm', as they called it. They suggested practical solutions. They worked in women's shelters and for community organisations. They were women of a type I had never met before. I admired and feared them in equal parts.

My natural academic tendencies were toward the literary and creative rather than the political and philosophical, but I began enrolling in units that would give me language to engage (one didn't talk anymore) with the academic, critical-theory-driven women who debated with anyone who would argue with them, which, at university, was just about everyone.

I also began dressing and acting differently. One night, after several helpings of port-from-a-box, I cut off my still-permed hair in the carpark of the Willagee Shopping Centre, then used the last of my disposable razor blades to finish the job at home. After shaving my head, I abandoned the use of razor blades, disposable or otherwise (no plastics were recyclable in 1990), deodorant, and make-up. I wore cheesecloth pants I borrowed from Bridget or second-hand coloured jeans. I abandoned dresses except when worn ironically with Doc Martens and sported a rainbow scarf around my shorn head. I protested in the forests and was arrested for chaining myself to a sheep ship. The latter was most memorable because my wharfie stepfather prevented a regular wharfie from stepping on my fingers, which were wrapped around the railing I was chained to, by barking, 'Oi, leave off, that's me stepdaughter.' I made thin soy milk, to which I added volumes of honey and vanilla to make it palatable, and tried to become a vegan.

And I fell into a full obsession – I would like to say love, but that would give the feeling a dignity it did not have – with a woman.

21

The object of my passion, for a time unrequited and forever uneven, was eight years older, five inches shorter, good looking, charismatic and unkempt, with a pealing and infectious laugh. I first saw her at a university student union meeting in a lecture theatre, where she was berating commerce students over something, perhaps about being commerce students. The content of what she said mattered less than the way in which she said it. She was articulate, passionate, fearless. She also had a halo of fine, knotted hair and a misbuttoned shirt, both of which were charming to my twenty-year-old bedazzled eyes. With so many important arguments to be had, ignoring personal grooming was gallant and a requirement of the revolution. I was smitten.

'Who is that?' I whispered to Boudicca, who had brought me to the meeting.

'Annie,' she said.

'Is she a lesbian?'

'She's the Women's Officer,' Boudicca said, as if lesbianism formed part of the job requirements.

From that point I took up the playbook I'd written for myself when I was fourteen. I found out what subjects Annie was doing, what meetings she was going to attend, and when she would be at the university social club. I joined the student union and began frequenting the Women's Room, which I soon learned was the place I was most likely to encounter her.

One Sunday, we were invited to Annie's house in the nightclub and migrant district of Northbridge to make badges for the upcoming Reclaim the Night rally. Her abode was one half of a duplex, with a long, lino-covered passageway off which there were high-ceilinged bedrooms, a lounge room in the middle of the house containing shabby couches and low tables covered in books, record sleeves and coffee cups, then a tiny kitchen at the back next to the bathroom. At the very rear of the block was an outdoor toilet reachable by a slabbed pathway. Sunflowers taller than us filled the sandy yard, and their heads were scattered inside, waiting to be dried to extract the seeds for the next plantings. There were no flyscreens, and the doors and windows were all propped open to let in the air. The dish rack was piled with a Jenga-arrangement of cups, plates, and bowls. I was struck by this as it seemed a symbol of a liberation from the housekeeping methods my grandmother Violet had drilled into us: first glasses, then cups, then plates stacked according to size, and lastly pots and pans. Pots and pans were not in evidence for the good reason that nobody in the house stooped to something so symbolic of female oppression as cooking.

One of the women in the badge-making group talked about the politics of design vis-a-vis the duplex. In the period it was built, women were meant to be out of sight, hence their relegation to the back quarters. I remember being surprised that there could be a politics of architecture, but I was fast learning there could be a politics of anything. The assembled women cut up letters, magazines, whatever we had to hand, to make badges we could both adorn ourselves with and use to educate passers-by as to our cause. Mine proclaimed *Other* on a yellow background. There were ankhs and drawings of fists. Annie cut up an original photograph of herself and her mother. I was shocked at the audacity of blithely taking scissors to a black-and-white original print. We drank herbal tea and began discussing the likelihood of an upcoming revolution, Marxism versus post-structuralism, colonisation, rights for sex workers, childcare at university, and then, when our political talk was expended, our personal lives.

At the badge-making Annie was in her element. Her laugh made everyone laugh. She recounted extravagant tales of the things she'd done, including propositioning her current lover when drunk. This had involved her sneezing capsicum through her nose and inquiring whether he found her sexually attractive, capsicum still dangling from a nostril, to which the lover answered, 'Sometimes.' The anecdote was funny to everybody except for me at the gut-dropping realisation that said lover was a male.

However, I wasn't going to let anything as pesky as heterosexuality stand in the way of trying to seduce her. I felt I was far worthier of Annie's wondrousness than any male could be, surely, and being straight was a contradiction of her otherwise liberatory attitude to convention.

One evening Boudicca and I had ridden to a women's dance in Northbridge with me perched, thrilled and terrified, on the back of her motorbike as we rushed down the freeway on a warm October evening. Later we rode on to Annie's house, with Boudicca announcing our arrival by revving the 750 outside the door. Annie yelled to come in, and so Boudicca revved the bike, mounted the pavement and rode through the front door, down the long passageway and into the living room. Annie and her housemate, Rose, watched our progression, shrieking with delight.

The utter coolness of such a stunt made Annie warm to me. I had already declared my undying and extravagant love, which was met with interest but not reciprocation, but as Boudicca disappeared into Annie's housemate's room, Annie asked if I would like to stay the night.

One of the things Annie said after this first encounter was, 'People historically have a difficult time with me.' She informed me that she had a selection of lovers in train: she didn't do relationships, relationships being bourgeois and retrograde, so I could forget all of that, in case I had any ideas. She even warned me that there was one male who was more regularly around than others (the recipient of the capsicum sneeze). In the heady morning-after, I pronounced I didn't care. Annie did everything except instruct me to flee the house if I wanted to have anything other than the type of relationship that would have rendered the Marquis de Sade nervous.

So the warning signs were there, lined up in a row and flashing fit to be seen from space, but I ignored them. I was convinced, with the certainty only available to twenty-year-olds and people on very strong medication, that this would be different. I would be different. I was young, pure, enthusiastic, and had been reading Great Literature for years about the desirability of impossible and/or difficult love (blithely ignoring the endings of Madame Bovary, Anna Karenina, Catherine and Heathcliff). I was eager for tragic, impossible love. As in *Wuthering Heights*, there was the boring mundane reality on one side, and the uniting of destined souls on the other.

I was a flag bearer for impossible love. Not content to merely overcome metaphorical obstacles I would, whenever drunk and nearby, hoist myself through Annie's window onto the couch, waiting for the object of my obsession to return and comfort my wounded heart.

The only problem with this impulse was that Annie was in no way prepared to provide comfort of this or any kind. Her responses to this behaviour, quite understandably, varied between impatience and irritation. In time Annie would make jokes of the incidents, but in their immediate aftermath I found more sympathetic comfort provided by her housemate, Rose, who was in the midst of experiencing passion similarly unrequited by Boudicca.

When I was not drunk and defenestrating myself, and when she was not detached or defending herself against the emotional onslaught of my passion, Annie was charismatic, unpredictable, fun to be around, and utterly fearless. Her house was filled with types of people I'd never met before, who appeared to enjoy shocking me with their tall tales, unconventional critiques of life, and heroic bingeing. She slept with the windows open in the middle of Northbridge, rarely bothered with underwear, and invited homeless people to come in for a cup of tea or to sleep on the couch on the verandah. One night a man snuck down the back of the house and peeped in the bathroom window, where Rose was taking a bath. An infuriated Annie, who was pushing five feet two inches in shoes, chased the man up the street and through an unlit Hyde Park, a haven for drug dealers and the site of many a sexual assault, yelling at him to keep the fuck away from her house.

Regardless of my pining and her reluctance, we embarked upon a torrid, widely witnessed, push-pull relationship of sorts. To observers, I seemed to regularly lose my senses. I possessed no other subject than my passion, and bored my friends with the latest incident or wounded feeling. It was not a relationship in which I could feel settled or content or creative. I had other girlfriends during this time, who also suffered from my inability to find any boundary with Annie, and the alacrity with which I disappeared back to her when beckoned.

When I went to England not long after my twenty-first birthday, in part hoping that the tyranny of distance would release me from the tyranny of my own feelings, I wrote rambling letters in which I attempted to be witty and detached on one page, but more often descended into introspective and melodramatic proclamations on the subsequent nine. I sat on the smelly mattress in the laundry room in Brixton, playing my steel-string guitar and wailing Indigo Girls and Sinead O'Connor songs until my housemates begged me to desist. I used the scarce resource of pound coins to call her from phone boxes in the snow, often miscalculating the time and waking her at 3am, which did nothing to endear me to her from ten thousand miles away. But the sound of her voice calmed me enough to quell whatever longing I had until the longing re-emerged and made me insensible to getting a grip on myself.

It was the kind of relationship one has in one's teens or early twenties, the kind which a person can normally look back upon with a fond what-was-I-thinking perspective. In usual circumstances, I would have moved on to other relationships, and the cringing neediness I had displayed would have receded to memory, or perhaps, mercifully, have exited my brain.

This indulgent perspective turned out, through every fault of my own, to be difficult to achieve.

22

The first time I met John was unremarkable. He was sitting in Annie's house, smoking a rollie and reading a book, and was unperturbed by being introduced to his sister's young lesbian lover. He was twelve years older than me, which meant he seemed of a different, alien generation. He had spent much of his youth in groups of anarchist, anti-nuclear protestors, playing pool and drinking quantities of beer in seedy pubs, experimenting with new drugs like ecstasy, and trying to find an alternative way to exist that avoided conventional things like marriage, children, or paid work. The Annie who had gushed over the amazing qualities of this brother was now serious and tried to engage him in conversation; toward these attempts he seemed equivocal at best. I could not discern the charisma I'd heard so much about. He seemed acceptably good-looking, for a male, and he was not my type, even if my type had been male. It was an inauspicious introduction.

The second time I met John was with Annie's housemate, Rose. We met in the Lebanese joint favoured by the angsty left and discussed Rose's latest heartbreak. John listened attentively, then delivered some wisdom about the clarifying nature of anger that was superbly articulated. He was newly sober and newly free of cigarettes. He was doing a twelve-step program and exuded calmness. I left pondering how together he had appeared, how this must be the version of the brother that had attracted comment. Finally, I could see why Annie thought so highly of him.

At our third meeting, Rose, Annie, John and I were wandering around the city, looking for a camera repair shop. John and I fell behind and started talking. Almost as soon as we started talking, we started laughing.

Every time we met after that, we laughed more and more. John was irreverently witty, and his eyes twinkled appealingly with the pleasure of making me laugh. I particularly enjoyed the irreverent comments he made about his sister, against whom I hurled my heart over and over again. He seemed to have all the qualities of his sister, but I did not feel compelled to rend myself open to him, or for him to fix my unending anxieties with his love.

If only he was a woman, I used to think.

. . .

After the 1993 horse-riding accident, when I was twenty-three, I divided the people I knew into two. The first group were the ones who visited me in hospital, took me out in my wheelchair despite the inconvenience involved, and did not immediately start talking about their sore back or the time they broke their arm on the monkey bars in the playground if I mentioned my pain levels were high. The second group comprised everyone else.

The recasting of those I knew also led to me changing the way I felt and behaved. I was able to stop my habitual haemorrhaging of emotion. I required all my energy to knit my bones and repair my damaged flesh, and it left little room for superfluous or extravagant feelings. I was, for the first time in my life, emotionally contained. I stopped wildly adopting this philosophy or that philosophy. This meant I could finally be friends with Annie. There is a photograph of us from that time, with me in the living room in her Northbridge house, my feet on her lap as her neighbour regaled us with some story of academia. We look comfortable together, and for a short time we were.

The pain sharpened my awareness of the chook raffle of existence, and whatever existence allows. Had I fallen a fraction harder, I would have been paralysed, as happened to Christopher Reeve in an alarmingly similar accident not long after mine. At the same time as I was recovering and recalibrating my world view, my nineteen-year-old cousin Konrad was in the last throes of futile treatment for his brain tumour. I apologised to him for never having visited him in hospital after his various operations. We discussed how pain twists the lens through which you see others, the world. I was ashamed of my former self-centredness and promised myself I would be kinder.

It was at this point that John became more than the twelve-years-older brother of my ex-girlfriend who I laughed with. Now, he became attentive and kind. He was not afraid of the pain I was experiencing. Nor did he dismiss the fear and anxiety that went with it, and which also accompanied being twenty-three, unqualified, temporarily disabled by my injuries, and broke. He was going out with a woman his own age who had a daughter still in primary school. He didn't talk much about this girlfriend-arrangement, except to indicate that it was an open and non-possessive relationship, typical of the anti-war, protesting, leftist crowd of the time.

When my ankle had healed, John and I took to walking into Fremantle from his place in a housing co-operative he'd helped establish in the mid 80s. We laughed, drank hot chocolate, and spent a lot of time in the New Edition bookshop, flipping through the latest *Black & White* magazine, or *Granta*, or books about tattoos or anarchism, or those by Marguerite Duras or Ian McEwan, reading appealing sentences to each other. By this time John had maintained sobriety for several years, ran ten kilometres each day, and was so protective of his personal space that he would often not answer the phone or respond to a knock at the door for a week or two at a time. Despite his fierce intelligence, he had no worldly ambition, which at the time I viewed as a Zen-like quality. His house in the middle of the co-op was sparse but peaceful. He also took care of his girlfriend-type's daughter once a week. He was devoted to the little girl and prioritised her over anything else in his life. I was impressed.

'You'd be a good sperm donor,' I said one day as we walked.

'You could move in and we could co-parent,' he replied.

'I could write and you could stay home and take care of the baby,' I said.

'All I need is a coffee and newspaper allowance,' he said.

Not long after this conversation, my then girlfriend-type took me to a party. John and his girlfriend-type were there. When John and I saw each other, we hugged and chatted delightedly. On the way home my girlfriend-type asked sternly if there was something between John and me.

'No!' I said, shocked. 'We're just good friends.'

This was met with a scepticism that I pondered. Maybe there was something there. Maybe John was more than my ex-girlfriend's brother, or should be, and maybe the fact of him being my ex-girlfriend's brother was stopping me from seeing it.

And so I started looking at John in a different way. When we were walking back from the bookshop one evening, I said that I thought I could smell myrrh burning, or perhaps frankincense. We took this as a sign, a blessing from the night sky. We walked close, as we always did, my arm around his shoulders to accommodate my greater height. We gently bumped hips as we walked.

...

That night, and for some time afterward, I was comforted by similarities in the surroundings favoured by this male sibling: the futon mattress made up with white sheets, a scattering of well-worn books on the floor nearby, bookshelves constructed of planks and bricks, comfortable couches covered in patterned Indian cloths. I was also comforted that with this male sibling I was not prone to hysterical outpourings of feeling and was quite content to disappear from John's life and back into my own for weeks at a time. I was nervous that the transition to a physical relationship would ruin the affection and regard we had for each other but relieved it was gloriously free of the high drama that had attended the time in which I had been around Annie.

I wasn't sure whether, when the fact became public, the bigger deal would be my sleeping with a male (being, as I was, a visible, card-carrying, head-shaving, dockers-wearing, protesting lesbian in the 90s lesbian community of Perth) or having slept with Annie's brother, given that most of the aforementioned community had witnessed my emotional states and many had listened to my endless recounting of her wondrousness, our difficulties, my extreme passions. In relation to the fact of his being Annie's brother, I reassured myself that I had the good parts of Annie without the difficult bits. Sure, the male aspect took a bit of getting used to again, but it was giddily pleasant.

The more immediately difficult part was that my then girlfriend-type, whom I'd just broken up with, viewed my running off with a boy as a betrayal not only of her specifically but also of the sisterhood generally, the nature of which she detailed in a very long and very expletive-laden answering machine message. Unsurprisingly too, Annie was not enamoured at my continuing boundaryless behaviour, and we did not speak for many years.

These reactions continued my pattern of ensuring explosive beginnings and endings to relationships. If there wasn't drama, obsession, and gossip, it wasn't worth doing.

But although hurtful to some and inexplicable to others, beginnings and endings of relationships at least had the benefit of being short in duration.

It was other ways of being, of establishing a relationship, that turned out to cause longer lasting problems. These resulted from deeper grooves and fissures that, being obscured, were easy to fall into, hard to recognise, and requiring more than mere understanding to climb free of.

23

I did understand the baffled reaction I got from other people to my changing sexual orientation, let alone changing sexual orientation with members of the same family.

It had taken some effort to elicit understanding from friends and family when I had declared myself a lesbian, after all. Gwen, whose unusual sexual appetites I had thought might make her sympathetic to mine, wailed when I revealed my lesbian state. Her biggest complaint was that she wanted a grandchild, a notion I had never before heard and certainly one I had never encouraged her to hold. Nevertheless, now that unarticulated hope had been dashed, and she was almost as distressed as when she'd found my cupboards stuffed with stolen items when I was fifteen during my kleptomaniac phase. When she calmed down, she proceeded to give me birthday cards with images of busty women in compromising poses. Perhaps provocatively, I brought various girlfriends, including Annie, to Sunday lunches at Frank and Violet's, inducing stiff politeness in all present, which I was prepared to accept in lieu of actual acceptance. However, when I announced I was now in a relationship with a male, Gwen gave me a look of pained tolerance no doubt similar to those Frank had produced when meeting all of the Allans, Mikes and Steves over the years.

To my friends, my 180-degree swing was viewed as being on a continuum with my general chaotic conduct in the world, having been twice in a mental hospital, twice dropped out of high school, three times changed university courses, shaved my head, been arrested chaining myself to a sheep ship, and so on. They merely considered this a new and expanded way in which I careened through life.

As for John himself, my friends only ever saw the best side of him, if they saw him at all. From the start very few of them saw us together, as he didn't like going out and loathed formal occasions. My friends relied on what I told them, and I told them that John was, by comparison, much easier to deal with than my previous relationships with women had been. He was always happy to see me. He pedalled enthusiastically from his house to the train station, on two train lines, to arrive at my share house with his own peanut paste and muesli, required due to his excessive exercise regime. He was witty and well read, and an enthusiastic conversationalist and debater. He was sure of his opinions and could back them up. He was outwardly lacking emotional and existential angst.

He sounded great, my friends agreed. I seemed calmer than when I'd been with Annie. He was so much older than me: maybe that was a good thing, as he'd had time to mature, unlike men in their twenties. They accepted that he was not social. We believed that relationships did not need to be conventional, that a person who did not bend to conventional goals, such as a career or a family, displayed the courage of their convictions. Keen to find ways of living outside The System, we admired others who managed to find a way around it.

If they had any misgivings about John and our relationship, they kept them to themselves as completely as I did.

...

In my memory, there was a stark contrast between John as he was when we were going out, without any actual plan to have a child, and how he became later. But that's not quite accurate. When I look back, I realise I had misgivings from the start, but I neither articulated them to anyone nor was able to admit them to myself.

Some of my misgivings were minor. There was the age thing, for one. John's friends were so much older, and we shared little pop culture or music, despite both growing up in Perth. He appeared mildly condescending toward the life struggles my friends and I were engaged in, such as finding satisfying jobs or creative fulfilment. Apart from lurking around bookshops, we did not have mutually compatible daily lives. He never came to see me perform in the comedy group that increasingly took up a large part of my life because he didn't like going out at night, and comedy wasn't his thing. I had no interest in the softball games or tennis he enjoyed, or the gym he spent time at, or watching Australian Rules football, so I figured that was okay. Wasn't it?

John went incommunicado from time to time, but I knew this was because he needed space from everybody, not just me. Sure, due to the lack of ambition I so admired, he didn't have a regular job – at thirty-five, he lived by not needing much, residing in a rent-controlled co-operative housing estate in Fremantle he'd helped establish, on a mixture of social security benefits and cash-in-hand cleaning work. I was only keen to have a job that would fit my creative pursuits, such as writing and performing, so I didn't mind that. Sure, he was damaged, but he'd done twelve-step programs and was even counselling in them, so that meant he was aware of his damage and how to manage it. He didn't witter on and on about his problems as I and most of my friends did. So that was all right too. Wasn't it?

The other aspect of the beginning of our relationship was that it was not, by anyone's definition, a relationship in the traditional sense. That is, while I was not seeing anyone else, John continued – without saying or me asking whether he was or wasn't – the relationship he'd been in with his girlfriend-type. I had been so thoroughly schooled in the smash-the-patriarchy school of feminism by this stage that any concern I had about this I blamed on my own conventional thinking. People did not own each other. Jealousy was something we had been taught to feel as a way of keeping women pinned to traditional roles. So I did not feel it was my place to ask the status of the arrangements he might have had elsewhere. I called what John and I were in 'lover-friendship'. John was sweet to me, and that was all that mattered. Wasn't it?

Then there were the other things.

One evening in 1993, some six months after we started going out, John and I were sitting with my new housemates Nikki and Shaun in our lounge room. The television was on, as it often was, which John had criticised privately to me before. I'd never been much of a television watcher, having had several years of my youth without one, but now I was being introduced to *Twin Peaks*, *Star Trek* Next Gen, and the pleasures of communing around a screen. It was interactive television-watching in any case – there was a running commentary of queries or criticism between Nikki, Shaun and me, prompted by whatever was appearing on the screen.

I wasn't paying that much attention to what was on this particular evening. Later it turned out it was the football, or a commentary on football, or something football-related. Given the usual lively debate that was occurring between John and Shaun about world politics and ideology, it wasn't clear to me there was anything invested in the show that was on. It could have been live, it could have been a replay for all I knew. So in the commercial break, I turned the channel over to something else.

When I changed the channel, John didn't say anything. If anybody else even noticed, they didn't comment. Conversation continued in a normal way. We all chatted for a while and later on went to bed.

John came into my room and shut the door. I was expecting him to turn around with his usual anticipatory grin, but instead came closer to me and hissed, in a hostile voice I'd never heard from him before, 'What did you do that for?'

'Do what?' I said lightly. I thought through the evening and tried to remember if there'd been anything noteworthy or anything that might have been upsetting to anybody.

'Turn the show off,' he said. 'You changed the channel, right in the middle of it.'

'Did I?' I said, searching his face for a sign that he was kidding, that he would revert to his usual lighthearted way, that it was some strange practical joke.

But he did not. His face was red. His complete change in demeanour shocked me.

I protested that I hadn't thought it was a big deal. John began to talk insistently, in what I soon realised was a quiet rage. He told me how disrespectful I'd been, how embarrassing it was, how it showed utter disregard for him, for Shaun, for normal social interaction. Then he questioned me: why would I do such a thing? How could I not know that not only had I upset him, I'd also ruined his and Shaun's banter, he'd come all the way there and been treated like that, who did I think I was?

To each question he demanded an answer. When I answered – protested my innocence of the heinous intent he ascribed – he said I was lying. He went over and over the sequence of events until I agreed with how he described it. Changing the television channel was wrong and I was wrong for not realising it. If I raised the pitch of my protests even a fraction, he told me to keep my voice down.

Eventually I began crying out of confusion, out of frustration, feeling falsely accused and being unable to defend myself, as if I were trapped in a Kafka story. Then I began sobbing. I sat on the floor and he sat on the edge of my bed, pointing at me, his torrent of fury unabating as I wept into my hands. He did not stop, even as I begged him to. I did not care who was right or wrong. I just wanted it to stop.

When, after some hours, he exhausted himself, he refused to leave my house. It was too late, there were no trains. He slept with his back to me. I did not sleep but did not dare leave the bed, in case he got up and resumed his accusations.

The next morning John was frosty toward me but behaved normally toward Nikki and Shaun. He left early, and after he left, I asked Nikki if Shaun had been upset by me turning over the channel the previous night. She didn't know what I was talking about, and I didn't explain further.

I remained shocked at this behaviour but also sufficiently ashamed by it that I did not speak of it to anyone. In my diary I called it a 'yuck'. I do not remember whether I contemplated ending the relationship. It may well have been that because the relationship was so loosely defined I felt there was no need for anything as official as ending it. I took comfort that our lives were separate and saw no way that the separation would be changed by anything.

And then, he phoned, or I did. Probably it was me. The pattern begun that night meant he usually extracted my acknowledgement that yes, I had done the wrong thing, and only then would he say, 'I was stressed because of x, I was having a bad time because of y, what you did reminded me of z.' Then he would make me laugh, and it was the end of it. For a time.

What I realise now, and what did not occur to me because at the time I did not know, was that John was separating from the open relationship that had been sputtering to an end even before I came on the scene. For years afterward I puzzled about how he could have been so sweet for so many months initially then change so suddenly. He said all the right things. He loved being with me. He was attentive and kind. He massaged my back, still painful from spinal fractures, with apricot oil.

Now I suspect that the other relationship had absorbed a side of John. It spared me from the flaring temper, the vituperative words and unabated fury that emerged when he was not dividing his private self. His periods of being incommunicado were part of his experiencing and recovering from the storming of emotion which was being visited elsewhere. But once there was no buffer, I suddenly experienced his full spectrum of emotion and expression.

I didn't record in my diary what happened after the channel-changing, and I rarely recorded the similar incidents that happened afterward. My diary was otherwise the repository for every thought, emotion, dream, event I experienced, often in cringe-worthy detail. But the references I made to these outbursts, as I thought of them, were made long afterward, when I referred to us being in harmony again, which implied that we must have fought. If I did reflect on them in my diary, I usually blamed myself. I had triggered him, I had to be more careful. Once, a year after we started going out, I noted how concerned I was about my own responses to conflict: *I shrink*, I wrote to myself. *I literally experience myself as getting smaller.*

24

In the second year of my relationship with John, I embarked on a second lover-friendship – with a woman.

This running-off-with-a-woman took place not long after what I considered the aberrant John began appearing more and more, and not long after I learned that he had continued his open relationship without being open with me about it.

However, I couldn't explain to myself why I was suddenly so driven to get away from John, because I couldn't acknowledge that I – the formerly fierce, card-carrying women's rights marcher, the one who had hurt so many women by running off with a man in the first place – was now in a relationship with someone who belittled me, dismissed me, and regularly put me on edge when I saw him.

To me, I was acting on my new understanding that our lover-friendship was commitment-free.

When I casually mentioned the new addition to my lover-friendships on a visit to his house in Fremantle one day, I half expected – and perhaps half wanted – John to be so furious that he broke it off. Instead, he displayed a deep woundedness. He was utterly hurt. He had never loved anybody the way he loved me, he told me, and now I was disregarding his feelings. Did I not understand that although he'd continued the previous relationship, he wanted to be exclusively with me and thought I had reciprocated this desire? Did I not understand that he had given the heart he had callously withheld from all previous lovers to me? He was a new man, turning over a new leaf.

I had ruined everything.

I drove back from Fremantle, feeling ashamed and guilty. I had, it seemed, misjudged everything. He was a fragile man who had never trusted before he trusted me, and now I'd broken him. He had never once been so hurt. I was so powerful that I had done this to him. I had misused my power, and now, look! My explanations about my new lover-friendship being different because it was a woman, about me never having said that I had become entirely straight, about wanting to be free now I was in less physical pain – none could match the depth of his woundedness.

Afterward, I wrote a long letter to him, trying to explain – but the letter sounded false, and to him it became further evidence of how I did not appreciate the heinousness of what I had done.

In the next few months I vacillated between being relieved at my freedom and wondering if I had done the right thing. I understood that what I'd done was barely conscious and tried without success to get to the bones of my desire to escape the relationship with John. I analysed myself and my actions in painful and fruitless detail. If I had spent a fraction of the time analysing John and John's actions, I might have been able to express what I could not at that point think. Every time I approached the subject of John's explosiveness and savageness, I veered away into the more well-worn path of blaming myself.

And because I didn't have the words for it, it was too easy to get back together again, six months later. A condition of us reuniting was that I had to concede that everything was my fault. And of course I did, because of course, it was. Wasn't it?

. . .

At the beginning of 1996, when I was twenty-six, everything changed.

Having spent much of the previous few years as a practising lesbian, I was a little rusty with the concept of birth control.

One minute, I was working on contract as a teacher of English to refugees, had recently returned from two successful comedy tours to fringe festivals in Hong Kong and Adelaide with a female comedy trio, and was the owner of a mortgage on a one-bedroom flat. The next, after peeing on a stick in a public toilet at Cloisters Arcade one lunchtime, I was expecting.

Even though I wasn't expecting to be expecting, on seeing the two faint blue parallel lines appear in the tiny window, my first feeling was joy, which rose like a warm balloon in my chest.

The balloon deflated somewhat on announcing my state to John. We were not living together. I lived in Maylands, he lived in Fremantle. He caught the train down and we discussed the practicalities of having a child. Again, having spent most of the previous several years around lesbians before lesbians had access to IVF, I had no idea what having a child might entail. I had pleasant visions of walking around with the baby in a pram, writing while it slept, singing to it, and teaching it how to read. People had babies all the time. How hard could it be?

I was firm that I was keeping the baby. John's only decision was how much he was going to be involved.

It didn't get off to a good start. He complained about me complaining about the sickness that I wished were only confined to mornings. He informed me he wasn't sure if I would cope with a child. He tired of hearing me complain about how the nausea was making my teaching work difficult.

Then, after he'd had some time to ponder, he decided he wanted us to be together.

If we were going to raise a child, this was how we were to do it. I would sell my flat at a loss, move in with him in Fremantle in the rent-controlled housing co-operative, and we would be a family. We would have separate ends of his unit, a concession to our mutual requirements for solitude. I agreed it made sense. I was nervous about selling my flat, but I could not afford to keep it if I moved, rent-controlled new space or not. Plus, I wanted our child to have the best possible start to life. We weren't going to get married, but surely it was best for a child to have two parents, united in love for their baby, no matter the differences in their lives before?

Within weeks I had left my former life for my new one as a partner, as a parent-to-be. The unit was small but light, with high ceilings, surrounded by native trees and shrubs and nasturtium patches in winter. Our child would be raised in a community, there was a park next door, there were other children who would save it from being an introverted singleton. Lying on my new bed, I could see the sky through the high window under the apex of the roof.

John and I took to walking on Port Beach each morning as my stomach expanded. The water of the Indian Ocean broke on the shore and whooshed over our feet as we wandered and talked and laughed. We liked the idea of our child, in its own salty waters, hearing the hiss and suck of the waves.

Some days a wave gathered up and teetered, its lip shimmering for an extended moment, and in the curve of the suspended glassy water darted silvery schools of baitfish. Then I would swim out past the break line, float on my back in the water, weightless under the blue skies that rarely held cloud, listening to the muted echoey sounds of the water moving over the ribbed soft sand beneath me.

In those months we read in a frenzy, preparing for the state of parenthood that would soon be upon us. We read books on attachment parenting with biblical reverence. We read about Montessori schooling and philosophies of learning. I read books about natural childbirth. We discussed what we had read and the damage we'd endured in our own childhoods, blighted as they had been by the ignorance of our parents and the cultural disregard for children and their feelings. We were in total accord. We would protect this child from all the malevolent forces in the world, including the dysfunction of our own families. With the compensation I received from the horse-riding accident, I bought an old Volvo, a washing machine, and a bed big enough to accommodate me and our baby, with cotton sheets in calming pastels. There would be no cot for this child. This child would never feel alone or abandoned.

Then there were more practical matters.

One day we were lying on the bed, discussing baby names on a hot day in December. Outside the large window, the hot easterly breeze stirred the Geraldton wax that was blooming there. My pale blooming stomach rose firmly, like a mound of sand patted into a pleasing shape at the beach. I was convinced I was having a boy; we settled easily on a boy's name.

'But what,' I said, 'if it's a girl?'

We silently contemplated for a moment, and then John said, 'I know – let's call her Annie!'

We exploded with laughter. We laughed and laughed until I became concerned the laughing was bringing on a contraction. I had to lie on my side in order to be able to laugh and breathe, the baby taking up all space south of my lungs.

And at the end of the laughter, wiping away our mirthful tears, we looked at each other.

'Okay,' I said. 'Let's.'

And so we named our baby girl after my ex-girlfriend and John's sister. It was part irony, part homage, part hope that a new child would bring about unity, understanding, and forgiveness.

SURPRISE! FIND YOURSELF LIVING WITH A STREET ANGEL, HOME DEVIL

25

It was the end of 1996. A vigorous easterly wind rustled the overhead canopies, bringing hot weather and sneeze-producing wheat dust from the recent harvest, as John and I trod the deserted footpaths of the co-op in the middle of the night, trying to hasten the contractions that remained stubbornly at a you-don't-need-to-come-in-yet distance apart. Images of women rushing to hospital to immediately give birth in television shows bore no resemblance to the interminable hours we spent waiting. The child had already shown a reluctance to leave the womb by being ten days overdue. When I'd had a scan to make sure all was in order, the report came back: 'VERY active baby'. The baby's in-utero kickboxing and half pikes with twists, however, did not translate to any desire to exit its enclosed comfort. I began to wonder if the child would emerge at all or whether I was having a very convincing phantom pregnancy.

All the things I had thought I would want at the birth – all my close friends, a masseuse, gentle music playing in the background, to be in water, to endure without pain relief – were the opposite of what I actually wanted when my body started the work required to expel the baby from its watery home and into the world. John eagerly responded to my demands for medicine balls, apple juice, a receptacle to vomit in, but I regarded him balefully, he being responsible for me being in this predicament in the first place, and I was relieved each time he went off to nap on the couch. Gwen, in contrast, was completely present and knew exactly what words to say when, for perhaps the only time in my life. She left the room only once, to sob because the sounds I made birthing resembled the sounds Frank had made dying.

There was no comfort to be had during labour: it was labour spiritual, emotional, and physical. I entered the birthing tub only to immediately leave it, as the still water intensified the pain of contractions and the warm water added to the already unbearable overheating. I vomited without caring I was vomiting, or where. I could not stop the diarrhoea which was no doubt worsened by the castor oil I'd taken to hasten this very event, so spent most of the second half of labour alternating between standing in the shower and sitting on the toilet. When the midwife inserted her entire arm up my vagina, like a vet into the rear end of a cow in *All Creatures Great and Small*, to see how I was progressing, I could not have cared less. When she intoned approvingly 'roomy pelvis' upon retracting her limb, I felt re-energised with pride. I was built for doing this. I would never care about anything ever again. All the other activities and concerns of my life – writing, relationships, education, work, endlessly agonising over this thing and that thing – fell away. There was nothing beyond this. All human history and human endeavour, I was convinced, culminated in this act. I understood why men were obsessed with creating their own brain children, ideas of Übermensch, of domination through violence and war. In the face of this, men were powerless and pointless.

These lofty considerations, as well as certainty and concern for dignity, fell away when the transition to the final stage of labour began and the pain took on an all-encompassing dimension that I naively believed had already been reached. When I inquired, 'Is it too late for some pethidine?' I already knew the answer and had a brief reflection on all the women before me who had died in childbirth. I understood now the extremity of being required for this ordinary act. These women were heroes. They fought and they lost, but the point was the fighting.

I was sitting on the toilet, resting in between the only thing that now existed in the world – the tense-and-release of pain – when the midwife suggested now might be a good time to stand up. I was surprised to feel, when I reached an inquiring hand down, a warm cantaloupe-shape protruding from my nether regions. As speedily as the preceding ten months had gone slowly, the baby was caught by the midwife and placed, bloody, purplish and whole, on my lap.

For a second the baby was still, and then with a jerk it reared back, took air, and yelled.

I stared at this fully formed human I had produced. I looked from the black-haired infant to John and Gwen, who were both crying, united in astonishment.

'Is it a boy or a girl?' Gwen asked, when she could.

'Oh,' I said. I lifted the chubby knee a little and said, 'It's a girl. I think.'

Some time later – after the afterbirth, the stitching, the first suckling – John and I gazed in wonder at the swaddled infant.

'Ba-ba-ba-ba,' John crooned, as he had been crooning at my stomach for months.

I tried to tally this curled-up collection of limbs, spine, shoulders with the unknown shapes I had felt under my stretched skin. Outside, I would have to learn the shape of this baby anew. Then I felt the side of her foot and recognised what I had felt beneath my ribcage. I had massaged this nub of flesh and felt it push back in response. If I closed my eyes and massaged the foot under the swaddling, I found myself reassured by this edge, this relic of familiarity between one state and the next.

'Baby Annie,' I said. 'Hello.'

...

As foreshadowed by the ultrasound report, Annie came out a VERY active baby. She was alert, interested in all movement, and ready to be amused.

Baby Annie did not take to sleep, mostly because this interrupted access to her supply of milk, which she extracted voraciously, and also because it robbed her of the opportunity to be involved in whatever was going on.

And in the early days, there was a lot going on. Despite John's general loathing of visitors, visitors were welcomed to view this perfect arrangement of baby flesh: the milk-stained lips, the deep-green eyes gazing out from cheeks that invited marvel at their soft density. Gwen visited regularly. Derek, my stepmother Olvi, and my seven- and five-year-old sisters, Luci and Alice, were eager to meet her and doted on her from the start; Annie introduced herself to Luci by ejecting a stream of milky vomit into her glass of water. My friends visited, marvelling at me having produced my ex-girlfriend's eponymous niece. Even the ex-girlfriend came, pleased at this extraordinary demonstration of acknowledging her central role in the production of this baby by providing the baby with her name. As if in determination to mend family fractures, Annie had also contrived to be born on my religious uncle's birthday. He had disapproved of my getting pregnant out of wedlock, as he had thirty years previously disapproved of Gwen, but he and my aunty visited with a congratulatory present and gazed down on his great-niece as lovingly as we all did.

John and I took baby Annie on pram rides around Fremantle. The Italian grandmothers outside tending their tomato plants cooed over her, then tightened her bunny rugs despite the sweltering weather. 'Too young to be out!' they chastised us. But even in her early babyhood, Annie was keen for movement and changes of scenery. John and I watched her face when we lifted her out of her capsule on her first outing at the beach. She listened intently to the whooshing of waves below then wriggled with excitement.

I would sit outside in the mornings with baby Annie on my lap, under the shade of the eaves, the scribbly gum drooping nearby, the nasturtium leaves a pillow of green. I found myself singing the songs Gwen had sung to me as a child: 'A You're Adorable', 'Somewhere Over the Rainbow', 'Close to You'. She would smile and kick her legs, and I felt a comforting continuity with my female bloodline that I had never before experienced. In these mornings, breathing in clean air, staring in wonder at this miracle of flesh, I felt content.

. . .

John and I were united over our love for this wriggling bundle of humanity we had produced. We discussed each new development: her head swivelling to follow voices, making long diphthong sounds to test her voice, the way her eyes disappeared into her squeezable cheeks when she smiled or laughed. John stayed up with her in the evening so I could get some hours of uninterrupted sleep, lighting candles and running water in the bathroom to soothe her. We were both outraged when Gwen said, in response to me mentioning being woken up continually by four-week-old Annie, 'You're making a rod for your own back. I'd just feed you, change your nappy, put you in your cot and close the door. You didn't cry for long. She's just putting it on.'

The usual stresses of new parenthood, however, such as sleep deprivation and accommodating a new human into one's psychological constellation, caused the fissures that might have remained unnoticed, or at least unremarked upon, in our relationship. But early on there were other stresses less usual that also required accommodation.

My body, which had so valiantly managed to grow a human and push it out without intervention of any kind, was displaying serial signs of protest. Firstly, less than a week after Annie's birth, I began haemorrhaging again – having already haemorrhaged after the birth – and feeling delirious. It was a uterine infection, the kind that used to see women off in the days before antibiotics. Antibiotics in hand, I returned from hospital but never succeeded in feeling well, only moderately less sick.

Along with the hallucinatory haze of sleep deprivation, I began to feel feverish and achy. When I stood up after a night feed, I felt as if I were walking on thumbtacks. My hands and knees reddened and swelled. My shoulders and hips ached as if someone had attempted to pull my limbs from my torso. I couldn't chew properly because my jaw was so sore. Picking up a cup of coffee in the morning was painful.

'Jules, this isn't right,' John said. At first he'd been impatient with my complaining about the soreness, but the impatience had turned to worry. 'Go to your doctor.'

'Everyone says it's normal, after having a baby,' I said.

'Just find out,' he said.

At the questioning of the doctor, I explained my collection of symptoms.

'And now I can't even change her nappies in the morning,' I said. 'I need to soak my hands in warm water first.'

The concern on the doctor's face alarmed me almost as much as my throbbing joints.

'Does anyone in your family have rheumatoid arthritis?' she asked.

I thought I had misheard. I was twenty-seven. Who gets arthritis at twenty-seven?

'It's an inflammatory disease,' she said. 'I'll refer you to a rheumatologist.'

'Will it get better?' I said.

'Talk to your rheumatologist,' she said. 'I've heard this one is good.'

I was sent home with pamphlets in those just-before-internet days, and when I read them, I understood the concern my doctor had tried to conceal. Rheumatoid arthritis is unrelated to osteoarthritis, which is associated with ageing. Your body attacks itself: cartilage, tissue, organs. Untreated, rheumatoid arthritis eats away at the joints. Untreated, it does most of its damage in its early years. Those pictures of deformed, gnarled hands you have seen, twisted by the ravages of unchecked inflammation – that is rheumatoid arthritis. An early name for it was arthritis deformans.

When I told Gwen, she said, 'Oh yes, that's what Grandma had.' This time I paid attention when she told me about her grandmother's knotted fingers, her being in a wheelchair from the age of thirty-five, her early death from pain and exhaustion. Her inability to undertake the heavy labours of pre-appliance country living meant her daughters left school as soon as they could, creating the martyrdom Violet had perfected and taught to her progeny.

When I saw the rheumatologist, armed with the results of blood tests he'd requested I obtain, he took my history in what I soon understood was his characteristic calm and unhurried manner.

After a time he finessed the diagnosis. It was not just rheumatoid arthritis, he said, but severe rheumatoid arthritis due to its suddenness and extremity. He asked whether I had noticed anything, pre-birth.

'The joint damage in rheumatoid arthritis occurs early,' he said. 'Some people have moderate symptoms, and by the time they seek treatment, the damage is done. But because yours is so sudden, we have a chance to get on top of it.'

'How much of a chance?'

He said, 'We have a number of options to try.'

And so I tried them. I began the standard treatment of sulphur drugs, which enabled me to keep breastfeeding. These were the drugs my great-grandmother would have had. When they didn't help me to walk or wake up without crippling pain, any more than they had for my great-grandmother, I went onto hydroxychloroquine, which worked on me about as well as it prevents COVID-19. Finally, when Annie was three, I was given methotrexate, an immune suppressant that finally gave me some reliable relief.

At every appointment my rheumatologist examined my joints, and most particularly my fingers.

'We want to keep these nice and straight,' he would say.

'Will I be able to write?' I asked. I had not written much apart from my diary for some time. I'd written short fiction and started doing honours in creative writing, but I could not work out what I wanted to say or how to say it. Now there was a risk of not doing it, I was gripped by a fear that I would never find out.

'We will do what we can,' he would answer.

26

Living in alternative Fremantle and in an ultra-alternative housing co-operative to boot, I was given much unsolicited advice on rheumatoid arthritis. It could be cured by green-lipped mussels, fish oil, glucosamine, avoiding nightshades, avoiding nuts and legumes, eating nuts and legumes, a vegan diet, a protein-only diet, fasting. Rheumatoid arthritis was caused by stress. It was caused by sugar. It was caused by a fault in my thinking, my beliefs. My cells had been listening to my unconscious belief patterns. I was resentful of authority and missed opportunities. I had to reframe my thinking. If I didn't reframe my thinking, I would remain ill.

I tried various remedies and elimination diets. After each one, my rheumatologist asked me how it went. When I reported that there was no improvement, he would say, 'My other patients also report this.'

It was also true that I was stressed. I was in pain and sleep-deprived, living in a new environment, in John's environment, away from my friends. I loved the baby but felt panicked at the weight of the responsibility I now had. After her early promise as a grandparent, Gwen was now too busy with her new business to help. She only once babysat during Annie's entire childhood. The compensation I'd received from the horse-riding accident had been spent on baby necessities, and John had decided that he was too overwhelmed to continue his casual cleaning jobs, so we were living on welfare. My position teaching English to refugees had been defunded by the incoming conservative government. The collection of things that had propped up my selfhood had gone.

And I now had to rely on John to meet the most basic of physical needs. We could not afford a wheelchair and did not have the space for it even if we could have, so I scooted around the unit on my office chair on the days when my joints were most painful. I had to get him to put Annie in the baby capsule on the days I was well enough to walk up to the carpark and get her out again when we returned home. I could not carry shopping, or cut vegetables, or clean the bathroom. Mostly he would do these things for me with good grace. But not always.

. . .

Because he was so good with children and had been such a dedicated father-figure for his former girlfriend's daughter, I had counted on John being a great dad. I felt I knew this as completely as I knew anything. And for a time my understanding remained undisturbed.

Everybody could see how much John adored his baby daughter. He took her around the co-op for her to be cooed over by older children and their parents. He took her to the park next door, sitting with her on a bench in the shade so her eyes learned to focus against the stretch of violent green under the benevolent blue sky, so she could clap her starfish hands as she watched the neighbourhood kids race each other to the swings, jump off the sandstone rocks that peppered the park. When she developed colic, which worsened at night, he lit candles in the bathroom, slung her over his forearm and swayed her back and forth until she became floppy with sleep.

As soon as she could hold her head upright, he hauled her around in a baby backpack, and her eyes would disappear as she grinned with pleasure while he ran, twirled, and hopped with her in tow. 'From the Lawrinson collection,' he intoned as he walked toward me and spun around in our narrow living area, now crammed with the detritus of small-babyhood.

John's primary aim as a parent for her first three years was to make Annie laugh or to otherwise entertain her. To this end, he catapulted over the wall that divided the bedroom and living room, commando-crawled under the bed, and slid down the passageway Tom-Cruise-style to enter the room in a way that Annie would never expect, causing her to lose her balance laughing. Later, he pretended to be the voice of the stop sign outside the co-op at night: even though she could see John's stocky body behind the sign, she believed it was conversing with her. In the echoey hall in the centre of the co-op he took Annie for screaming practice, which was a duet of screams of varying lengths and pitches, until the staff at day care requested he desist due to Annie's inability to differentiate the co-op hall from the day care rooms. At night he drew stories on her back about a character called Annie Panny

Piddly Pop Doop Doop Wop Wop Bip. He made up songs about her, about us, all requiring her active participation:

> We're going back to our nice new house
> Where there's hardly even a single mouse
> And certainly not any
> [cue Annie] RATS

> We're going back to our nice new home
> Where Mummy's writing a book on her own
> Because that makes her
> [cue Annie] HAPPY

> We're going back to our nice new spot
> Where Daddy can mooch around a lot
> Because that makes him
> [cue Annie] HAPPY

These were the times John was expansive, witty, comfortable in himself, and reminiscent of the side of John I fell in love with and continued to admire. I was relieved when it returned to the fore.

27

Through everything that was to come, John rarely lost his desire to make people laugh. It was the chief and most reliable satisfaction of his life, of which I was a daily beneficiary. It was an impulse I could rely on, and for which I forgave him many other things. When things were difficult, his humour could be mordant. Mostly, though, he would deliver an unexpected, perfectly described and perfectly timed observation which so delighted both him and his listeners.

Since becoming an unbiddable teenager, John had infuriated his mother generally and specifically, but it was she who provoked in him his desire to make women laugh. His mother was testy and critical toward him. Until the end of her days – she persisted into her nineties in spite of her drinking of acidic wine, and smoking cigarettes she resorted to cutting in half to prevent her consuming them in their entirety – she was adamant that she should not have had any of her four children, and that the only one she'd loved was the one who had early on cut off contact with the family. She'd got married late for her time, but her Catholicism meant that children were the inevitable result of marriage. It was only in despair after her fourth infant that she begged her doctor to prescribe her the new contraceptive medication to prevent any more.

As the eldest, and the boy, John felt himself both favoured by his mother and the subject of her excessive expectations. He developed a stubborn resistance to expectations of any kind in response, and her disapproval of his life and activities was constant, until Annie was born.

In spite of their at times mutual irritation and impatience, John took Annie to visit his mother – Ma – regularly. Ma softened with delight at her only granddaughter, but her expression remained closed in disapproval at John himself. In the face of her resistance, he would deliver one-liner after one-liner, testing to see what would make her, against her will, laugh.

Usually the winning quip was accompanied by a kind of stillness as

Ma processed the witty observation or vulgar description. He would be rewarded by the sight of his mother's otherwise stern eyes, on understanding the witticism, widen. She would cross her arms over her chest as if arming herself against her response and then put her hand to her laughing face to try to shield him from the satisfaction he'd earned.

'Oh, John,' she'd wheeze. 'That's not funny.'

The other women John enjoyed charming – day care workers, Annie's teachers, mothers at school, tennis companions, me – would show the same concentration as we listened to John's banter, littered, as we came to expect it, with his left-field or salacious commentary. As our wit caught up with what he had just said, we would explode into helpless laughter at the incongruous image, the vulgar characterisation, John watching our faces with pleasure, laughing along with us.

...

Pre-Annie, the best times John and I had arose when our contact was limited. Our relationship was at its richest when we could talk about books and writing, laugh at John's barbs about the people we knew, argue about politics, and then retreat. We were never a couple where each person could relax into quietness together. John was possessive of his space and wanted to protect his being from others, whom he habitually saw as a threat. And I always found myself in need of solitude to rebalance myself, to re-centre after being pulled off balance by the views of others.

And now, the part of John disturbed by his childhood experiences, the one that would suddenly switch from sanguine to the savaging responses I'd first met in 1993, began to reappear. This part of him had been kept in check when he'd lived alone, when he could shut himself off from the world. I had understood that the weeks-long silences were often the times he was haunted by the past, when it unsettled and unbalanced him. I understood because I too had times when the past nudged into the present, when it pushed me off balance for days at a time.

Every morning John woke up anxious. Seeing him in the mornings, his face riven with the memory of disturbing dreams that stained his waking consciousness with their horror, was like seeing my own daily disturbance unmasked. I was able to cover over the dismay I regularly felt on waking. I could dispel it through getting up and writing – writing novels, writing in my diary, writing the tedious details of nightmares I could never bear to re-read – but he could not. He could not loosen the grip of the unsettled sleeping that led him to wail in the night hours, as if realising he could not escape the ghostly fingers around his wrists, or the ghostly figures pursuing him.

John's worst time was dusk. Dusk was the time when the veil between the worlds was at its thinnest, he said: it gave him the horrors. When he was a single person, he used to run at this time, run on the oval high on a Fremantle hill, running until the sun had sunk behind the Indian Ocean.

Now he could not run. And nor could I.

28

Even now, for every description of what he said and did, I want to add – 'though', 'as well'. I want to preface it with 'one time'. Because the events I will describe felt like things that happened separately, slightly apart from the daily routines of life. I could put them to one side, mostly. When my fingers were not aflame with pain, I continued writing in the diary I'd kept since my teenage years. Every time I read back on these now, when I can bear to, I am surprised – every time – by what I did record, and what I was able to forget as soon as I closed the covers with their spiral binding and deposited them into their waiting drawer.

One time. Though, as well. One time.

There were, at first, only a few areas where I felt the limitations of our support for each other's experiences. One of them was that John had no more tolerance of me being in discomfort or pain after the birth than he was before it. If I complained of being tired, he'd snap, 'Well, I'm tired too. We've got a baby.' As I had begun experiencing pain in inverse proportions to sleep, his lack of sympathy for my discomfort soon became a point of tension. *He does not have patience with me*, I wrote to myself. *But he's a great dad, and we love Annie.*

Then there were domestic matters – minor matters, I knew. Everyone fights over control of space – don't they? It was his house, and he was particular. The table and benches had to be clear when they weren't being used. The floor had to be vacuumed and mopped every day. Everything had to be put away because it was a small house and it could not accommodate mess or clutter. One time, an explosion occurred because I had missed a bean on the floor when I was cleaning up after a meal. Another time, I hadn't done the washing up quickly enough. I'd put too much salt in the food or used too much oil. I'd left mess on the table overnight. Sometimes it was because I didn't apologise sufficiently for the failing he'd identified. Sometimes it was because I argued back. In the early days I could see no warning signs. Later

I learned the signs of the build-up, like the humidity in the air that thickened before Perth received the relief of whirling cyclonic rains from the Pilbara.

Pain was one limit; money was another. If I worried about money, he would tell me that we were richer than most of the people on the planet, he'd worked hard to get us into a rent-controlled house, there was nothing to worry about. He criticised anyone I spoke to for support, especially if the person happened to be my mother or his sister. When I told him I'd mentioned to one of his friends who had been visiting regularly that I was having a hard time, he was incandescent with rage. I was never to complain about him to anyone, did I understand?

Once, in frustration, I said I was so miserable I was going to leave.

'Don't you ever say you're going to leave me unless you mean it,' he said. 'That's a terrible thing to do, threatening to take my baby away from me.'

I phoned various services for new mothers to see if I could get help because of the morning stiffness and the problems with changing nappies. The conversation was awkward:

'Are you a single mother?'

'No.'

'Is your husband at work?'

'No.'

'Why can't he help you?'

'Because he is asleep.'

'Sorry?'

'He sleeps late.'

I was advised that I should get him up: that would solve the problem. I was too ashamed to tell the woman how anxious and irritable John was in the mornings and getting him up would double rather than halve my problems. And he was tired because he'd stayed up at first with Annie, and then because he needed space, and the quiet night hours were the only time he got them. That was reasonable, wasn't it?

After one argument, I called a women's refuge. I got an address, but I didn't go. It wasn't bad enough. They'd wonder what I was doing there. I'd have to explain to everyone.

I spoke to a friend, quietly, when John was out and baby Annie asleep.

She asked concerned questions, and then: 'Does he hit you?'

'No,' I said reluctantly.

And he didn't. Which meant, in my mind, that it wasn't bad enough. If it was bad enough, people would tell me to leave. And they didn't, quite.

I thought, sometimes, of the drama that our getting together had generated. Having a baby had shut some people up. It wasn't just me hooking up with my ex-girlfriend's brother, which on its own suggested some kind of pathology. No, now it was serious. It legitimised our relationship and made me seem less unbalanced than otherwise might be the case. So if I left now, I undid all of that. I would appear cruel to John and to be carrying on my usual tendencies to run away from relationships the minute they were less than satisfying.

I also thought of Gwen, who always said to me that she was concerned that I couldn't stick at anything. She'd said it when I couldn't decide between ballet, judo, and horse riding, when I gave up clarinet, when I dropped out of school, when I kept leaving jobs and moving houses. The only thing I'd stuck at was my degree. The thought of explaining to her that I couldn't even stay with the father of my child for a year made me shudder.

And the good outweighed the bad.

In my diary I mostly recorded Annie's latest milestones and the state of my rheumatoid symptoms. But sometimes I also recorded the distance I felt from John. After we'd had them, I described how we would have spats and then talk our way back to harmony. When we talked, it felt as if we were uncovering new understandings of each other, finding the depths we would need as parents, together. It smoothed the jagged edges of the arguments, made them fit into the regularity that was, at least in the first few years, the majority of it. It wasn't that bad. Was it?

We loved Annie's every new skill, her early propensity for smiling and laughing. We still talked about the books we were reading. He encouraged my writing. I didn't know what I wanted to write, only that I needed to after the diagnosis of rheumatoid arthritis, so I began writing poetry, short stories, and eventually longer fiction for the child and teenager I had been. He cheered when I placed stories in local magazines or won second place in competitions. I was suffering self-doubt as crippling as the disease that made my joints hot to touch, but because I trusted John's intelligence and judgement of the written word, his faith in my work meant everything to me and buoyed me when the enterprise of publishing seemed indifferent from my ideas and efforts.

Now I understand that the yearning I'd felt in childhood to be understood, and the loneliness that arose from my otherness, led me to seek out and hold on to anyone who offered recognition. If a person *saw* me, I was prepared to submit to any demand they might make on me, no matter how disproportionate, for the gift of their understanding. If someone understood me, they must – surely – have my best interests in mind. Surely it could not be that in the easy warmth of their sympathy, I allowed myself to yield all else to them. The Scientologist uncle, the psychiatrist with his wandering hands, and on into adulthood.

So the other John was the price I paid for the part I valued, the one I felt I needed. Most of the time I thought it was a fair exchange.

...

After fighting we regularly tried to work things out. John found it hard to believe he was at fault. The only concession he would make was that it was both of us. In one of these discussions John asked, 'What am I difficult in relation to?' I responded, with feeling, 'Any stimuli.'

At the end of Annie's first year, we sat on the floor of the kitchen in the co-op. All the units in the co-op had cork floors that regularly needed sanding and resealing with a glue so toxic you had to leave the house for a day so the fumes had time to subside. Our neighbours had taken Annie for an hour. It was, unusually for us, a planned time for discussion.

'I can't do this,' I said to John. 'The fighting is exhausting me. I feel alienated from you. If we separate now, Annie won't know the difference. I can't live like this.'

I can't remember what led to the conversation, only that I felt I had reached a point where I could not go on. It might have been the frequency of the arguments or their increasing severity. I had taken heed of him telling me not to threaten leaving unless I meant it. So now, I meant it.

'It's been hard, losing my self-care practices,' he said. 'But I love you and the baby more than anything. We need to work this out, Jules.'

John had been having a 'day off' a week all year, where he had no obligations to me or Annie. Now I demanded that I have one too, a day to write, to go out, to have John take Annie out. John agreed. He'd see if we could move into a bigger house in the co-op. And we would talk to each other when we were feeling tense.

I was relieved. I did not want to leave. I still did not know where I would go if I left, but I'd been prepared to find something, somehow.

There was a time of peace, and I was relieved that peace was possible. When we celebrated Annie's first birthday at Christmas-time 1997, I was giddy to have made it through the year. It had been hard. But in the new year we would move to a bigger house in the co-op, which would be our house. It would have a study, a room for me to write in. The rheumatoid arthritis was not settled, but I no longer needed to wheel myself around the house on the office chair. And in the new year, Annie was going to start day care. It would give her the socialisation I had missed out on and would give John and me time together, as well as space to do other things. It was a turning point that held promise.

...

On Annie's first day at day care we carried her in to meet the staff and the children. The smell of the meal in preparation was delicious. The day care centre boasted staff from many countries, and the Spanish cook relished her job and the children she was surrounded by each day. Annie's head swivelled this way and that at the bright colours and the cheerful mayhem of children playing inside and out. We handed her over to tall, young, kind Lara, and Annie gave a brief wave to us as she disappeared, rapt, into the new, vibrant atmosphere. Lara would soon become the subject of a new song that John and Annie sang together in a swing patter:

Lara, from International Day Care
She's coming nearer, than far-er
That's Lara!

We received daily reports, printed on yellow sheets, of Annie's food intake, naps, and general mood ('Was a little bit sensitive today' was code for 'Tried to injure other children if they looked sideways at her'). At the end of the day John picked her up. Annie could hear the blue 1982 Volvo from the play area and rushed outside to see him, calling, 'Daddy! Daddy!' joyfully at his approach. One time, to the delight of the children and the consternation of staff, John vaulted the fence to the play area, booming, 'Annie!' and holding his arms out for her to leap into.

John and I took advantage of day care by driving down to Port Beach each morning. We walked on the fine white sand, firm if the tide was out, thigh-wearyingly soft if it was in and we were forced to trudge the sloping shore that the water reaches only in winter storms. On these mornings we talked for the hour our walk took us, the water sparkling silver in the morning light, hats on if it was warm, layered in matching flannelette shirts that could be stripped off and knotted around our waists in warmer weather.

We talked about the dreams or nightmares we'd had the night before, about co-op meetings and how they reminded him of his family, about Gwen and how stressed and angry she had become with her new real estate business, about the pieces of writing I was working on, and always about Annie. We repeated to each other the funny things that she'd said; discussed her developing, passionate friendships with kids at day care; wondered when she, and therefore I, would finally sleep through the night. We noticed the schools of baitfish darting in the waves, the seagulls gathering where other schools of bigger fish were pulsing underneath the surface of the water further out, invisible to us. The seagulls bobbed in circular formations, occasionally darting down.

'Jules, have you noticed what happens when we talk out here?' John said. 'At the end, I always feel like a load has been lifted.'

'The words dissolve in the salty air,' I said.

'In the house, it's like they get trapped, don't you reckon?' he said.

'Maybe we should only talk outdoors,' I suggested, and we laughed.

On days too wet or windy to walk, John slept in. I wrote in the spare room on the computer that I'd bought with the last of my horse-riding accident money. When we both ended up in the kitchen for our midmorning coffees, there was often a slightly formal air. We talked it away, but it took longer than on the beach.

In the new spaciousness of the second house, with Annie at day care more and more, I began to plan. I would go back to university in 1999, do honours in creative writing, and see if I could get a scholarship to do a PhD in writing. I began doing casual work, teaching English as a Second Language, to supplement the benefits we were on, entering a workplace full of young, intelligent, kind, and curious colleagues. They had all lived and taught overseas: in Korea, Oman, Mexico, Colombia, the Czech Republic, Japan, the US. I felt different, older, even though I was not quite thirty myself, but I also felt myself expanding with the conversations that were the pleasure of the days. Our students were largely Swiss and Japanese, and the occasional tedium of teaching the difference between 'will' and 'going to' was tempered by my enjoyment of watching cultural difference in play. In winter, for example, Japanese students would snort back their post-flu mucus, while the Swiss students shuddered. When the Swiss students blew their noses and put the tissues in their pockets, the Japanese students recoiled.

I didn't notice, at the time, that while my world expanded, John's did not. And before long, because of the contrast between us, or because of his ennui, or because, perhaps, of early symptoms of what would show later, we returned to where we had been.

. . .

On cassette tapes, John recorded the *Sunday Morning Coming Down* program on the community radio station. As well as Johnny Cash, the show featured a mixture of alternative, folksy music, such as Leo Kottke, Mongolian throat singing, Kirsty MacColl, Bob Dylan ('Tangled Up in Blue' and 'Subterranean Homesick Blues'), and Irish music such as The Wolfe Tones. He selected the songs he liked and copied them onto a second tape. He called these tapes 'Annie and Daddy's Favourites No. 1', 'Annie and Daddy's Favourites No. 2' etc., which he played in the old 1982 Volvo whenever he ferried Annie about. Annie and John loved to shout their favourite lines about snort forts and shoes and the devil being dead and buried in Killarney.

John believed he was tone-deaf. The belief gave him pain, and he hoped that Annie would inherit my musical ear, muted though it was compared to Gwen's. Among John's unwaveringly good grades from primary school to when he dropped out in Year Eleven, there was an F for music. But he broadened my musical tastes through his discoveries from community radio, and when he sang within his range, he sang on key. And he and Annie kept building up their favourite tapes until 2007, when Annie was eleven and the new car we bought no longer contained a cassette player.

Just before he turned fifty, he brought home all of his school reports. All of his primary reports are contained in a plastic-covered, soft-paged book, with Koonawarra School and John's name written neatly on the front. The reports ended in Year Seven, with the comment *Set your sights high, John! First place in class.*

The offending music grade was there too, from Year Two. The grades for reading, writing, oral expression, speech, spelling, writing, arithmetic (oral and written), social studies, elementary science, art, and health are all marked V.G., with comments like *well above average, fluent* and *confident*. Music alone is an F. But what John had never noticed, until that moment, was the key glued into the front of the book. The key explains that the rating F is not *fail*, but *fair*.

'Oh, Jules,' he said, holding the report out at the exculpatory page. 'I believed it was a fail. All those years, I believed it.'

Our understandings of ourselves came from what we thought others believed of us, we agreed.

It wasn't the only set of childhood experiences we shared.

John had as a child been subject to sexual abuse by someone in authority: his primary school headmaster, Mr Buddee, at a school camp attended by selected boys, which had included John. He reported the incident – he'd told me there was only one – to his mother, who'd told his teacher father, who'd gone to the education department, who'd got Mr Buddee suddenly and permanently moved.

Not long afterward, John developed twitches and tics. When he blinked, he screwed up his whole face. Sometimes it looked as if he was winking at people. He only knew he was doing it when other people winked back.

His mother took him to allergy specialists. He had X-rays taken of his face and head and was given various medications. He still twitched.

...

Valiantly we tried to prevent Annie from suffering what we had. We did not want her to be anxious, as we were. We protected her from the obvious things that might cause her injury. She stayed in a car seat until there were none big enough to accommodate her. Sleepovers were rare and carefully vetted. We listened with interest to all her pronouncements, but also because we did not want her to be the keeper of secrets. I never discussed weight or dieting. Everything was framed by its healthiness or otherwise. We encouraged her in all things, celebrated her fearlessness, her liveliness – most especially in those first three crucial years, according to the theory of attachment parenting.

The problem was that we still believed what we read. Or perhaps it was that you cannot overcome the things you are not properly conscious of.

What I am trying to say is: we both thought we were doing the right thing. That's how it started off, anyway.

...

In the year Annie turned three, early one evening, I asked John to do the washing up, and he refused. He was already tense. I can't remember why, or maybe there wasn't a reason. But his face took on the stony aspect it did when he was displeased.

Annie was playing on the large blue rug nearby, chatting with her imaginary friend, Boop, and showing her this thing or that thing. John hated music or television in the evening, so early on Annie learned to play with Boop at these times; not long afterward she would become her own leaping, twirling, haunch-sitting creation, Jungle Girl.

'Mummy,' she said. 'I will never get bored in my life, because I can always be Jungle Girl!'

On this day I was preparing dinner, or maybe we'd had dinner; I can't remember the order of it. But part of my reasoning was that if I was cooking, it followed that he should wash up.

'I never agreed to that,' he said. 'Why should I do that?'

'Because it's fair,' I said. I found myself suddenly confused about something I'd thought was akin to natural law that the person who cooks is relieved of washing-up responsibilities. I'd taken this shared understanding for granted, but now I wondered if this was something odd. Gwen's family had always been very particular about domestic tasks. You washed up in order – glasses, cups, plates and cutlery, pots and pans – rinsed and stacked them neatly, dried everything immediately. When you hung out clean clothes, you pegged things by the part of the garment where peg marks would be least visible. When you mopped the floor, you also needed to extract your old toothbrush to scrub dirt from every crevice, and you must never – the way John did – use bath towels to dry it. I might not have been properly socialised, but I knew how to iron crisp seams into a pant leg.

'Don't tell me what's fair and what's not,' he said. 'It's not your house, it's our house, and I'll do what I want.'

'So you're not going to wash up?'

'I'll wash up if I want to wash up,' he said. 'Not when you tell me to.'

I thought it was important to hold my ground. What he was saying didn't make sense. We were supposed to share the load. I'd just cooked – or was cooking – something requiring pots and pans, plates and colanders. There were dirty plates. How was asking for them to be washed up unreasonable? And now it seemed he wanted me to cook and wash up, and do most of the childcare, come to that?

'I'm asking you to do it now,' I said.

John stared at me, the whites of his eyes turning the peculiar red that was always the barometer of his fury.

'Don't take that bossy fucking tone with me,' he said.

'It's a simple thing,' I said. 'Why do you have to make such a problem out of it?'

We were yelling, or had voices raised. Now we were at the edges of the co-op, John no longer cared about keeping his voice down. He yelled, we yelled, with Annie still there, there playing with Boop and in full view, not asleep. But I was not looking at her. I was looking at John.

In one movement, John lifted the dirty plates from the sideboard, hoisted them head height, and slammed them on the floor at my feet. They broke into uneven pieces, sending chips of white porcelain across the kitchen. The breaking was a dull thud, muffled by the cork floor.

'There,' he said. 'Happy now?'

I scooped Annie up and took her to her room. I don't remember if she was crying or if she was like me, silent with shock. We retreated to the end of the house, to the room we shared. I remember afterward, sweeping up shards, making sure there were none left that would pierce her feet.

I don't remember if we resolved it the next morning or whether it was after a couple of silent days, days when we took care of Annie, separately, spent time away from the house. Apart from the physical breaking of crockery, apart from Annie being there, there was nothing in this outburst that was different from any of the others that happened before or afterward. No doubt we'd have come to some agreement about how I should ask him things. He always insisted that I come up with the solution to a problem. 'You're smart,' he'd say, after I'd protested that I was out of ideas. 'You'll think of something.'

But after that I never expected that he would do the washing up after I'd cooked. If I wanted clean dishes, I did them myself.

And if I ever tried to explain John's behaviour to Annie, when she was older, or excuse myself on the basis he hadn't hit me or her, she'd say, 'Remember him smashing plates, Mum?' She'd shake her head. 'I do.'

. . .

John's frustration kept growing, even though we had a bigger house, more time to ourselves thanks to day care, and more money thanks to my working.

We decided that the problem was the co-op.

John had been a founding member of the co-op in the 80s. Its idea was to provide stable housing to people on low incomes, housing over which they had control, so that the residents could spend their time working in their communities instead of being wage slaves. At first the idea was to secure a government loan so the co-op would eventually become filled with owner-occupiers, but the interest rates, which rose to seventeen percent after Australia floated the dollar in the late 80s, put paid to that. So the co-op was owned by the government but managed by the tenants. John was disappointed that the original vision had been so tempered by reality and spoke in scathing terms about his fellow founders, whose original socialist fervour had been blunted by self-interest and the lull of comfort that he had expected to enable revolution.

Each month the co-op held meetings that required consensus decision-making to plan for matters of maintenance and finance. If there was ever a dispute – and it seemed there always was – John got decisions made in his favour because he alone would block anything he didn't support, and he had no fear of continuing an argument outside the confines of the meeting, which eventually wore down any opposition. The others in the co-op said John was bullying them. Most didn't seem to like me, perhaps because I took John's part, as I was instructed, in the meetings and elsewhere.

John began to complain that living in the co-op reminded him of his family. Indeed, there remained living there one of his actual sisters, whom he had forbidden from visiting our house after I had complained to her about John in the early days. Another was his ex-girlfriend, one he'd gone out with when I'd run off with a woman and broken his heart. And with everyone else, they had experienced the souring of relationships that regularly occurred with those with whom John was closely involved for any length of time.

In this period – 1998, 1999, and into 2000 – John was so wound up after each monthly meeting that he did not sleep, staying up at night, stewing over slights he'd detected, railing over former wrongs I only vaguely understood. He focused most of his fury on his sister and his ex-girlfriend. He explained to me that they wanted to get him out of the co-op. They were after him, no doubt about it. One day John and I were on the verandah of the co-op hall with Annie, and she was pointing her chubby fingers at this thing or that thing.

'She's got the point from her father,' one of the residents laughed.

John handed Annie to me and went over to the unwitting resident, who was returning to his unit with his wife.

'What did you say, mate?' John said.

When the man turned around, John pointed at him then pushed him in the chest with his pointing finger.

'Did you say something about my daughter?' John said. 'What was it? What is it you're trying to say?'

'I was only joking, John,' the man said, hands up. 'Settle down.'

'Don't you dare even look at my daughter again, do you hear me,' he said. 'If you've got something to say, I'm right here. Got it?'

'Yes, John,' the man said.

'You'd better fucking get it,' John said.

He also felt slighted by his ex-girlfriend. He began throwing rocks on her roof at night, until he missed and sent one through the window of our neighbour, who had only just come out of hospital after having a liver transplant. He felt so terrible about that that he made sure all his further actions were specifically directed at the ex-girlfriend, so there could be no other accidental intermediary. To this end, he smeared the inside of her letterbox with mince every few days, so it attracted ants. On another occasion, he smeared it with fresh dog shit. Every few weeks he began to beckon her dog, who would be delighted at John's attention. John would take the dog's collar off, take the dog to the park next door, and call the ranger, knowing the dog was unregistered and that a fine would have to be paid each time the dog was retrieved.

I watched and wondered if John was going to venture from nuisance behaviour into criminality. He could not let go of the things that upset him. I feared the intensity of his fury would give him an aneurism.

One night, after a co-op meeting, John would not stop raging. We poured some stout and sat at the kitchen table while he recounted every expression, every phrase, every movement designed to irritate him. He was particularly outraged by something his sister had said and explained exactly why it was angled to try to make him so unsafe he'd leave the co-op. He'd fought so hard to get her into the co-op in the first place, he said, and now this, this betrayal.

I was tired. I listened and agreed, but at some point I failed to support his outrage with the required enthusiasm. So he began on me, asking me what I was really thinking, questioning my loyalty to him, saying it was all on him, us being in this rent-controlled environment with these toxic people, and the least I could do was back him up one hundred percent.

I tried to defend myself. Then, my guard lowered by the stout, I began to argue back.

'You know what your problem is?' I said. 'You're just like your sister.'

It was one of the only times I thought he was going to hit me. He came close to me, grabbed the tops of my arms so hard it felt as if his thumbs were pressing into my bones. Then he spat in my face.

'That's an awful thing to say,' he said.

Something has to change, I thought to myself after he'd slammed the door, after I'd wiped my face on my own discarded clothing, after I'd thought about how I'd been pushed to insulting him so, after I lay down and put my hand on the torso of our sleeping daughter. We cannot go on like this. The co-op was the problem.

He could not change or make it change, but I could.

. . .

Not long after the spitting incident, I received first-class honours in writing. I rewrote the young adult novel, some of which had formed part of the thesis, based on the feedback from my markers. I'd been sending out a middle-grade novel all year and had got many we-like-it-but responses. The young adult novel was about a girl growing up in a suburb called Kenwood who had a crush on another girl who was the lead in the high school musical. Apart from that, I made it all up. I imaginatively titled it *Obsession*.

I applied for and secured a scholarship for the newly established qualification of a PhD in writing. The scholarship and an extra award for academic excellence, plus my work, meant that I could do what I had not been able to before: I applied for a house loan. John's mother gave us a deposit. She was always embarrassed by her son's failure to embrace paid employment, so he regarded this as his contribution. We would have to move to a distant suburb, far from everyone we knew, because it was all we could afford. But it would be our home, away from the co-op, the people who were stressing John out so much.

Gwen had become a real estate principal after ten miserable years as an accountant in the public sector. After drilling into me the fear of the type of choice-removing poverty I'd grown up in post-divorce, she exhorted the transformative value of home ownership. She was pleased that I was studying, but she was more pleased at me taking out a loan.

'You won't know yourself, Jules,' she said.

This prediction turned out to be truer than I could have imagined.

29

When we moved into our own house in the year 2000, Annie was three and a half. It was a modest brick-and-tile house near the towering pairs of powerlines that you could hear humming as you walked beneath them, in a suburb named after the swampy lakes it was built around. From the backyard you could hear the low buzz of traffic on the freeway that lay a kilometre to the south-east.

John had lived in Fremantle for fifteen years. He was used to walking down to the cappuccino strip in the morning, reading the paper and chatting to the old Italian women en route, even after Annie was born. He loved the light of Fremantle, its proximity to the ocean he loved to fish in and walk alongside, its wide skies and buildings of pale sandstone dug out of the quarry that the co-op was later built in. He was known as witty and friendly by casual acquaintances, of which he had many. He had enjoyed showing off Annie, enjoyed demonstrating his transition from Fremantle Lost Boy to doting father.

Before, John's cyclical surges of unhappiness, frustration and fury had been aimed solely at the co-op, and at me. If Annie had been there, it was accidental.

We had not yet arranged the furniture in the new house when Annie became fractious at dinnertime.

'Eat your food and be quiet,' John said.

'But I don't like this,' Annie said.

'I don't care whether you like it or not,' John said calmly.

'Can't I have toast?'

'Just do what you're told and stop arguing the toss,' he said.

'But Daddy, I—'

'Stop winding me up,' he said.

'But—'

'Go to your room,' he said.

The chair scraped as John stood suddenly up.

'I said,' he yelled, making us both jump, 'get out of that chair and go to your fucking room!'

Annie began wailing.

'Honey,' I said. 'Don't talk to her like that.'

John hissed at me. 'She won't fucking listen. I'm sick of it. I haven't had any space and I just want to have a quiet fucking meal and she won't leave it alone.'

Annie continued to wail. I took her by the shoulder – I could not carry her, because of my joints – and ushered her to my room. I dragged her mattress in, dropped it on the floor, and closed the door. She lay on the floor and cried herself to sleep while I lay with her, saying he was just grumpy, telling her not to worry about it. He'd never yelled at her before. She saw and heard him yelling at me, speaking to me with impatience and derision, but this was something different. I was almost as shocked at him yelling at her as I had been when he'd yelled at me over the channel-changing all those years ago.

I lay next to Annie, listening to the strange noises of a new house. I thought about what it had taken to get here. There was little money left over from my scholarship after paying the mortgage. I thought about how I'd appealed to John's mother to help us with the deposit. I'd told her I was worried about how stressed he was, being at war with the people with whom he had lived for a decade. And she agreed it would be better to be away from the co-op, for us to be in our own house; she'd expressed mild shame at the continuing disharmony among her offspring. But now, John getting a mortgage, having a child: these were the things that his mother never thought she'd see. She credited me for changing him.

If I left now, I would have to admit it hadn't worked. That I hadn't been able to change him after all.

So I was trapped. That's what I thought, lying next to Annie, looking out into the dark, trying to make out shapes in the unfamiliar room.

. . .

Annie's in-utero activity and her babyhood wakefulness translated into unceasing movement once she found her feet. If she sat on your lap, you knew she was sickening; mostly, she was off and running, dancing, jumping up and down. She was the opposite to my quiet, introverted, clinging childhood self. She was wildly social and loved talking to anybody. She liked being read poems and stories so that she could look at the pictures but was not interested in the writing underneath or beside them – at preschool we discovered this was because she was so severely long-sighted and astigmatic, the words were likely a grey blur. When she was four I took her on a train one day, and she struck up a conversation with a large, shy man sitting on the train behind us.

'What's your name?' she asked.

'My name's Mel,' the man said.

'Hello, Melon,' she said. 'Do you have any sisters?'

Her sociability and chattiness did not take well to the constraints of a schoolroom. She could not sit still long enough to concentrate; the only time she sat still was when she was drawing or painting. Her desire for constant conversation meant that early on she had passionate friendships, and had teachers and classmates who either adored her or were driven to distraction by her. Her sunny disposition could be twisted into defiance if she was thwarted by being required to rein herself in, either socially or in the classroom.

At her first school, one older girl took exception to Annie and began taunting her about a range of things: her thick glasses with the patch put over one eye to correct her nearly double vision; the car seat John required her still to sit in for safety; and most loudly on account of the cuts of crumbly parmesan cheese she'd adored since my Italian stepmother had introduced her to them. The older and taller girl complained about this stinky cheese, until five-year-old Annie picked up a wedge and held it close to the girl's face, backing her against the fence and saying, 'Cheese for sale! Cheese for sale!' From then, Annie was left to eat her lunch in peace.

...

As adherents to attachment parenting, John and I believed that so long as the first three years of a child's life are full of comfort, reassurance, and the meeting of needs, they would be able to weather whatever else came their way. John and I blamed our own anxieties on our mothers both smoking through their pregnancies, which reportedly caused anxiety through foetal oxygen-deprivation, and then failing to be available to us as babies and infants. So in the three-year formative time, we'd made sure we were available to Annie. She breastfed until her third birthday, when the new drugs I had to take for rheumatoid arthritis necessitated weaning. She had co-slept with me. And, aside from when Annie had witnessed John throwing plates at my feet or heard him yelling at me, her life was generally filled with positive social interactions at day care, in the co-op, and at home.

Annie loved me, but the person who could match her energy and enthusiasm was John.

John took her to tennis lessons and to gymnastics. He took her down to the ocean, where they could run down the beach or bounce on the clumps of glistening seaweed that banked up in winter months, or make sandcastles, or spot shells and the carcasses of crabs, or press into the squeaky foam-like texture of cuttlefish.

But as she grew and developed her own personality, and after we moved to the house in the suburbs, the endless patience with Annie that John had had in her early years was regularly replaced with something different.

For example, once she was old enough to understand, John instructed Annie not to speak with him in the car unless he asked her a question. He explained that it would be dangerous for her to ask him anything if he were crossing a road, or concentrating, and that because she did not know whether his concentration was required, she should remain silent. Because he drove her to gymnastics, to school, and to tennis, Annie was expected to be silent a lot of the time. She wasn't allowed to have screens or her Tamagotchi or anything to distract her. She was just supposed to be quiet.

There were only two problems with this. One, Annie was lively and energetic and talkative, and being constrained in a car seat was enough of a challenge without the requirement for her also to remain silent. The other was that John, if he was in a good mood, would chat with Annie as they drove, or they would sing to Daddy and Annie's Favourites. If Annie was allowed to start chatting, she assumed that she might be able to keep on. But then John would say, 'That's enough. I need to concentrate now,' and if she didn't shift from chatty to silent immediately, he would – once on the other side of the intersection, or through the traffic jam, or the 40-kilometre-an-hour section – yell until his face turned purple, glaring at her in the rear-view mirror.

I knew of these events because if I was home, I would be alerted by the sounds of the car doors slamming with a particular force, and then Annie would enter, weeping.

'I didn't do anything!' she'd protest.

'Go to your room,' John would say. 'I told you. You were just shitting me.'

'I wasn't, Daddy!'

'Go!'

Each afternoon, once she started at school, John expected Annie to tell him everything about what had happened during her day. He wanted to know who she had talked to, what she had eaten (to check she hadn't illicitly consumed anything salty, fatty, or sweet), whether she had drunk her required volume of water, and whether she had worn her hat and sunscreen when she'd gone out into the playground.

And if she argued with him, or brushed off his questions, or didn't immediately tell him what he felt was the whole truth, John would chastise her harshly and send her to her room.

If I was concerned about the way John treated Annie, I told myself that she was as feisty as he was, and was tough in ways that I was not as a child. She did not seem wounded by his yelling at her. She would yell back until he sent her to her room, where she would cry and then, later, they would make up. I felt, often, that I was watching a battle of wills between the two of them.

Sometimes I would wonder why John couldn't seem to rein in his impatience or his frustration. Sometimes I tried to talk him around. If I gave him my focused attention, if I asked for, or listened to, the full story of whatever it was that had driven him wild that day with Annie, he might calm down. Sometimes I delicately tried to suggest that his manner with his daughter was not having the desired effect. Perhaps giving vent to his frustrations through criticising her, through yelling at her, through monitoring what she said and ate and did at every moment, was not the best way?

But no matter how carefully I broached it, he would say that it was all right for me, being at work and away from it. How dare I criticise him, when he was doing his best in such a trying situation? I did not know what it was like, being with her all the time, so argumentative, so tiring. What was he supposed to do?

Once she'd stopped weeping and raging, Annie, confined to her room for hours, would make a drawing demonstrating her penitence. She would feed it under her doorway, so it was visible in the corridor, and wait for John's response.

'Why are you sorry?' John would say to her. 'You're just bullshitting me, you're not sorry. You just want to get out of your room.'

So Annie began to add to her drawings these notes:

To Daddy. Sorry I ruined your day yesterday. I feel really bad. I was too wound up about that silly raspberry tea. I'm gonna give you some space this weekend coz I know and understand you won't forgive me straight away until I prove to you I will be good. I hope this card has made you feel a bit better. Love from Annie.

Daddy. Sorry that I was being grumpy this morning. I will be more organised next time. I love you.

To Daddykins. I'm sorry for once again ruining your Friday. I was wound up in the car and today you were right and I was wrong and as you pointed out I said, 'I don't think so' which said to Mrs Durack basically 'No'. I have been thinking about it and did realise that you were right. I hope you know you are the best dad ever.

I'm so sorry Daddy. I know writing a note to you every time I go into my room might seem a bit suspicious but I just want to make you feel a bit better. I will stop with the attitude. I can get really grumpy as you know. We both do! If I'm feeling grumpy I will stay away from you, I promise. I'm really really sorry. I do know you're sick and I shouldn't be giving you a hard time. I will let you relax without me annoying you. Luv Annie.

To Daddy, I'm sorry I was difficult and rude today down at the cliffs. I know you wanted a relaxing time and all. I promise I won't give you any more problems this holidays. Xxx Annie. PS I will give you time to forgive me.

To my dearest darling Daddy. I'm as you know extremely grateful to you for pouring your money and time towards my plate. You have taken me to the orthodontist god knows how many times so I am not in pain and you have been extremely sympathetic towards me when it hurt. I'm sorry I have been such an arse and I will go along with my punishments that I deserve and I will be a saint for the rest of me living here. I love you.

Dear Daddy, Sorry for talking over you today and not letting you finish your sentence. Love you lots more than anything, from Annie.

To Daddy, I'm really sorry that I was so difficult in the car today. I was very hysterical because I was excited to see Jaz. Now that I realise what I did I feel really bad. I can tell how tired you are from driving. You're the best dad and I know that you're really angry with me (I don't blame you) and I really apologise for ruining your day. I love you so much about what I did you always know in my heart you're the bestest dad a girl could have. I love you from your daughter Annie. I'm sorry. Sorry Sorry Sorry Sorry Sorry.

Dear Daddy, I'm sorry I have been ear thumping today. I will never again insert a poo-bag down your checkered, red button-up shirt (I think it is cotton). I love you and deep down somewhere I know you love me too. Thank you for letting me know what I did. Love Annie.

I began taking comfort in what I imagined would happen when Annie became a teenager. Once she was a teenager, she would argue back. She would not be shut in her room then. Then, he'd reap what he was sowing. I could not fix this. But in time, Annie might.

Besides, I could explain away the side of John that yelled at me, broke plates, threw video recorders, banished Annie to her room, could not find patience within himself for his only child, because I understood his twitch-provoking anxiety, the feelings of horror he woke up with, the fear that disturbed his unconscious so much he would wail in the night. I understood this because I experienced those things too. I could channel the anxiety into study and work, and while the disturbances I felt made me want to give shape to them with words and narrative structure, John did not have these things. He could not work with other people. He could not suppress the anger his uncomfortable feelings produced, and if he could not avoid the source of his irritation – that is, his child – he lashed out. He could not rein in his fury nor his terrors. John's outlets for his deep discomforts were tennis, chess, and gardening. And they weren't enough.

John told me he'd been dux of his primary school and had excelled at high school until he'd decided not to. When he'd announced to his primary school class that he wanted to be a fisherman, the resultant laughter offended him deeply. They'd laughed, according to him, because he was top of the class and therefore expected to be something exalted, to achieve. His response to this laughter was to become determined to confound their expectations, which mirrored those his mother also held. He went through the rest of his life stubbornly refusing to achieve anything that was expected of him by dint of the values of mainstream society.

John had loved *The Story of Ferdinand* as a child. *The Story of Ferdinand* was a 1936 children's book about a young bull who grew to be the biggest in his herd, perhaps an ironic object of admiration for a person who failed to exceed the height of five feet four in adulthood. Expected to enter the bullfighting ring, Ferdinand instead preferred to sit alone and sniff flowers. When Ferdinand was stung by a bee one day, he roared, reared up, and was mistaken as a fierce bull worthy of the ring.

No doubt Ferdinand's story was provided to young John by his pacifist and left-leaning father, who later also furnished him with a copy of Mao's *Little Red Book*. John's version of sniffing flowers was holing up in his room reading. From an early age this was where he could be found when he wasn't wandering with his friends among the pine forests of Como until forced by dimming daylight to return to the unhappy home he grew up in, full of tension, fighting between parents and siblings all, and a Catholicism that rendered him angsty with guilt and shame.

I understood that Annie and I were inadvertent bees, and that the bucking, furious Ferdinand was not representative of Ferdinand's true nature. If only we would stop stinging him, he'd be fine.

30

Because I could see no way of changing it, I tried to ignore the difficulties that grew between Annie and John, with me and John. And often, it was easy enough to be lulled into something close to contentment by the benign day-to-day activities that were the bulk of our times.

In the beginning our new house-in-the-suburbs had lush soft grass back and front, carefully landscaped, which John regarded as a sign of the bourgeois: eventually I gave up either begging him to mow it or asking someone else to. But he loved the native bushes and trees around the perimeter of the house that bloomed at different times of the year, attracting a constant stream of chattering birds and bees with their low and long Gregorian sounds. We both loved the old red ironbark that was there before the house. I used to disdain gardening the way John disdained lawn, but once he showed me how to fertilise and mulch, how to propagate, and which plants belonged together, I was hooked. Together we dug up the back yard, laid out long garden beds, created compost heaps and worm farms. We grew onions and garlic, tomatoes, cucumbers and peas, herbs in pots. Annie tripped over pumpkin vines, chasing Hecta the Jack Russell through the back yard, when he arrived in 2007, and I learned to make baba ganoush so we had something to do with all the eggplants.

John and I never slept in the same bed – we were both too unsettled as sleepers for that – but in the evening, after Annie was in her room, John and I would cuddle for a while and then take turns drawing pictures on each other's backs. We drew soothing scenes of the beach, with us walking on it, or of the trail around Bibra Lake, with its darting ducks and blue-breasted robins and black swans in formation on the water like chess pieces mid-game. Sometimes we played noughts-and-crosses, in which John claimed extra squares I swear were already filled. The main aim of the premium back tickle was to include the widest range of dots, dashes, sweeping lines, circles, flicks, taps, and jiggles possible in a single story. And at the end we swept our fingers back and forth across the back, making it blank, dissolving the story to allow the person to dissolve into sleep.

Occasionally I became frustrated with John's reluctance to do housework other than the washing up. He would respond that he did the shopping and chopping, and the transportation of the child. What else could I want? And, for a period, to assuage my irritation, he did the vacuuming – still not frequently, but he undertook the task donned in my nightie, bra, and knickers, Sadie-the-cleaning-lady gloves, his smile lipsticked on. If ever after that I asked him to clean the floors, he'd say, 'Hang on, I'll just go get myself ready.'

In the late afternoon in dry Perth springs and summers, John would go outside and water the vegetable patches while the sky ran through its array of pastels. Hecta would dart through the undergrowth near the fence, with the occasional flurry of activity indicating he'd successfully tracked down a cat lurking for birds. The cat would leap to safety on the fence and regard Hecta balefully while the diminutive dog barked and leapt at his feline tormentor. In the house, Annie and I would be able to talk without interruption while I made dinner, or the two of us ate together. John rarely ate with us. After a few early attempts to eat together, he preferred eating in his room, reading a book.

And books too, until the end, united us. I admired his flashy intelligence, evidenced by his fast humour, chess skills, and his ability to describe and dissect information on a wide range of topics, but I was more impressed by the depth and breadth of his reading. His excellent memory of the arguments of the political thinkers he was keen on – Christopher Hitchens, George Monbiot, Edward Said, Tariq Ali, Richard Dawkins, Sam Harris, Noam Chomsky – lent authority to his views about the flaws in Western society and its power structures. We shared a love of the fiction of Jane Gardam, Ian McEwan, Don DeLillo: *White Noise* was his all-time favourite book. He introduced me to Hemingway, and I introduced him to Graham Greene's *A Burnt-Out Case*, with its Catholic themes of redemption through suffering.

I did have times of wondering why John could not see that Annie's childhood time was fleeting, that the time he lost in impatience and frustration stopped him from seeing the wonder of his own daughter. He'd spent much of his own life railing against the explosions of his father and the coldness of his mother, who until she died said that she rued having her four children. Could he not see that Annie would rail against him in the same way?

Also in the same way, I could not see that I was re-enacting the placating I'd seen my grandmother do with my grandfather, the silence with which the entire family responded to his temper, his impatience, his violence. If John was recreating the dynamics of his family of origin without a glimmer of recognition of it, so was I.

. . .

When there was first talk of a pandemic in 2005, with bird flu, John started trawling the internet for all the information on it that he could find.

'Jules,' he said. 'We have to prepare. Governments are ignoring it, and by the time they do anything, it'll be too late.'

So our shed became filled with tins of kidney beans and lentils, packets of seeds for all type of vegetables, bags of soil enricher, bottles of liquid fertiliser. We bought a water tank that John filled up from the tap because he didn't trust that the water from the eaves would be clean enough. The kitchen drawers were filled with N95 masks, and we each had a full-face ventilator.

'You can't go to work, once we get an outbreak here,' John said. 'You've got to explain to them about your immunity.'

He was referring to the medication I was on to keep the rheumatoid arthritis in check.

'I will,' I said.

'No, now,' he said. 'You'll need to stay home. I'll go to the supermarket, if we need to. You and Annie stay here.'

I was working at the health department by then, in the office of its director general. I told John that each day the chief medical officer walked by, I would read his face for signs of anxiety or concern as the bird flu outbreak spread in Canada and China and report back to John.

'If something was happening, he'd know,' I said. 'He seems pretty relaxed at the moment.'

'They're not prepared,' he said. 'We have to be.'

Part of me thought John was taking it too far. If we had to stay home for months and grow our own food, we'd be sharing it with the neighbours, if it got to that. If we didn't, people would be helping themselves. In his planning, we would be living as if nobody else around us existed. He'd told me that when he was a kid, playing in the pine forests of Manning with his friends, he'd imagine that they were there, alone, and the rest of civilisation had been mysteriously wiped out. I asked if the idea alarmed him. 'No,' he said. 'They were the happiest times of my life.'

But there was part of me that thought John might be on to something. If something disastrous was going to happen, it didn't hurt to be prepared.

...

Another aspect of my relationship with John was that, at least at first, we told each other about our feelings, our thoughts, the things we'd experienced. But that began to change.

Shortly after we moved into the house in the suburbs, John found out his old headmaster, Mr Buddee, was in a nursing home. He didn't tell me how he'd found out or who it was who might be sharing the information. It's possible that he found him through the internet. Mr Buddee had gone on to write children's books in the early 70s and a book about the Parkhurst boys in 1984. The Parkhurst boys were juvenile offenders sent out to the colonies between 1842 and 1861, pardoned in exchange for their labours, of which Western Australia made great use. Buddee had donated his research into the Parkhurst boys to the State Library of Western Australia. His preoccupation with prepubescent boys remained undiminished.

John paid Mr Buddee a visit, placing himself on a wheezing vinyl armchair.

'Do you remember me?' he said to the old man sitting with a crocheted rug on his lap.

Mr Buddee smiled. 'Were you one of my students?'

When John told him his name, Mr Buddee stopped smiling. His name was the same as his father's name.

'Do you remember Andrew C.?' John said.

Mr Buddee nodded warily.

'He drove his car into a tree when he was nineteen,' John said. 'What about Neil M.? Remember him?'

'I don't know what you want,' Mr Buddee said.

'Neil became an alcoholic,' John said. 'He choked to death on his own vomit.'

John went on and on, example after example. Then he asked, 'Do you remember what you did to us?'

'I didn't hurt any of you,' Mr Buddee said.

John leaned in and poked the bony chest with his forefinger. He could smell the mustiness of age, the antiseptic tang of the recently cleaned floor.

'I know what you are,' he said. 'And I'm going to make sure you never forget.'

Mr Buddee was still protesting as John walked away from him.

John waited for the feeling of satisfaction to come, but it didn't. Instead there was an uneasiness that revived his twitching, and a shrinking in his chest, a bit like shame.

John didn't tell me about the visit until many weeks afterward. We were walking at dusk one day when he said suddenly, 'I went and saw Paul Buddee.'

He didn't look at me.

'Really? When?' I tried to hide my shock. I still told John before I did anything important or challenging. We tested scenarios, worked out the best options, and I almost always listened to his advice. I'd assumed that he did the same.

'He went on as if nothing had happened,' he said. 'All he did was move schools. He was never punished.'

'But he knows you know,' I said.

'I told him I'd be back,' John said.

'Will you?'

'He thinks I will.'

'You've scared him.'

'He said he didn't hurt us.'

'They used to think children didn't have feelings.'

'As if nothing had happened,' John repeated.

I'd been aware that there were some things that I kept from John – my discomfort about his temper, for example, unless I was shouting about it during an argument. But that was the first time I realised that there was plenty he was capable of keeping from me too.

...

One day, when she was six and I had just finished my PhD, Annie was in her room, screaming and yelling in protest at her latest incarceration. She yelled and screamed and yelled some more. Then the pitch of the screaming changed.

'Something's wrong,' I said as I wrenched open the lock. Inside I saw Annie leaning forward, arms wide, blood streaming from her face. I could not tell if it was her mouth or her nose, only that the blood would not stop coming. John got towels and I sat in the back with her as we sped to the emergency department at Fremantle Hospital.

As Annie waited in the cubicle to be seen, the doctors questioned John and me separately and together. What had happened? Did she have these kinds of accidents often? Then they asked me: why is her surname different from his? Is he her stepfather?

I realised then they were asking if John hit her, if he'd caused the injuries we were seeking treatment for. I was horrified. No, of course not, I told them.

Annie, once the bleeding had been staunched, explained that she had jumped up and down on the chair, yelling, when she'd lost her footing and smashed her face on the back of it.

Eventually they believed her, and us, and we returned home. On the way John said, 'We should get married.'

I did not immediately respond. We were not married because neither of us believed in the institution. We did not want to have a wedding. John rarely came to family Christmases and birthdays because he did not like to be at social events he could not quickly escape from, so the idea of a wedding, of bringing our family members together, had never been seriously entertained.

'If we were married, they wouldn't question us like that,' he said. 'That was awful.'

He did not like to be accused, he said, but he was glad they interrogated him. There were men out there who would do such things, he knew.

'Okay,' I said. 'We'll get married then. At a registry office.'

I thought John would forget about his suggestion. I did not raise it again, but he did. We were going to stay together anyway, he said, so why not get married?

I agreed with him, even if my enthusiasm didn't quite meet his. We may as well. We were as good as married anyway. It was just a formality.

So it was decided. We would get married.

. . .

As soon as my health stabilised and Annie began kindergarten, so that neither required the level of preoccupation they had formerly required, I started to find solace in activities that allowed me to escape the daily life that I was less and less sure about wanting.

Some of the activities were aimed at creating a new life for myself through using my love of language and learning.

Once rheumatoid scared me into writing, I had carried on in a frenzy, keeping my door closed when I woke early and typing furiously for half an hour before John or Annie stirred. My first novel won a premier's prize. I wrote a thesis to accompany my second novel, *Skating the Edge*, which explored experiences in a hospital similar to the one I'd been in with Carita, and featured a Carita-like protagonist. In the years following, I published one or two novels a year, sometimes for children but mostly for teenagers, whose angst I still related to. In 2004 I was awarded an Australia Council grant to write a historical novel based on Gwen's teenage pregnancy. It would become *Bye, Beautiful*, published by Penguin, and it went on to be used in high schools for two decades. I relished worrying over plot points and character development, the fleshing out of the details of scenes, reading dialogue to myself to make sure its rhythms were true.

Writing and study were the more positive outcomes of my tendency toward preoccupation, introspection, and solitude. But alongside these ran mental tendencies, conveniently invisible, which I'd early developed as a means of distancing myself from quotidian discomforts, especially those

I could not articulate the causes of.

Now I found myself regularly falling into preoccupations with other people. As soon as I was well enough to resume working, I also resumed having passions – chaste – for people who were not John. I allowed myself to feel the longing and dissatisfaction I had with my current circumstance through the conduit of the unreachable object of my desire, much in the way I had escaped the chaos of my teenage years with Gwen through my focus on Karen.

I felt bad that I did not feel, or no longer felt, such desire for John. I reasoned that it was not in my nature to be monogamous or heterosexual. As I had in high school, and then university, I found myself rent with this longing, channelling feeling through my divided heart. It was not John, I told myself. It was just that I wanted to be elsewhere or, at best, two places at once. I wanted to feel liberated, now the medication had finally loosened my joints. I was chairing the board of an arts organisation and an arts assessment panel, so I was often out at night, seeing plays, going to exhibition openings. John never wanted to come, and besides, someone had to stay home with Annie. After the plays or the exhibition I would go out dancing, temporarily young, temporarily free. I would dance, thinking of whoever it was I was currently in thrall to, imagining we could be free together.

This state of affairs – or lack of them – was fine when the object of my desire was unreachable. But a few years after we had moved into the suburb by the lake, the latest object of my desire was a person, and a male, unusually, with whom I was doing contract work while I was finishing my PhD. He was the same age as John, with not dissimilar humour, but he was tall, confident, ambitious. We had a small office, and we were often alone. He was in a long-term relationship with someone, and I was about to get married.

'Why are you getting married?' he asked one day.

His question had an urgency, an interest, behind it. When I answered what I usually did – it was just a formality, we were going to be together forever anyway – it sounded like an excuse. It did not sound convincing, even to me.

And when my colleague looked at me, I began to suspect that I was not only choosing, formally, a life partner, but a certain type of life that I was not sure I wanted. But the suspicion was not enough to derail what was already in train, and easily quelled. Or so I told myself.

. . .

John and I married at the registry office, as planned. It was a wintry, windy day, raining on and off. Our friends, including Bridget and Shaun, were there, along with our families, it being the first time the families had met each other. Seven-year-old Annie and her cousins were in white flower-girl dresses, grinning with their gap-toothed smiles. We proceeded to a pub for lunch afterward. My cousin had snuck out of her motel the night before and stolen white flowers and foliage to scatter on the long tables. John kept breaking into impatience with Annie, who was so excited she couldn't contain herself. She had a pimple on her face, and John suggested to me she'd deliberately engineered it to appear on her face on the day of the wedding. Apart from that, it was a good day. John enjoyed himself, was loquacious and witty, and the misgivings some of my family may have had about him were allayed.

But the next week I went to work. I told my colleague we'd had the wedding. He shook his head.

I began to feel trapped, anxious. I couldn't stop thinking of my colleague shaking his head. I had made a mistake. Everybody treated John and me differently because we were married. John delighted in this. I was dismayed. Suddenly our relationship had legitimacy. Even though we'd been living together, we'd had a child, and we lived in a jurisdiction where de facto relationships acquire the same legal standing as marriages after two years, our relationship had been kept at arms-length by others. And now I realised that I'd kept one foot propping open the door, that I too kept the idea of a permanent union, and what it implied, at arms-length.

Not long after this, my colleague and I were out at a dinner function. I had given him a lift. We were parked outside his place, laughing about something that had happened at the dinner, when he propositioned me.

'I can't,' I said.

'Why not?'

'Because John would kill you,' I said.

'John doesn't need to know,' he replied.

'It would throw my life into chaos,' I said. 'I just got married.'

'Kiss me,' he said.

'If we kiss we may as well have sex,' I said.

'You're not saying you don't want to.'

'Of course I want to,' I said. 'But I can't.'

He nodded, as if I'd told him all he needed to know, and got out of the car.

We did not mention the conversation again for some time. It played in my mind as something impossible, like my former, impossible crushes, except this one, dangerously, was not. I found that I was able to carve off this what-if fantasy from the rest of my existence. The difficulty I was having getting a permanent job after my PhD. The endless bickering between John and Annie, the constant efforts I made to get Annie away from the house, to Derek and Olvi's and to my cousin Lou in Binningup. The haunting I felt, writing about Gwen's family in *Bye, Beautiful*. The uncertainty of whether the effort I put into writing was worth it. And, most of all, the crush separated me from the panic I had to push down, now being married when I did not want to be. I had made a vow I had not understood the implication of.

To separate myself from all these things, I could think about myself and my colleague. I could imagine waking up at his house on a Sunday morning. I could imagine our children meeting, playing, laughing. I could be myself with him in a way I could no longer be myself with John. It was all possible, if only I held it a little to one side, if I ignored the other, real fact of being married, of having a mortgage and a child and a husband subject to volatile mood swings. If I ignored having no permanent job and a husband who did not work and the constant financial stress this caused.

...

For a time the fantasy sustained me. And then, when I did allow the kissing – no sex, that was the rule, only kissing, and maybe some other things – the two states could no longer be separated. But neither could they be merged.

...

It didn't last for long. The frisson created by the danger of my new situation was an excitement in itself – I felt, for those times I was with my colleague, entirely separate from my regular life with this delicious, dangerous secret.

In a twist familiar to all cheaters, I was suddenly filled with new dissatisfaction with John. Some of it was dissatisfaction that I had not otherwise let myself properly feel. But some was a projection of my own guilt at not just coming out and saying that I did not want to be with him. I began to fantasise that it wasn't that hard, that I could leave. Once I was with my colleague, what could he do? He would have to accept the situation. Of course he would be angry, for a time, but would he prefer that I was miserable with him instead of happy with someone else?

My colleague and I had agreed that we absolutely would not say anything to anybody. As a person whose natural tendency is to describe and explain and analyse every shade of human behaviour and motivation, I always knew this would be a temporary arrangement. Already I had told my friend Sarah, who was also the only person who knew the detail of my trials with John, and my friend Lencie, who had known me since university and therefore was entirely unsurprised by my revelation. My faith in the clarifying power of Truth also meant that dissembling did not become me. And then there was the impulsiveness that had led me to this situation in the first place. Gwen's general parental advice to me on any matter was 'Go for it'. So when, one evening, the tension between what I felt and my daily situation became unbearable, I convinced myself that it was time to speak.

...

I was cooking pasta for dinner, drinking cheap wine that made my mouth shrivel with its acidity. Annie was staying at a friend's house. I stirred the sauce, chunky with the fresh tomato pieces I had cooked down. I drained the pasta into the metal colander, turned off the sauce, and said to John, 'I need to tell you something.'

I started crying, serving the pasta with the clawed pasta scoop. John was concerned: what was wrong? He made me sit down. He listened, completely silent, as I told him that I'd had a crush on my colleague. That he'd propositioned me. That, after resisting, we had kissed. Only kissed, but I was so confused.

As I was trying to explain, John's stillness and silence told me I had made a mistake. I should have kept my churning feelings to myself. I remembered, too late, some quote about the truth being a bludgeon.

Very, very quietly, John asked, 'What do you want?'

'I don't know,' I replied. 'I love you. But I have feelings for him.'

'Are you leaving me?'

'No!' It was automatic. I remembered his early warning. Don't threaten to leave unless you mean it.

Then he began. His eyes turned red, his face almost purpled. Flecks of spit gathered in the corner of his mouth as he demanded to know exactly what we had said, how it had happened, know who had kissed who first. He wanted to know how I felt, how it felt, every detail. He wanted to know if I wanted to have sex with my colleague.

'Yes,' I said.

'Did you have sex?'

'No,' I said.

'You're lying,' he said.

'I'm not lying,' I said. 'I swear on anything. I didn't.'

'I don't believe you,' he said.

'Well don't,' I said. 'I didn't.'

'If you are lying,' he said, 'you're going to feel guilty for the rest of your life.'

'I didn't, so I won't.'

'Are you sure you're not leaving me?'

'No,' I said. 'You and Annie are my family.'

'If you leave me,' he said, 'I'll get custody of Annie.'

'I'm not leaving you.'

'I'm young enough to find someone else,' he said. 'So if you're going to go, do it now.'

'I'm not,' I said.

Then he asked for my colleague's number. As I went to my room for my phone, I texted quickly: *John knows, I'm sorry.* I wrote his home number on a scrap of paper and handed it to John.

John made me come and sit by the phone while he called. I heard my colleague's familiar, cheerful voice answer through the receiver. He mustn't have got the text.

'You fucking low-life scumbag. You want to fuck my wife, you fucking arsehole. You go anywhere near her again, you speak to her again, and I'll fucking come for you. I know where you live and where you work. When you least expect it, I'll wait for you, some night, and I'll smash your knees with a baseball bat. I'll take your fucking legs out from under you and you'll wish you'd never seen her. If you ever go anywhere near her again, I swear I'll kneecap you, you cowardly cunt. Do you understand me? What? Do you? Good.'

When he slammed the receiver down, he said, 'You should be glad I'm directing it at him, or else I'd be directing it at you.'

I nodded. I deserved this response and everything that came after it, I understood this. I deserved all of it.

'Now, where does he live?'

'You can't go there,' I said.

'You should have thought of all this earlier,' he said.

'His kids will be there,' I lied.

John hesitated for a second, then took the keys and the metal baseball bat he kept under the bed. 'Don't you tell him I'm coming,' he said, and slammed the door so hard the windows rattled.

On my phone I saw my colleague's text in reply.

Why'd you tell him?

I messaged that John was coming over. Then I deleted everything: that message, his numbers, the sweet, cryptic texts we'd sent each other over the months.

When John came home, he was still raging. He wouldn't tell me what had happened, but the baseball bat was unbloodied. He insisted on having sex. I submitted. I thought about my colleague the whole time.

. . .

Afterward I tried to measure whether the honesty had been worth it. I reasoned that it was a way of stopping myself from going too far with my colleague. If I'd actually slept with him, I knew it would have been over with John. And I wasn't ready for it to be over with John. Or I lacked the courage. I wasn't sure which it was.

I worried about Annie, about John and I separating at the same age I had been when my parents split up. I worried about my own unconscious desire to replay my own childhood, which I'd tried so hard to avoid. And I knew John's threat to get custody was real, and that, once I was the enemy, he would stop at nothing to make my life difficult, the post-marriage, post-dependent-child version of throwing stones on a roof. I did not, at the time, think about the other effects on Annie, the effects of being with edgy, arguing parents, the effects of being raised with a controlling, uncontrolled father. That came later.

31

After the almost-affair, John agreed to marriage counselling. I had suggested this many times before, after our fights had left me hollowed out and alienated from both him and myself, but he always refused. The problem was not with us, with the fighting. It had been with the small house, with a bright, argumentative daughter who could not sit still, with the uncertainty of our finances when it was just the PhD scholarship and my teaching keeping us afloat, with my anxiety or his anxiety, separately.

We made an appointment with a marriage counsellor. After my confession, John had alternated between being stonily silent and being furious with me. I had no reason to object to his rages now. It really was all my fault now. And I had agreed to stay with him, so I must. He gave me an ultimatum, and I chose. I could not change my mind.

The waiting room of the counselling service was studiously neutral. Greys, pastels, prints of landscapes that could be anywhere. John and I sat in chairs spaced apart and completed our pre-counselling questionnaire. The questionnaire was in three parts. The first part inquired about my family background, our marital status and history, how many children we had, my health and financial status. The second asked about how I am: trouble sleeping? Loss of appetite? Feelings of worthlessness? The third asked about what prompted us to embark on counselling.

The receptionist came and took the questionnaire and delivered it into the room where we were waiting outside.

John walked comfortably in when the woman ushered us in, some ten minutes later. John was always confident of his charms with women. He said that because he was short, he could therefore apply his wit and banter to full effect without appearing sleazy. As we sat down, the woman offered us a smile as neutral as the interior decorating.

'Could you tell me why you're here today?' the counsellor asked.

She looked at me. I shrugged and gestured toward John.

'I can tell you why,' John said. 'Jules is the love of my life – she knows that, everybody knows that – we've been together for ten years. We got married in June, we've got a daughter, and my dad's died. Then she has this – thing – with a bloke she works with.'

'I see,' she said. 'And how do you feel about that?'

John almost-laughed. 'Well,' he said, 'I feel betrayed. Obviously.'

The counsellor turned to me. 'And why do you think you're here today?'

'Because of what John said,' I said. 'I feel really guilty. And now we're either not talking or we're fighting.'

'Do you try to talk?'

'Yes,' I said. 'But it ends up with us fighting. And then we end up not talking again.'

'And what do you fight about?'

'Me having the affair-thing,' I said.

'And that's all?'

'Well, sometimes it's about housework,' I said. 'But it's really about the affair.'

The counsellor was quiet for a moment. John was drumming his fingers on the arm of the chair, and his leg was jiggling.

'So the man you were involved with,' the counsellor said. 'You work with him?'

'Worked,' I said. 'I'm getting another job now.'

'And what do you do?'

'I've just finished my PhD,' I said. 'I used to teach, but now I'm trying to find a regular job, in the public sector or arts administration or something.'

'And you, John?'

'Excuse me?'

'What do you do?'

'I'm a house husband,' he said. 'I edit her books and do most of the running around with Annie.'

'How old is Annie?'

'Eight this month,' he said. 'She's the apple of our eye, isn't she, Jules?'

'She is,' I smiled.

'And she was a planned baby?' the counsellor asked.

'Not exactly,' I said.

'She was,' John said. 'We were always going to have a baby together, we just hadn't quite planned on her popping up right when she did. But it would have happened sooner or later.'

'And any complications with the birth?'

'Jules was magnificent,' John beamed. 'No drugs, but she was so calm, and then out came Annie. It was astonishing.'

'And how did Annie settle, as a baby?'

'She didn't sleep for three years,' I said. 'Well, I mean, she woke up during the night for three years.'

'She didn't want to miss out on anything,' John said. 'I used to walk her around the co-op in the middle of the night, so Jules could get some sleep.'

'Any postnatal depression?'

'I was too sick to be depressed,' I said.

'I made her go to the doctor,' John said.

'The pregnancy triggered rheumatoid arthritis,' I explained.

'Right,' the counsellor said. 'How is it now?'

'I've gone on drugs that do the trick,' I said.

The counsellor nodded. She looked as if she might ask something more about Annie, so her next question surprised me. 'So, John, before Annie was born, what did you used to do? Work-wise.'

'I was a drug and alcohol counsellor for a bit,' he said. 'A bit of cleaning, a bit of cash work. I was doing an arts degree when Jules got pregnant.'

'He got straight high distinctions,' I said. 'Of course.'

'And you haven't gone back to it?'

'It was a bit hard with everything going on,' he said. 'Jules was really sick, like she said, and so I needed to take care of her and Annie.'

The counsellor nodded again. 'Julia, how do you feel about John not doing paid work?'

'Fine,' I said. 'He supports me with what I'm doing. My writing is the most important thing, and he's a really fantastic editor. And when I go to work I don't need to worry about getting Annie sorted out.'

The counsellor looked as if she was thinking carefully about what her next question would be. But before she formed it, John cut in.

'What's this about?' John said. 'Jules and I came here to work out how we go on with this situation. How are we going to do that?'

'I'm trying to understand the dynamics of your relationship,' the counsellor said. 'You seem a little defensive about that.'

I could tell that John was about to erupt in a fury. He went still. His eyes appeared to change colour. Under one eye, a cheek twitched.

'I just want to know what the parameters are,' he said. 'You seem to be pushing a particular agenda, and that's not what we're here for.'

In the pause while the counsellor appeared to be deciding what approach she was going to take to John challenging her skills and professionalism, I moved in to relieve her of having to.

'I want to talk about the affair too,' I said. 'I'm horrified by what I almost let happen to our family. But I can't pretend I didn't have those feelings either.'

I'm not sure what caused me the most shame: talking about the turmoil that led me to my colleague's arms or the knowing/not knowing that I was supporting John's ability to avoid discussing the imbalance in our marriage, one that was only going to get worse in the coming years. But I also knew it was not the counsellor who would shortly be in the car with John as he railed against her and her agenda, and how she seemed to want to make my lack of faith, my betrayal, into his responsibility. This is why he's never wanted to go to relationship counselling, he'd declare. He knew it would be like that. She wasn't aware of her own bias, did I see? She couldn't even tolerate being asked about it.

We were intelligent, analytical people. We loved each other. We had been through difficult times and we had come through them. We would work it out ourselves.

32

In the middle of this unhappiness, after six months of applications, I got a job in the public sector, one that promised stability and promotion. John was resentful. Why should he be happy for anything after what I'd done, my true duplicitous nature hidden behind my achievements?

I was anxious about working full-time. My writing career was flourishing. I had been picked up by Penguin, I was beginning to be invited to festivals and schools. How would I write, working thirty-eight hours a week, travelling nearly an hour each way? Since Annie was born I'd managed to find teaching contracts with breaks in between, and then the PhD scholarship allowed me to teach less and write more. John had sporadic attempts at working, always part-time, cleaning jobs, selling jobs, but he always took issue with his employer – and of course, he was always right, he was right to quit, he was being treated terribly.

But working, it turned out, had its own benefits, not least of which were financial. I found my skills were recognised, encouraged, sought after. Soon I was appointed as a speechwriter for a director general and a minister. I was being paid to write. And I was away from home.

John vacillated between being glad that there was more money and resentful at the additional obligations it placed on him. He would call me in the mornings and afternoons at work, complaining about being left with Annie, about how badly behaved she was, about how she wouldn't stop winding him up. When I came home, John would send Annie to her room and continue the same complaints while I cooked dinner. He was always so tired, all the domestics, all the childcare; if I mentioned that I was tired, working, he'd say, 'At least you get to be around adults! I'm just around *her* all the time!' Once I'd calmed him down I'd sneak into her room, tell her not to worry about him, tell her we would go to my dad's place on the weekend, that we would go on holiday together. Once I asked why he hadn't videotaped a show I'd asked him to. In response, he ripped the video from the television and smashed it on the floor. I remember being at work one day, early in my public sector career, exhausted because John had kept me up in a flare-up of his resentment about my (now former) colleague. I was thinking how nobody at work would guess how John spoke to me at home. How competent I was at work, how inept at managing my private life. John told me only he knew me, only he knew my true self. Now, when we fought, he would spit, 'Who do you think you are?'

I did not think of myself as a victim. I never started a fight, but I was no longer the twenty-three-year-old who wept as he yelled. I argued back. Once, I left the house, yelling out the window, 'Cunt! You're a fucking cunt!' But I returned when I concluded I had nowhere to go. When the fighting got bad once, I did ask Derek if there was any chance he was going to finish the granny flat he was building out the side of his house, his house being full of my younger stepbrother and stepsisters. Originally, he was building it for Gran to move into, but Gran had sickened and died some years before, and the granny flat still had concrete floors, raw brick interiors, the sky still visible through the tiles beneath which huntsman spiders lurked and redbacks nested. Derek inquired as to my interest. I told him Annie and I might need it. When he next asked, I said it was okay, we'd sorted things out.

. . .

In 2007 I applied for a job at the Western Australian Parliament as a principal research advisor for the Legislative Assembly committees. Because I thought I had no chance to win such a prestigious position, I was breezy and confident in the interview, making the panellists laugh. I hadn't realised that parliamentary positions were not part of the public sector, so when the panel inquired whether I belonged to a political party I was surprised. In the public sector, this was a question akin to asking if you were planning on having babies or whether you believed the Second Coming was nigh. I collected myself enough to say, 'Yes. But nobody would be able to guess which one,' after which they asked whether I would be prepared to cancel my membership if I were successful. My shallowness of political conviction made it easy to agree. These questions also alerted me to the fact that at Parliament, things were done differently.

When I was offered the job I had an anxious moment, having to explain away my 1990 arrest for chaining myself to a sheep ship, worrying it would be construed as an employment-limiting political protest. However, the human resources person I emailed with my concern replied, 'As long as you've had a good wash since then, you should be all right.'

Less than a year after I started at Parliament, I was promoted to Sergeant-at-Arms, which came with a piece of medieval weaponry known as a mace. I worked in the house of Parliament proper, announcing the arrival of the Speaker at the commencement of each sitting day and trying not to drop the gold-plated and very expensive bit of kit as I balanced it on its brackets, where it signified that Parliament was sitting.

Parliament bore no resemblance to any workplace I'd previously experienced. The plush carpets muffled the well-shod steps of Members of Parliament and the people who sought their favour. The jarrah panelling through the building was so extensive there were no fire sprinklers, as the only recommended action in event of fire was to get out and away. There was even a shoe-polishing machine in the ladies' toilets. There were generous Christmas lunches with free-flowing wine. There was a bar and a wine club. There might have been sexist comments made by senior parliamentary officers and Members of Parliament that would have been the subject of an investigation and disciplinary action in the public sector, but such trifles were not a cause for concern. Parliament wasn't a workplace. It was a world unto itself. And I was happy to step into it.

· · ·

After Annie started high school, in 2009, there was a shift in my relationship with John.

Because Annie was now independently catching the bus to school, John got a job as a traffic warden, ushering children safely across roads morning and afternoon. It wasn't much, but it was something, and I hoped this would be a harbinger for something more. He began to spend a lot of time playing online chess, now he wasn't coaching the chess team at Annie's primary school, and he was happily absorbed in chess strategies and verbally sparring with his opponents.

Each morning I brought John our sweet, milky coffees to his room. I placed his on the bedside table, nudging aside his pile of books. I put mine on the desk in front of the window and drew open the blackout curtains. Through the window we would look out onto the day: the quiet cul-de-sac, the untrimmed grevillea whose heavy, cone-shaped flowers drew honeyeaters with their flecks of yellow brightening their black and tan feathers, the Albany woolly bush that recalled the one at the co-op under which we buried Annie's placenta when I realised my attempts at earth-mothering would not extend to me eating frozen squares of it, no matter how nourishing. There used to be a lawn at the front, but that had been converted to a garden bed edged with limestone blocks. Corn grew there, then potatoes, then something blighted the patch and it became threaded with weeds. As we'd done on Port Beach when Annie was in day care, we talked about the dreams we'd had, the books we were reading, about Annie. Hecta would join us, wriggling and rolling on the once-cream carpet before taking off outside to see what may have dared to enter his yard overnight.

The man who had never wanted to go out to eat because sitting at a table reminded him of tense childhood dinners also began coming out to various restaurants with me for lunch on weekends. One of my friends was a food blogger, so we drove around the suburbs newly settled with students or migrants, sampling noodle soups, roti bread dipped in Malaysian curry sauces, chicken rice. John had stopped obsessing over the fat and salt content of everything he ate, and we talked and laughed amid the clattering cutlery and animated, incomprehensible conversations of those around us.

As the sun melted into the ocean on evenings warm and cool, we took to walking at Woodman Point with Hecta. If people were fishing, John would go and see what was in their buckets, talk about what fish were running, while I would watch the pelicans that gathered. They were almost as tall as I was, with hairpin-curved necks, and they would turn their heads and fix Hecta with one black eye to make sure he wasn't competition for the baitfish they might be thrown. I loved how pelicans were ungainly on land, but with an awkward flapping of wings they could launch themselves up, angling this way and that before settling into a glide, a majestic expanse of wings finding balance in the air.

Other evenings we would sit out the back, John drinking a mid-strength stubby of beer, me drinking a wine, looking out over our chaotic but productive garden beds full of onions, kale, garlic, and trailing pumpkin vines, compost bins where our vegetable scraps rotted and were mixed with seaweed we hauled off winter beaches to fertilise the new season's soil before planting.

It was a sweet time. I didn't know what had caused this mellowing, but it was a relief. John's prickly edges softened, the sturm und drang of our daily life blessedly becalmed. This is what people meant, I thought, when they talked about marriage being something worked on, something that develops and changes, if only you have patience and willingness. I was glad, finally, that I hadn't walked away in 2004. This was its own, subtle reward.

...

In 2009 I was sent on an attachment to the House of Commons. There was a Commonwealth Serjeant-at-Arms (as they spell it in the UK) conference due to be held, peopled with my fellow constables of the parliaments of Canada, the other states of Australia, New Zealand, India, Bangladesh, Singapore, Barbados, Mauritius, and various African countries. I was to spend several weeks in the houses of Parliament before the conference, to make sure I got an educational bang for the parliamentary buck. When I was living in Brixton in 1991, and after narrowly escaping being blown up by an IRA bomb at Victoria Station one morning, I always took the longer but above-ground double-decker bus to work in the West End, climbing upstairs to sit as close to the front window as practicable. Every time the bus crossed the Thames, I stared in wonderment at the majestic Palace of Westminster, previously only known to me through shots of *Yes Minister* and *The Goodies*. Now, eighteen years later, I would have my own office there for three whole weeks.

As John was disinclined to leaving home and was not a good traveller even when he did, twelve-year-old Annie was to accompany me as my partner. Apart from the odd antipodean exception, and the rather more notable one of Jill Pay in the House of Commons itself, most of the serjeants were male and straight, so Annie became one of the wives in the spousal contingent. She was the youngest person ever to have her own access-all-areas pass to the UK Parliament, her pre-teen face grinning out from the rigid plastic badge.

Annie and I had an apartment in Dolphin Square, Pimlico. From there I walked each humid summer's morning to the House of Commons along the Thames, bouncing along as I marvelled at my own good luck, while Annie stayed in the apartment to do her homework. I entered the parliamentary estate through the hammer-beamed majesty of Westminster Hall, where the trials of King Charles I and William Wallace, among others, had been held, and made my way to my office in the serjeant's section of the Palace of Westminster. Through the open window at my desk I could see the Clock Tower, commonly known as Big Ben, the iron roofs and the smog-stained limestone walls that were forever in the process of being scrubbed clean, section by section.

My job for the attachment comprised ensuring that international harmony was maintained by the seating arrangement for the conference, an act of high diplomacy requiring me to make sure delegates from African countries were seated as far apart from each other as possible to prevent possible outbreaks of unparliamentary exchanges.

As part of my professional development I was given tours of the Houses. As a republican with a penchant for the Royal Family, I was much taken with the robing room in which the Queen used to prepare before each opening of Parliament: reportedly, even she still became nervous, balancing the heft of her crown on her head while following the Usher to the Commons each opening day. I met with the plummy-voiced clerks who were generous with their knowledge of their particular area of parliamentary procedure, if rather more conservative than I was used to parliamentary staff being in Australia. When I told one clerk that my friend Nobbly, who'd moved to the UK when we were twenty-one, had been arrested outside for protesting fox hunting, she responded stiffly, 'I run hounds. What is wrong with running hounds?' I regularly offered to do errands and would be overjoyed to find myself completely lost in some ancient corridor of the beautiful building. The immense tiled lobby to the Commons was my north star: if I found my way back there, I could find my way to the serjeant's quarters. I got to watch the last sitting day of the session, with Jill Pay balancing a mace almost as tall as she was on her diminutive but strong shoulders.

My fascination with and alienation from this ancient, privileged realm was complete when the serjeants and their partners were invited to the serjeant's house, which was provided as part of her role, for a lunch on the final day of the conference.

I had thought that perhaps this would be a modest dwelling, akin to that of a groundskeeper in a public park. Instead we were led through a secret tunnel under the street, around the corner, and into the basement of a four-storey house filled with cream carpets and tasteful ornaments that would have cost more than my annual salary, and into the top room looking out to the bustling London street, its noise silenced by double glazing.

There we sat on brocaded couches and were brought quintessentially English finger food. I hissed at Annie not to drop anything, before a well-oiled sardine slipped from my own Wedgwood plate I was balancing and onto the brocade. The humiliation I felt was akin to that I'd felt the previous week, when, at a small lunch held at a parliamentary restaurant overlooking the Thames, the effect of three weeks of English food resulted in an essential mid-cleavage button popping from my blouse and toward the serjeant as she was in the middle of a thank-you-all-for-your-work speech. 'You Australians,' one of the sympathetic staff said to me as he lent me a jacket. 'You're very natural.'

The final serjeants' party was held on a cruise boat that glided down the murky, magnificent Thames in the summer sunset that lasted for hours. The falsetto voice of the recently dead Michael Jackson got everyone on the dance floor after canapés and champagne. The roof above the dance floor opened, and as we went under each of the bridges on the way back from the Thames loch we danced and waved our hands at the people on the bridges above who were watching our procession, at the stars that were hidden by the bright lights of London, at our own good fortune, being there, dancing on the water and under each concrete-and-metal span uniting the south and north of the city, and which made our gleeful shouts echo temporarily. Annie and I grinned at each other, at the marvel of it, at the infective cheerfulness of the fast tempo and the high voice whoo-hoo-ing almost as much as we were. Annie and I danced and laughed and didn't think of home, not once.

33

Not long after we arrived home from London, John began having various, non-specific physical symptoms that escalated into the following year, 2010. His bladder wouldn't empty properly, so he went on medication to help ease the discomfort. His cholesterol suddenly increased, so he went on medication to help that. His eyesight bothered him, so he got new glasses. Then he began to experience a climbing of anxiety, for which he refused to contemplate medication. He attributed the anxiety to his physical difficulties and to a spiritual malaise, a loss of purpose, now that he was not the dad who took Annie to primary school, or a chess coach. It was anxiety both explainable and familiar.

So as suddenly as the household quiet had been ushered in, John's escalating anxiety ended it.

One weekend in February 2011 I bought Annie a tin of chocolate Nesquik during the weekly shop. When John spied it, he began one of his tirades.

'How dare you buy this shit for our daughter?' he said, his face reddening, spit gathering at the sides of his mouth. 'We've agreed not to have shit food in this house. Haven't we?'

'But honey,' I said. 'It's just a small tin. Besides, she's fourteen now, she's only having it sometimes.'

'Why would you do that?' he spat. 'Nobody fucking listens to me in this house!'

He took the tin out the back. I got out of the house, figuring it would give him time to calm down.

The strange part of this interaction was not John's ranting about the Nesquik. The strange part was that it was not referred to, over and over again afterward, until I had apologised with a tone he accepted. It did not cause a mood that lingered for days. The house did not become silent, in case a trigger set off another spray of insult, with Annie and me signalling to each other when John had vacated the kitchen or living area, only speaking in low tones behind our closed doors.

After it happened, John appeared to have forgotten it entirely.

I mentioned the incident to a friend at work. She looked at me with concern.

'Babe,' she said. 'That is really extreme.'

'I know,' I said. 'He's never forgotten a fight before.'

'Not that,' she said. 'I mean his reaction. To you buying Nesquik?'

'Well, yeah,' I said. 'It's sugar. We don't have it in the house. But him forgetting about it? That's weird.'

She did not say anything else, but her reaction brought to consciousness what I had spent fifteen years hiving off to an unexamined corner of my mind, shoving into outbreaks of indignant diary entries, and otherwise forgetting. The part of my brain where I had relegated spitting, angry, video-throwing John, characterising that John as an aberration from the witty one, the true one, the one I had loved and continued to love, could no longer lie dormant.

What might have happened, had things unfolded differently, is that I would have taken stock and realised that in spite of the lull of the previous year or two, John was not going to change. The threats he had previously made about having custody of Annie if I ever left him no longer mattered. Now she was a teenager, she was already beginning to understand her father in a different way. John would try to control me, to financially hurt me, to be vicious in private and civil in public. I would have realised it was long overdue that Annie and I deserved better. I would have gathered all the courage I would need – and it would need a lot – and I would start a new life.

Instead I was shortly to find myself stuck in an entirely new way, at the same time formerly suppressed feelings were inconveniently released and now became uncontainable.

FIND OUT WHY YOUR HUSBAND IS URINATING IN THE KITCHEN OF AN EVENING

34

It is 2011.

I'm not sure what wakes me up: the sound of the opening door, the dim light from somewhere in the dark house, or the muttering. The dog's claws tap on the passage tiles, then on the bare concrete of my room. We recently had an extension built – ostensibly to make the small house bigger, but really it was my idea, to put more distance between John and Annie. The matching mortgage extension didn't cover flooring, painting, or fixing the torn-up back yard. I, as usual, am in the middle, between John's room and Annie's.

My nightmares lately have, as well as becoming more frequent, taken on a hallucinatory quality. I find myself sitting up, trying to get a spider web off my face, or to shoo the blank-eyed white cat from the bottom of my bed, or to fight off the man who is standing over me, his hand over my face or at my throat. Annie reports that when she or John come in after I've been yelling, I am sitting up, terrified, wailing that it/he's over there, can't you see? And then I wake up properly, and I can't tell whether the web or the cat or the man is real, or my fourteen-year-old daughter or fifty-two-year-old husband. It takes some time before I realise it's the latter, and everything is all right, or at least not as dire as first suspected.

But now, actually, there is a man in my room. I can see him in the light, standing near my computer desk, facing the window with its imperfectly closed curtains. He is at the end of my bed, but he's facing away. I hear muttering, and the tap-tap of the dog coming closer to him. Then I hear the surprisingly heavy splashing, and I leap out of bed.

'Honey!' I say, snapping on the light. 'This isn't the toilet!'

John is standing there, alarmed, but he can't stop pissing. He looks disoriented and surprised that I am there, in my own room.

I approach him from behind, grab him by the shoulders that are strong from tennis and gardening, and turn him around. There is a large and spreading puddle of piss next to my computer desk.

'The toilet's there, honey,' I say in as calm a voice as I can muster at 2am.

'Oh,' he says.

'I'll clean it up,' I say, although he hasn't expressed concern. He is docile, as if he's sleepwalking. Maybe he is.

I guide him back to his room. He sits on the side of the bed for a moment then lies down. He turns away from me, pulls the sheet over his shoulder, and goes straight back to sleep.

I go to the laundry and fill up the bucket, squirt some disinfectant, soak the mop.

As I approach my door I hear a rhythmic rasping. Hecta is licking the floor, his tail wagging. His Jack Russell beard has turned a faint yellow, and he produces the dog version of a grin as he sees me.

He's done a good job. You'd never know what had happened, but for the faint cooked-asparagus scent in the air.

When I tell people about this – or about John's middle-of-the-night pissing in the living room, which he has also started doing – they ask if he is drinking a lot.

'Yes,' I say. Since resuming alcohol consumption seven months after Annie was born, John has religiously limited himself to three mid-strength middies of beer each day, no more, no less, apart from our stint of stout-drinking in Annie's toddler years. But lately I've been finding bottles of scotch everywhere – in the garden, under his bed, in the bottom of the laundry basket. Some are full, some are almost empty. When I throw them out, John never mentions them again.

'It's definitely booze-related,' people nod. 'I know someone who does exactly that. It's a sign of alcoholism.'

I let this comfort me, even though John does this when I know he hasn't had anything more than his three middies. I am beginning to look for comfort wherever I can get it.

...

The reason I needed comfort was because, aside from forgetting arguments about the purchase of Nesquik, John had been displaying changes in conduct that were beginning to trouble me, practised as I might have usually been at putting John's behavioural foibles to one side.

First of all, there was the driving.

John took great pride in his pristine driving record and extended his civility to others who also drove well, letting people in, waving gallantly as he did so. He also, sometimes on the same journey, took loud and threatening exception to others who in his view caused danger on the road, through speeding or cutting him off, or pulling out in front of him. He forced people off the road so he could berate them, waving a finger at them while Annie and I sat in the car. If he noticed me looking askance, he'd say, 'You and Annie are the most important things in my life. That dickhead was putting you in danger!' It was a logic hard to argue against.

But after we got back from London, John's driving confidence and navigational ability began to diminish.

He took to poring over road maps whenever he was driving anywhere. We had never had a satellite navigation system, as we were both good with directions and familiar with most of the suburbs of Perth. Now he drew lines through suburbs, over pages, and frowned at them before he went anywhere new. He located the blue P for parking areas nearby and circled them. If there was a tennis tournament or other appointment he had to get to, he did a test run first. At the time I thought this was an extension of the anxiety he had always suffered, and which seemed to be worsening.

In late 2010, John was driving Annie to her best friend's house, a place he'd visited countless times, when he became gripped by panic.

'Where do I go?' he asked her.

'I don't know,' she said. 'That way?'

'Which way?' he said. 'Tell me which way!'

When Annie told me this, I imagined John peering ahead, the streets rearranging themselves into something unfamiliar, disorienting, like finding yourself on the wrong floor of the building you work in. Everything looks as if it should be familiar, but nothing is where it should be, and where have all your colleagues gone?

Annie pointed John in the right direction, and he said, 'I knew that, I knew that.'

Soon afterward, he was driving on the freeway, this time delivering Annie to a birthday lunch, and when he stopped at the exit he began to bang the gear console.

'How do I drive this thing?' he said. 'What do I do?'

'I don't know, Dad, I'm fourteen,' she said.

'What am I supposed to do?' he said.

'Call Mum,' Annie suggested.

'No!' he said. 'Don't you dare!'

The mystery of how to achieve forward motion – release foot from the brake, press down right foot on the accelerator – eventually revealed itself, and Annie fled from the car to the birthday gathering. The console never quite recovered, and resisted being placed into gear ever after.

John started sleeping in the car after dropping Annie at her dance lessons, even though the hall was only five minutes from home. Annie reported having to wake him up when she stepped out in her leotard and ballet flats into the dark winter nights.

'It's weird,' she said. 'Nobody else's dad does that.'

'I'm just tired,' John said, when I asked. It wasn't until much later that I realised that he was worried about getting lost, driving in the dark. And of all the other things that he'd started doing, getting lost was the last thing I thought to be concerned about.

...

One day I came home to find John rummaging frantically through every drawer in the house. I could see where he'd been already – drawers were hanging out, their contents on the floor or spilling over the sides. It looked as if we'd been burgled.

'What's wrong, honey?' I said.

'I've lost my wallet,' he said. 'I've been looking everywhere. I've got the shopping money in there.'

I glanced over to the round pine table. We'd reversed roles recently. I'd become the one always telling John to keep the table clear, to minimal effect. Next to the fruit bowl, piles of books, a stack of unopened mail, and a scattering of pens was his ratty leather wallet.

'There it is,' I pointed.

'I need new glasses!' he said, rushing over, putting the wallet in the pocket of his King Gee shorts, which he's taken to wearing with thick black socks and white sneakers. 'Thanks, honey.'

He extracted a beer from the fridge, whistled to Hecta, and went outside to the garden. I put everything back in the drawers and poured myself a glass of wine. I sat at the table and watched John watering the thirty-year-old gum tree. I wanted to cry, but I wasn't sure why. Instead, I took a large swallow of wine, until the knot in my throat loosened, for now.

. . .

To the outside world, John remained social, gregarious, and witty, with a prodigious, if selective, memory for detail. He had been known for remembering not only the names of people's brothers and sisters and parents, even when met in passing, but also their dogs. Once he irritated an ex-girlfriend by forgetting she'd been in a serious car accident when they'd been going out some fifteen years prior but remembering the name of her long-since-dead beagle.

Now he retained the veneer of sociability and was able to use it to ward off queries about his behaviour, his lack of ability to retain information. At my forty-first birthday lunch he was chatting to Gwen's brother, whom we'd recently had at our house to fix guttering. Afterward he turned to me and said, 'So how does that man know Gwen?' He would greet tennis buddies, neighbours, and acquaintances in the supermarket, chatting away, but as soon as they had gone he'd ask me, 'Who was that?'

In early 2011 we were walking the dog around the lake. Hecta strained at every dark dot of duck shit, and jerked at the end of the lead from side to side, searching for a dropped chicken bone or ant-animated piece of discarded sandwich or biscuit or otherwise unidentifiable piece of matter deemed worth a swallow. John began talking about his sister's husband and asking about when we would be seeing him next.

'Honey,' I said. 'He died two years ago, in England. Remember?'

John's brother-in-law, a gentle man plagued by mental illness, had disappeared some years previously while travelling in the UK. After his photograph appeared on the back of milk cartons across England, pleading for help to locate the missing man, his remains were found in a forest near his family home, propped against a tree. It was not the kind of event that would slip anyone's mind in normal circumstances.

John stared at me for a moment, as if I was bluffing, or being wantonly cruel, then he began sobbing.

'No,' he said, hands over his face. 'No. That's awful, Jules. It's awful!'

He also couldn't hold on to the fact that I was in the process of leaving one job and taking up another. I'd left the Legislative Assembly for a promotion, and for the best part of a year had been managing the hiring, firing, and administrative support in a government department. I managed the contracts for two government airplanes, a jet, and a turbo prop, which were on call in case urgent organ transportation was needed, which meant I was on call too. When I started suspecting something was wrong with John, after my colleague's chance comment about John's response to the Nesquik, I knew that the position was incompatible with whatever was coming. So I sought out a new job.

The new job was back at Parliament, this time in its upper house.

. . .

The Deputy Clerk of the Legislative Council, Nigel Lake, had been on my first interview panel when I'd applied for and got a job in the Legislative Assembly in 2007. We got on well from the start. His meticulousness and thoroughness in his job and person was admirable, and he was kind, generous, and drily funny. He had a commanding build, inherited from his Tongan biological father, that wouldn't have been out of place in a line-up of rugby forwards, and he held a similarly commanding authority with his methodical, logical application of parliamentary rules in the chamber. Members and staff alike were comforted that with Nigel around, everything was under control. He was as unflappable as he was fastidious in both his appearance and his work. Nigel's motto in all aspects of life was that if you were going to do something, you did it properly.

When Nigel heard I was looking for another job, he had called me. Was I interested in applying for the Usher of the Black Rod in the Legislative Council?

The Legislative Council aspect of the equation gave me some pause. The Western Australian Legislative Council had long had a history of its table officers going rogue. As early as 1932, the forty-year-old Usher of the Black Rod, Ernest A. Brown, was arrested for fraud (then known more charmingly as uttering) in the form of faking cheques. His arrest caused shock among parliamentarians, who liked and trusted the man employed by the Parliament for twenty-four years.

In a much fresher instance, the Legislative Council's long-standing Clerk, Laurie Marquet, was charged in 2005 after siphoning off more than two hundred thousand dollars from the Council to pay for methylamphetamine, as well as being charged for perverting the course of justice and possession of the drugs he hadn't yet had the opportunity to put in his arm. He promptly died, aged fifty-nine, before a conviction could be proven.

The next appointment had been the Parliament's first female Clerk, who lasted a total of nine months in the role before disappearing, never to darken the door of the Parliament again. There were whisperings she'd been the subject of a campaign to oust her: the whisperings were unproven, but contributed to the sense of intrigue with which the upper house was regarded by those outside it. The chamber was certainly a male-dominated affair, with the odd female in the lowest administrative roles. Legislative Assembly staff, on account of all of the foregoing, nicknamed the upper house the Dark Side.

In spite of my foreboding, which was after all my default feeling in most matters, I applied for and then accepted the position. I reasoned that although I was swapping stress with long hours and less pay, this would be a better option for dealing with whatever it was that was going on with John. I was also keen to work directly for Nigel. With a home life descending into chaos, working for someone predictable, steady, and patient seemed an excellent choice.

Also, who wouldn't want a job called Usher of the Black Rod?

. . .

My appointment as the first female Usher of the Black Rod meant I was featured in the state's newspaper, photographed in the red Council chamber with my bar jacket, gown, and jabot, wielding the black rod. Up until the

1950s, the rod had been a pool cue painted black, when a former member took pity and, in commemoration of Queen Elizabeth's 1954 visit, employed the Crown Jeweller to make one out of ebony, topped by a gold swan. The most visible duty of the Usher in Westminster-style democracies is to seek admission for the upper house members to enter the lower house at each opening of Parliament. This is achieved by the Usher leading the newly elected members from one chamber to the other, like a gothic and humourless Pied Piper, rapping thrice at the chamber door with the black rod, waiting while the door is cracked open by the Sergeant-at-Arms before being slammed in the Usher's face. The Sergeant then bellows to the Speaker, 'Black Rod seeks admission,' to which the traditional response is, 'Admit Black Rod,' occasionally causing less high-minded members of parliament to fall about laughing. One of my predecessors, beside himself with nervousness, got his rod ends mixed up and rapped the golden swan flat.

Despite the get-up, and my new position garnering a piece in the state's only newspaper, John could not remember that I'd changed jobs, let alone gone back to Parliament. Before this, I used to debrief at home about work-related goings on. Working near seats of power provides no end of anecdote suitable for provoking astonishment and outrage at the way organisations are run and the behaviour of those inside them. Even though he hadn't had a day job, John would comment wittily on this person or that situation. Now he did not. Now he only talked about what he'd done in the house, about Hecta the dog, about the chess tournaments he was playing online. And he was still regularly enraged by Annie's behaviour and tone, although by now she took advantage of her increasing independence and age by being home as little as possible.

I dismissed my concern at his slippery memory and tunnelling focus by reasoning that I was quite happy to keep my work and home separate, so it didn't matter that John didn't remember where I was employed. I was ecstatic at being in a job where the phone did not ring day and night, where my responsibility was limited to chamber security and the functioning of the administration office. I was reunited with my colleagues from the lower house, and Nigel was a calm and decisive manager. For a time, the Council followed through on its promise of routine and predictability.

My first inkling that life in the Council was not going to be quite as easy as I'd hoped was when a senior manager called me in and said, without meeting my eyes, that he'd told Nigel not to employ any more people from the Legislative Assembly. The second inkling was when a male colleague came into my office and casually observed that employing women in the chamber only led to trouble. Oh, he didn't mean me. He was just saying.

And then, just as I was gowning up for a sitting day, the barrier I'd been so keen to keep in place between home and work was breached. I'd got back to my desk as I had finished preparations for the day's sitting, which was about to commence, and found several missed calls on my personal phone.

'I can't get in!' John said in a panic when I called him back.

'Can't get in where?'

'The house, of course!'

'Where are your keys?'

'They're inside!'

I could hear Annie yelling at John in the background.

'I'm on my way,' I said.

I called past Nigel's office on the way, told him that I had to go to a family emergency, and would explain later.

When I arrived half an hour later, John and Annie were both in the back yard, much to the consternation of the dog, who was locked inside the house and barking in outrage at being separated from his humans in this manner. I unbolted the back door and Annie rushed past me in one direction, Hecta in the other.

'Daddy's such a fucking idiot,' she said. 'I told him not to, but he did.'

I looked outside. The shade cloth on the patio was hanging in shreds. John had climbed over the roof and kicked his way through the shade cloth, although he could have just jumped down onto the side garden and thence to the ground. Around the side of the house, the newly installed flywire screens from Annie's windows had been buckled by John's panicky extraction from their frames.

'The windows are key-locked, honey,' I said. 'You couldn't have got into them anyway.'

'She was yelling at me,' John said. 'I couldn't think.'

When I returned to work I was embarrassed and annoyed at feeling embarrassed. I sat on the well-upholstered Parliament chair across from the Clerk and Nigel and explained that, although I didn't know because John refused to go to a doctor, there was something wrong with my husband. He was acting strangely and forgetting things and getting into panics. I'd try not to let it affect my work, of course. I just needed them to know in case I had to disappear in the middle of a sitting day again.

Both the Clerk and Nigel said supportive things, not to worry, we'll work around it. Nigel in particular was soberly kind to me. I wanted to fold into that kindness, to lean into it, to have a weight taken off me, just for a moment. It was a wish that seemed as impossible as stopping what else was hurtling in my direction.

35

As 2011 wore on, John's odd behaviours escalated.

Once excessively neighbourly, John stood in front of a neighbour's car to prevent her leaving the cul-de-sac and yelled at her for using our bin for her excess lawn clippings. He hit a dog with the baseball bat he'd taken to carrying because the dog wouldn't back off and leave Hecta alone. He began talking to unknown children in the supermarket, saying, 'You're going to be the next prime minister of Australia, aren't you? Give me a high five!', to the alarmed looks of parents.

As well as urinating in my room during the night, he would find himself in the kitchen and begin to bellow for me, accompanying his yells with the dropping of crockery as he scrambled around, looking for whatever it was he thought he had lost.

'Why didn't you get me up?' John would yell, wide-eyed at 2am. 'It's time to go to work.'

'Not yet,' I would say in a calm voice. 'You can still sleep for a few more hours.'

'You're always doing this,' he'd say. 'What do you mean, you fucking fuck? I've got to get up!'

After each incident, he got up in the morning and donned his fluorescent attire for his job as a traffic warden. With his orange flags in hand, he was ready to usher children across the road and cheerily waved goodbye as I sat at the kitchen table, jittery with anxiety and wishing for the obliteration of memory that came so easily to him.

More disturbing was his sudden propensity to invite homeless men to our house, men he'd met when walking the dog. Mostly they were harmless. There were men living in public housing in the suburb, men affected by long years of alcohol abuse, men who had lost everything, or who had nothing to lose. They were quiet and polite and sad. But one young man with long lank hair, also called John, kept coming around and sitting in our kitchen while

John gave him beer and food. Then it turned out that John had been giving him his pay. One evening when I was at work, Annie got out of the shower and walked into her bedroom with a towel wrapped around her to find the guy staring at her. Annie started to scream, and he disappeared.

'Why did you let that guy in?' Annie said to her father when he rushed to her room.

'What guy?' he said.

The next evening, lank-haired John showed up again, but this time I was home. I yelled at him through the security screen, saying if he ever came back to the house again, or took money off John, or went near our daughter I'd call the police. I didn't know if he knew when I was working nights, or if he could tell how scared I was, or whether he would come back whether I yelled at him or not.

'All right, all right,' he said, holding his palms up, and slunk off.

'Why did you yell at him?' John said, once I closed and bolted the door. 'He was my friend.'

'It's not safe for Annie,' I snapped. 'You can't let him in. It's not safe.'

John looked confused. He used to aggressively confront anyone who put Annie in danger, physical or psychological – parents, teachers, men who looked the wrong way in public spaces and, of course, inconsiderate drivers. Now he said, 'You're upset, aren't you?'

'You have to remember,' I said, hoping something of my tone would stay in his head. 'Don't let any of those men in the house. It's not safe for Annie.'

'We've got to protect the kids,' John nodded. He wandered off toward the garden, stubby in hand, dog at his heels. I heard him repeating, 'The kids, the kids, the kids. We've got to protect the kids.'

. . .

John continued refusing to go to his doctor to discuss his behaviour, no matter how delicately I phrased it. Until this time, he attended the medical centre over every niggle he experienced, for tennis sprains, for prostate checks, to get his sugar levels tested, and, most recently, for repeat prescriptions of the cholesterol tablets the doctor had put him on.

I suggested that perhaps he needed some medical assistance with his anxiety, which was a symptom we could both agree was causing him some difficulty. There were some days now when John would start crying with the panic he could not articulate the parameters of. Before this, I had only seen John cry twice: once when Hecta was nearly mauled to death at the park, and the other time when his father died. Now he cried constantly.

'I'm just a bit vague,' he said.

He started substituting words. Clouds became fluffy stuff in the sky, dresses were cloths. Once we were walking the dog past a man with an intellectual disability who was waiting at a bus stop. 'That guy's a bit blunt, isn't he?' John said sympathetically.

I tried to take matters into my own hands. I spoke to his doctor, writing a letter explaining that I would be bringing John to see him on some false pretext, and I needed him to assess John's memory – without, I emphasised, mentioning why he was doing this, as he was so touchy.

'So, John,' the doctor said as soon as we'd sat down. 'Your wife tells me she's got some concerns about your memory.'

'I play chess every day, and I read, and I do all the housework,' John replied. 'There's nothing wrong with me.'

John endured a few more questions stiffly. He accepted another prescription for managing cholesterol. When we got home he yelled at me, 'How dare you! Who do you think you are? There's nothing wrong with me. Look at all the work I do! How could I do all that if I had problems with my memory?'

He was so outraged that, not for the first time, I wondered whether it was just me. After all, if I ever mentioned my concerns about John's behaviour to people who knew him, they brushed it off, saying how normal he seemed, how witty he was, and perhaps it was that he was drinking too much, or not getting enough of this vitamin or that vitamin, or that he was suffering from some physical ailment that manifested in odd behaviour at home. Other people recounted examples of similar behaviour in people with brain tumours or undetected stroke. These seemed to be the most plausible explanations. After all, he was only in his early fifties.

One thing he did remember was the insult that doctor had delivered. He never went back to him again.

I was in the familiar position of being aware that something was wrong but having to live as if it wasn't. If I could put off having a name attached to John's behaviour, perhaps it would mean that the behaviour was fleeting, or not a sign of something more sinister, or unfixable. I knew that I would have to force John to go to a new doctor, to do whatever needed to be done to get a diagnosis.

Normally my generalised undercurrent of anxiety would drive me to finish tasks before they were due, to write lists speedily dispatched, to anticipate, plan, and respond to any foreseeable situation. But I kept on delaying this particular conversation. I would intend to do it, then days and weeks went by, and the new doctor was not located, and no appointment was made. I remembered my aunty and Frank, both waiting five months before seeing a doctor for the blood in their stools, not wanting the diagnosis of cancer they knew was coming. Before, I never understood this avoidance. Now I did.

I no longer had the concentration to read, and struggled to write. But I sought out new activities and developed new habits that applied ice to my anxiety, at least temporarily.

I was unable to sleep without the aid of antihistamines. They made my nightmares worse, but at least I could fall asleep again afterward, instead of lying awake with a hammering heart. I began going to the gym to try to rid myself of the excessive nervous energy I had. I did not otherwise feel I could breathe properly, and panic felt always as if it were fluttering at my breastbone unless I was moving.

I began drinking wine at first regularly, and then in increasing amounts. This was assisted by having both a bar and a wine club at work, and no end of hard-drinking colleagues and parliamentarians to keep me company. I chased the fleeting and blessed ungripping between the first and second glasses of wine and the blurring of awareness that made me able to tolerate John's endless afternoon talking, repetitions about what the dog had done or what he'd seen at the ocean that day. If I didn't listen hard enough, if I didn't say 'that sounds great' or 'wow' at the right intervals, he would look at me anxiously and repeat whatever it was he'd said more loudly. Even at night his sleep was restless, and he muttered and moaned as if conversing with troublesome ghosts.

And I started looking at my boss with a newly appreciative eye.

. . .

I came home to hear the unusual sound of gentle lapping. It sounded as if Hecta was having a particularly long drink, except that Hecta appeared at the door, his stumpy tail batting from side to side as he licked my shins in greeting. There was also a low hissing accompanying the lapping.

I put my bag down on the table and realised I could smell the faintly metallic odour of freshly running water. When I turned to the kitchen, I saw it was awash, the water snaking into the passageway.

I rushed to the kitchen and tried to halt my rushing without skidding across the flooded floor. I leaned over the sink and shut off the taps, which were running on full. The water rushed into the plugged sink and cascaded down the laminated cupboard doors.

'Hi, honey!' John said, emerging from his room. Then he stood looking at the water I was wading through. 'What happened?'

'You left the taps on,' I said.

'Did I?' he said. 'I'm playing chess. I got caught up.'

John offered to help but I directed him back to his computer. I threw towels over the floor, then put them in the washing machine. Hecta watched with interest for a time, but to his disappointment the floor-cleaning did not result in a found bone or the emergence of any other type of foodstuff. He returned to his basket and leaned his chin on its edge.

Over the next weeks John flooded the kitchen repeatedly until the cupboard doors swelled with moisture and needed to be taken from their hinges. Eventually I started taking the plug with me when I left the house.

. . .

For months I had been paying attention to Nigel. As well as being authoritative and handsome, he had the added intrigue of being emotionally inscrutable. He looked extremely fetching in our sitting day attire of bar jackets, jabots, and court gowns. I had not appreciated the depth of his knowledge of parliamentary processes, garnered over his twenty years at Parliament, and his legendary attention to detail meant that no aspect of the running of the house was overlooked. He was modest about his skills. When presented with a complex question, he would say to the staff, members of Parliament or Presiding Officers alike, 'I'll get back to you on that.' Unlike my approach of providing an intuitive answer and reverse-engineering my reasoning to fit, Nigel's response would be a correct, fully considered response requiring no revision or calibration.

Nigel and I began playing online chess tournaments with two of our parliamentary services colleagues. Rather than my habit of becoming impatient, considering the endless permutations of a move, Nigel would sit and regard the chessboard with complete attention. On the strength of his play, we regularly won on behalf of the Legislative Council. I began asking for his opinion on my options on particular moves, and when he came into my office and stood behind my chair, I became aware of his warm physical presence, which did not aid my concentration at the chessboard.

I had always hung out with Nigel when we went away for professional development trips or during breaks on sitting nights, cadging the odd cigarette from him, smoking being the only vice of his I'd been able to detect. He'd always been a gentleman, drily funny, attentive, and utterly respectful. His life was ordered and deliberate, and appeared to be the product of choice rather than accident. And now, suddenly, all of these things seemed to be what was missing from my life.

But I couldn't. He was married. I was married, although I wasn't sure who I was married to. From that first flickering I knew that if I gave into that wanting, it would lead me to situations I could not yet imagine, and some of these situations would be highly undesirable. I wasn't beyond caring, so I tried to tamp out the feeling as quickly as it emerged.

I wasn't beyond caring, yet.

...

One Saturday afternoon in late 2011, John and I had an argument. He had put red wine vinegar over the ceiling to get rid of emerging mould patches.

In the previous week he'd put a single pair of underpants through a whole wash and then in the dryer. He'd bought another two containers of Seasol, to add to the twenty litres already cluttering the patio. Then there was another your-sink-runneth-over episode in the laundry. So after the red wine vinegar had left red splotches all over the ceiling, my voice carried the frustration of the week with it.

'Couldn't you see the colour of it?' I asked.

John exploded. 'I did what you asked me to do, I got the mould off! You're always picking on me, pick pick pick, all the time! I'm getting out of here!'

He took his car keys and wallet and stormed out of the house.

At first Annie and I were relieved. We had always preferred being in the house with only each other, not having to watch for John's unexpected shifts of mood, his sudden geysers of temper. Always, if John was going to be home for any length of time, I had taken Annie out – to my cousin's, to my dad and stepmother's, to her friends, to Fremantle. If he was going to be in the garden, outside, it was okay, but the three of us inside the house was tricky. Now, with his increasingly erratic behaviour, being in the house was tense for new reasons. So we relished being able to call out to each other, have music on, watch television, eat whatever we wanted to without wondering what his response was going to be.

But on this Saturday it was different. He remained gone past dinnertime, past bedtime. He had left his phone in the house, so I had no way of contacting him. Annie had a dress rehearsal for her Year Ten dance concert the next morning, so I told her to go to bed. Instead we sat up together as I called everybody I thought he might possibly visit. Most people told me not to worry. He was fine. He'd be back.

I was racked with guilt. I shouldn't have been impatient. I should have taken the red spots on the ceiling as merely another example of signs that he was not right.

'What if he dies?' Annie asked.

'I know,' I said. 'If he's not home soon, I'll call the police.'

Still he failed to arrive. I called a few more people, asked for advice. Eventually and reluctantly, I called the police, even though it was Saturday night and I knew they had other things to worry about.

'My husband has taken the car and hasn't come home,' I said. And then I said, 'I think he's got early-onset Alzheimer's disease.'

Annie, who had been listening nearby, stared at me. We had discussed that maybe he was developing what his father had had at a much more expected age. But I had never said it aloud before to somebody else, to strangers in official places. Saying it aloud made it real.

The police were helpful and patient. They asked about the car, what John was wearing, whether I had checked with friends and family. They put out a call to locate the car and an alert on the credit card transactions.

An hour later the police called back. The credit card had been used in a service station forty kilometres north of Perth.

In the middle of the night I saw car lights pull in the driveway. I was peering out the window, trying to work out if it was a police car or John, when he came sauntering in.

'Hi,' he said, bending down to greet the dog.

'Daddy!' Annie hugged him. 'I'm glad you're okay.'

'Petal,' he said. 'How was school?'

'It's Saturday night, Daddy,' Annie said.

'Oh,' he said. 'Have a good nap, petal.'

'Where have you been?' I said. 'I've been worried sick! I had to call the police!'

He waved his hand. 'I've been up the coast,' he said. 'Talking to some people.'

'That's it,' I said. 'You're going to the doctor next week.'

'I'm tired,' he said. 'I'm just going to go and lie down.'

One of the things John and I had always done together, happily, was talk. We used to discuss and analyse the world, people we knew, Annie. We laughed a lot. It occurred to me, looking at his closed door, that I couldn't remember the last time we had had a proper conversation.

I'd taken it for granted, that talking. And hadn't even noticed when it stopped.

...

I found new satisfaction in going to work. In the centuries-old rhythms of parliamentary sittings and processes, there was order and predictability. If some of the staff were threatened by having a female Usher of the Black Rod, I was able to ignore it, or hang out with my previous colleagues from The Other Place. We had meals in the dining room on sitting nights, and the staff canteen served excellent food at other times. There was a gym and a bar. I had my own office with thick carpets, custom-made shelving, and jarrah-panelled walls. When John and Annie weren't calling me in desperation and despair, I could pretend for whole hours that the chaos I lived in didn't exist, that I had no responsibilities beyond assisting in the smooth running of the upper house, that there was a world outside that I was part of. Sure, I burst into tears in my office at unexpected times, or occasionally stayed so late at the bar on Friday nights I was unfit to drive home, but mostly I was Just Fine.

The kindness and steadiness of Nigel at work also countered the chaos elsewhere. In the same way that I was able to block out my home situation at work, I was also able to block out the fact that Nigel too was married. From when I'd started at Parliament four years previously, staff had wondered about him and his wife, as the only thing they appeared to share was a now adult son. She was not someone you would mess with, it was agreed. Nigel, however, never gave anything away about his home life or his opinion about it. As far as I knew, he was happily married.

And then one day someone mentioned, after an afternoon at the bar, that Nigel had had an affair with another former colleague some years earlier.

'Does his wife know?' I asked.

She laughed. 'Nigel's still alive, isn't he?' She shook her head. 'That would be the thing that would put anyone off having an affair with him – the risk of his wife finding out.'

This information compelled me to reconsider my hesitation. Starting relationships in an atmosphere of drama and danger was one thing with which I was familiar. Not that I was looking for another relationship, no! I wanted, merely, distraction and fun, with someone who was safe and discreet, and magnetically handsome. The fact that he was the total opposite of John, aside from the chess-playing and intelligence, was pleasing. If I couldn't have the alternative life I was wishing I could lead, perhaps I could have an affair with someone who represented all of those things.

I was also able to put aside the fact that if I did have an affair with Nigel, it could well finish whatever career I had and put my job in jeopardy. I knew enough to know that it is always the woman who pays in these situations, particularly in parliamentary settings.

I decided I would proposition Nigel. If he rejected the proposition, it would be embarrassing but not fatal, because he prioritised work over all other things. Nothing I said, no matter how foolish, would interfere with the running of the Legislative Council. And I would frame it in a way he could politely decline and it would never be mentioned again.

...

In 2011 a diagnosis for a brain disease, unless it was a straightforward tumour or lesion or injury, was slow. There were numerous tests available, and which one you needed was about as predictable as a poker hand. The tests you would require depended on which type of specialist you saw: neurologist, gerontologist, general physician. Often each test required a previous step. To get a PET scan you must already have had a CT scan. To get an MRI you needed to have had a CT scan, a blood test, and a specialist's recommendation. As you grow increasingly desperate for an answer, each additional step is frustrating.

After the driving-up-the-coast incident I booked John in to see a new doctor, a lovely man with all the tact and understanding that our previous one had failed to display. This GP referred John to a general physician (CT and PET), who referred us to a geriatrician (more tests), who referred us to a neurologist (MRI). Each clinician required John to undertake a new Mini-Mental State Examination, in which he could easily recall the day of the week, the season, and who the prime minister was, but not how many sisters he had. Before each visit I had to coax him to attend, coax him to answer the questions, reassure him that they were just seeing if they could help his vagueness. I told the stories of why we were there over and over again, trying to speak in code about the urination, the driving, the anxiety, the mix-ups with words, the blank looks, the running taps.

'I do the washing up,' John would say. 'I play chess.'

In late January 2012, it was a general physician who called John and me in. Once we were seated, he spoke only to me. Unlike the previous visit, before the PET scan he now had the results of, the doctor did not smile or ask questions. His seriousness unnerved me even before he said what I knew he would say but which I had hoped and, despite everything, believed he would not.

'John's brain shows deterioration consistent with mild to moderate early-onset Alzheimer's disease,' he said.

He paused as my eyes burnt and my tightening throat made it difficult to breathe. Then he talked. He prescribed medications to treat John's anxiety. He took him off the cholesterol medication he'd been on.

'But his cholesterol is high,' I said.

'Cholesterol drugs worsen mood disturbances and hallucinations in people with dementia,' he said, to my considerable despair. 'He should never have been put on those.'

Then he prescribed a drug that might – might – slow down the progression of the disease.

'John,' he said. 'I was telling your wife you have early-onset Alzheimer's disease. Do you understand what that means?'

'Yes,' John said.

I remembered from my English as a Foreign Language teaching days: never ask students a yes or no answer. You have to test their knowledge, get them to paraphrase, or you'll never know if they understood. If you ask a one-answer question, a confused, fearful, or baffled student will always say yes.

'I'm going to prescribe you some tablets,' the doctor continued. 'You need to take them all, all right?'

'Sure,' John smiled. 'I garden too. I walk the dog. We have a Jack Russell, Hecta the protector.'

John tried, to this doctor and the ones that followed, to say: *Look, I can still do things. I am competent. I was once as smart as you are.*

But almost always, they looked past him to me. Their sober eyes told me that they had seen what I was about to go through. Empathy was all they could offer. On our way out, they would say in funereal tones, 'Best of luck.'

In the chemist we waited for John's medication. I tried to look through my blurring eyes at items on the shelves, things for cuts, wounds, indigestion, pains of various kinds. Inconveniences.

In the car, John said, 'There's no coming back from Alzheimer's, is there? That's why you're crying.'

Then a little while later, 'I won't be there for Annie when she grows up, will I?'

'I don't know, honey,' I lied – the first of the necessary lies. Before, John would become enraged if he thought I was lying to him. His family was full of lies and liars, he'd say. You have to tell me the truth.

He cried, then. We cried together.

And that was the last time we spoke about the future we thought we'd have, with Annie grown up, our present lives something to look back on. Early-onset Alzheimer's disease swallows any future you anticipated as surely and completely as it swallows the past.

36

At an away-day for Legislative Council staff, we had all taken a Myers–Briggs survey – the one where various personality characteristics and tendencies in decision-making are reduced to a set of binaries: thinking–feeling, sensing–intuition, judgement–perception, introversion–extroversion. These were then plotted on a butcher's-paper graph. The facilitator told us that for most organisations, a spread of characteristics on the spectrum was indicative of inclusive hiring practices and diversity of thinking. I, however, was regarding the plotted initials for other reasons.

Apart from our shared tendency toward introversion, his more pronounced than mine, Nigel and I were exact opposites. I thought this explained my interest in him, why we seemed to get on so well: our differences were profound and intriguing. What this also should have told me is that whatever I thought I knew about Nigel's motivations for doing anything was quite likely wrong, and I was similarly ill-equipped to make any interpretation of his behaviour.

I discovered this on the evening I finally summoned the courage to proposition Nigel. It was a Thursday sitting night, and I had come close to putting the question to him before we headed for our respective cars but failed. Finally, driving home in the dark, I dialled.

As we had only just parted on the back steps of Parliament, Nigel was, unsurprisingly, surprised to hear from me.

'Is everything all right?' he said.

'I wanted to ask you something,' I said.

'Sure,' he said.

'Would you have an affair with me?'

There was silence. In the silence I was left to conclude how wrong I had been to make the call. I contemplated the humiliation I would feel, turning up to work the next day, having abased myself by asking this of someone who clearly had not been displaying the interest I'd thought he had. I wondered if there would be disciplinary action. I wondered how I would stand the shame of having made such an egregious error of judgement. Driving down the freeway, overhead lights reflecting on the windscreen and illuminating my cringing face, I wondered how I was going to live with this at work, day after day.

These feelings were in no way assuaged when Nigel said, 'Jules, I'm really flattered. But I'll need to get back to you on that.'

'Okay,' I said. 'Sorry.'

'Talk to you tomorrow, all right?'

'Yep, bye.'

I drove the rest of the way home thanking goodness I hadn't asked him in person and witnessed the pitying look that would no doubt have accompanied the 'I'll need to get back to you on that'. If he'd wanted to have an affair, he would have just said yes. That 'I'm really flattered line'? Every girl who'd had a teenage crush on anyone possessing a skerrick of kindness was familiar with that one. I was being let down gently. Which was good, in that it likely meant no disciplinary action for hitting on a colleague, but jeepers.

Inside the house near the lake, illuminated by the lamp I now left on at night so John wouldn't become so disoriented when he woke, Hecta came over for an ear scratch before retreating into his basket. John muttered and called out in his sleep, the way he did every night. He used to be a heavy sleeper, but now the division between waking and dreaming seemed tenuous. I tiptoed past him and went to my own room, too demoralised even to have wine, and knocked myself out with a Phenergan in the hope that I could escape my humiliation.

The next day I steeled myself and turned up to work, pretending nothing had happened. When I first saw Nigel, he nodded and said good morning the way he normally did. Great, I thought. He would pretend, and I would pretend, and sooner or later we would pretend it into never having happened. But then he came to my office midmorning.

'I'm sorry I haven't been able to talk, but I've got something urgent on,' he said. 'Can I come and see you at two?'

'Of course,' I said.

All morning and in the early afternoon I saw him at the photocopier, then going back into his office and closing the door. I was confused. Surely, if he was going to say yes, I'd have got some kind of sign. Some kind of feeling. Some kind of anything.

At the promised time he came into my office and shut the door. He sat himself on the curved-back seat across from my desk, as if we were having a regular meeting about, say, the plaque displaying the names of members who'd served in the military at the back of the Council chamber, or the uniform allowance allocated to staff, or plans for the historical display in the public gallery. Instead we discussed logistics and parameters of a different nature. If we were to have an affair, how would we do it? What was I expecting? How would we ensure secrecy?

At the end of the conversation, we both stood up, as if to shake hands on a deal, and stood facing each other. Nigel smiled at me.

'Come here,' he said.

. . .

For the next few months, the John-related household chaos had an equally intense, but far more enjoyable, counterpoint in physical encounters with Nigel and their giddy aftermath. As anyone who has ever had an affair knows, part of their appeal is the risky nature of them. The workaday world recedes as the stakes increase, and concerns about the future are replaced by the need for the immediate situation to be concealed, and by the object sought by every meditator: be here now. When you are having an affair that could be discovered and ended at any moment, every undressing, every touch, every encounter and exchange balloons in its significance, pushing all other concerns aside.

As well as having our own lockable offices, Nigel and I knew every unregarded space throughout Parliament of which we could take advantage after parliamentary parties, or late sittings, or on weekends. We went to the occasional hotel, but work was the most convenient place. As Usher of the Black Rod, I knew where all the security cameras were. Because parliamentarians value discretion, if not secrecy, in their comings and goings, there were plenty of places security cameras weren't.

For me, the concern was not about John finding out – he was already well beyond being able to understand or care about anything not in his immediate vicinity. But the risk of being discovered by our colleagues or by Nigel's wife was real. Fortunately or otherwise, the part of my brain that would normally be troubled about this had been drowned in oxytocin.

As well as having the equivalent of danger-detection aphasia, my brain was also unable to keep hold of my determination for the affair to be a distraction, nothing more. I did not want a relationship and I really, really did not have the time or the inclination to let myself have *feelings*. Feelings were a luxury I could not indulge in. Besides, it could only be a rebound relationship. Besides, he was married. Besides, we were, as Myers–Briggs charted for us, completely opposite in all ways. I told myself this in no uncertain terms, but my sense of reason had atrophied as completely as John's memory.

Mere weeks after our affair had begun, Nigel took his wife on a cruise to Singapore for ten days. I was beside myself. I was at home, with John, without escape. Annie was spending more and more time with my sisters, with her friends, anywhere else but the home that was no longer home to us. It was at this point that I became uncomfortably aware that somewhere the distraction quotient vis-a-vis my affair with Nigel had diminished while the *feelings* quotient had crept up. I didn't just miss the distraction in action. I missed him.

This, I told myself to no avail, would not do.

I took to painting the house white. I cleared out what John had accumulated in the shed, where among other things I found the tin of Nesquik from twelve months ago, hidden and forgotten, while trying to assure John it was all right that we had fewer bags of compost, fewer lidless plastic containers full of nuts, bolts, and nails, fewer collections of plastic bags and rakes and brooms (every time he misplaced one, he bought more), fewer old bike frames and wheels and fishing rods and knotted tackle and collections of rusted tools, fewer plastic crates full of empty bottles, fewer random chairs, bookshelves, and drawers he'd hauled from suburb throw-outs, fewer tins of red kidney beans he'd bought when he thought bird flu was going to become an economy-stopping pandemic. I took boxes and boxes of books from our overflowing shelves to the op shop. I tried to create order. I tried to create a distraction that wouldn't bring its own chaos.

In this time I came to understand how adrift I was. How nothing would prevent what was happening to John, and now I had these pesky Nigel-related *feelings* to deal with. I was on a hiding to nothing. I cried, went to the gym, drank and danced with friends. When I did see Annie, all we did was talk about the strange and, for her, embarrassing new things John had started doing. I did not know what was going to happen, only that none of it was likely to be pleasant.

I also came to understand that my state of mind had no effect on the world. Having spent a lot of time in alternative circles, not to mention being brought up with the Judeo-Christian concept of damnation being caused by the father's sins being visited on the children, I had imbibed the belief that your thinking creates your world, that you get what you deserve. When you're living with someone disintegrating from early-onset Alzheimer's, which develops faster than other types, when you have minimal means and less practical support, when you're in the midst of realising that the same person currently disintegrating had been if not outright abusive to you and your daughter for the past fifteen years then perilously close to it – if there was a way of thinking myself out of it, I would have.

. . .

In my misplaced faith in the safety net of the Australian health and welfare system, I thought that there would be help, financial and practical, for a relatively young person with Alzheimer's who had a teenage daughter and working wife, with no other means to speak of.

In the beginning I was offered help by various people who took pity on our situation. When I actually asked for the offer to be translated to action, mostly those same people were unavailable. It was not from lack of care or willingness. They too worked and had families, or lived far away, or did not want to or could not commit to the regularity John needed.

Also, what people thought would be involved in taking care of a person with early-onset dementia was often quite different from the reality. The reality, in those early days, consisted of listening and responding to ceaseless repetitions, ceaseless finding-of-lost-things only for them to be lost again minutes later, ceaseless vigilance to stop him from setting fire to pans or boiling the kettle dry or letting the dog out.

Then there was the issue of money. We went to Centrelink, to see if he could apply for disability pension.

'He's too young to have Alzheimer's,' the assessor said to us.

'Ah, yes,' I said. 'That's why it's called early-onset.'

'I do the washing up,' John said. 'And do the gardening. And walk the dog.'

'He'll have to go on unemployment benefit,' she said.

I laughed. 'You want to send him for interviews?'

Then we found out that he wouldn't be eligible for anything, because I earned too much – not enough to pay for private care, or to comfortably pay for all the tests and specialist visits and medications he needed, thanks to being a one-income family for fifteen years, but too much to qualify for benefits.

I called the Aged Care Assessment Team in order to get John qualified for in-home help. Again, John was technically too young, but on this occasion they would make an exception. Then came the kicker: even if he was eligible for the highest level of assistance, John would only be entitled to sixteen hours of care a week.

'But I work thirty-eight hours a week,' I said. 'More, on sitting weeks. What happens the rest of the time?'

I went to a counsellor who specialised in dealing with families affected by dementia. I spent my weekly sessions with her weeping about John's past behaviour and despairing about his present conduct.

'If I quit work to take care of him, we'll lose the house,' I said.

'There is an option,' she said. 'Separate from him.'

I stared at her.

'If you do, he'll be taken care of by the state,' she said. 'It won't be your responsibility.'

On both counts she was wrong.

• • •

When Nigel returned from his cruise, our work offices were being recarpeted and we were both sharing an office with our colleagues. Our liaisons took on a different level of risk. There were brief kisses when others went to lunch, squeezed hands while passing each other in the corridor, chairs propped against meeting room doors. The level of opportunity decreased. The level of risk did the opposite.

One night Nigel's wife called as we were sitting on chairs in a locked office after a liaison. I could hear her from Nigel's phone: Where was he? Where was I? Why was my car the only one there? What were we doing? Nigel gave reassurances and explanations and then left, instructing me to stay until he got home and let me know the coast was clear.

I knew it would not be long until he was confronted. His wife had been suspicious of Nigel having affairs with people he hadn't had affairs with. How would she react if she found out that this time her suspicions were correct?

I asked what he would do. What I meant was this: Would he leave her? I knew that if he did, he wouldn't be leaving his wife for me. He was leaving his wife because it was past due.

'If it happens, I'll make a decision then,' he said.

One Monday morning I got a call from a number I didn't recognise. But I recognised her voice.

'Why have you been sending texts to my husband after work hours?'

'You know why. Have you asked Nigel?'

'Are you having an affair with my husband?'

'Yes,' I said.

'Who started it?'

'I did.'

'Why?'

'So many reasons. You need to speak to your husband, not me.'

She made it clear I should stay away from him before I hung up.

When Nigel walked into my office half an hour later, he was agitated and sporting a large red mark on his cheek. After phoning me, his wife had hidden her car near Parliament, waited until he parked his. She surprised him by getting in his passenger seat and repeating the question she'd been asking all weekend, since she'd intercepted a text from me: Are you having an affair? When he denied it, again, she punched him.

'I deserved it,' he told me.

We discussed what we did now. Or what he would do now.

'I don't know, Julesy,' he said. 'We can't see each other, and I can't promise you anything. I have to work this out first.'

For me, this meant an extended time of uncertainty, creating an addition to the flux I'd been wanting to be distracted from. Now, I had at home a confused and frustrated man, a frustrated and sad fifteen-year-old, and at work a reminder of what I wanted and could no longer have.

...

Over Easter my friend Kitty and I drove north to Carnarvon with our girls to visit another high school friend on her mango farm. John could still make coffee, get himself cereal, take Hecta for walks – although I suspected it was Hecta who knew the way around the lake. I asked John's sister to give him dinner and cajole him into taking his medication for the three nights we would be away.

We drove for ten hours through windswept scrubby expanses, through trees turned the colour of charcoal from recent fires, past orange-trunked trees with glossy leaves, through the moonscape of former ocean beds and worn-down mountains fringing the eastern horizon. The clear expanses uncoiled my thoughts.

We arrived at our friend's house in the burnished afternoon light, stretched our cramping limbs walking down a dry red riverbed, pelicans perched on the logs at its edge. Her husband handed me their pet Stimson's python. The trick with handling a python, I was told, is to relax as it twines around your hand, your arm, your neck, against all your instincts. If you startle it, if you grip its head or tail, it will bite. You let it glide and twine around your outstretched arms, your open hands, while you stand still, and all will be well.

In daylight we drove out to a steep bank of sand dunes that ran for kilometres, absent of people, the creases between them tufted with spinifex grass and blue-tongued, triangle-headed bobtails like plump sausages. They waggled away, patterning the sand with delicate tracks, and apprehended us from a distance with their black eyes. We let air out of the four-wheel drive's tyres so the vehicle could drive over the top of the fine white sand. I launched myself down a dune on a home-made sandboard, hissing when it built up speed as I descended, toppling over when I came to a sudden stop at the bottom, squealing with delight. My thighs burnt hotter than the Gascoyne sun as I climbed back up, dragging my board by its rope. Our friend's husband set up a shooting range, with cans set in the middle distance, and we laid belly down on blue tarp, squinted, and fired his rifle. In the coral lagoon I swam, seeing through a saucer-sized face mask the brightly coloured fish darting over nubs of coral, indifferent to the shade cast by me floating on the shimmering ocean surface, kicking my flippered feet to keep me in place.

When I got home to Perth there was glass from a dropped bottle shattered over the kitchen floor: John had forgotten it was there and it crunched as he walked over it in his sandshoes. He was irritable: 'Where have you been?' He was due to have his driving test that week. He could remember that if nothing else.

'I've never had an accident,' he said. 'I'm a good driver. Why are they doing this to me?'

'I know,' I said. 'The doctors say you have to.'

'They say I've got Alzheimer's,' he said. 'What would they know?' And then, 'Where have you been?'

37

For two months Nigel tried to sort things out with his wife through marriage counselling. He would not tell me how it was going, but every Monday morning he appeared drawn and unhappy.

Nigel's wife appeared at Parliament from time to time. Once, Nigel came racing into my office, telling me not to go to my car as she was waiting near it. Another time she appeared in the foyer as it was bustling with Directors-General and senior public servants preparing to appear in the Budget Estimates hearings. She was shouting about what kind of man Nigel was and what he'd been doing with 'that slut'. She had complained to our HR manager and the Clerk. She sent emails to our parliamentary colleagues across Australia and overseas, every contact of mine she could find on Facebook before I blocked her.

While I was not delighted by this turn of events, I accepted Nigel's wife's fury as the fair product of my behaviour. If I'd been her, I'd hate me too. Unlike the other things happening in my life, this was something for which I could accept full responsibility. I had done something outside acceptable norms, and this was my punishment. There was no mystery. Nigel's wife was a woman scorned, and I had caused the scorning.

It was a sign of Nigel's enduring sense of privacy and lack of spite that he did not tell me then what he had discovered during the months of counselling, which was that his wife had herself had several affairs during their marriage too. Nigel had suspected they were happening but did not confront her because he wanted to preserve the relationship for the sake of their son.

As for me, it felt almost noble, suffering the consequences of actions that I had chosen. Action and consequence, cause and effect, as neat as it came, sorely lacking elsewhere.

. . .

In Western Australia in 2012, there was no automatic driving disqualification for a diagnosis of Alzheimer's. It was explained to me that some people retain their driving faculties long after their diagnosis. After years of driving the reflexes are instinctual, and one of the last to recede in the early stages of the disease. I was not sure if this was true for early-onset Alzheimer's like John's, which indiscriminately ate memories old and new. I'd started hiding the keys to John's car and trying to distract him whenever he asked for them, but it became a constant point of tension. So I had to ask John's doctor to write a referral for a driving test with an occupational therapist.

John was outraged when I told him.

'It's just a check,' I said. 'But wouldn't it be okay, people driving you around?'

'There's nothing wrong with me!' he bellowed. 'I'm just a bit vague sometimes!'

The occupational therapist was young and kind. John was smiling and gregarious as we arrived, but his shirt gave off the penetrating odour of anxious sweat. I waited, pacing, at the assessment centre, while he drove the occupational therapist away.

When they walked back in, John was no longer smiling. The occupational therapist looked white. We were ushered into an office.

'I'm afraid, John, that we're going to need to suspend your licence,' she said.

'They made me get out of the car!' John said to me, pointing at the young woman. 'It was because you distracted me! How am I supposed to drive if you're distracting me?'

The occupational therapist said to John, 'I'm sorry.'

'I've never had an accident!' John said. 'Not one!'

The occupational therapist said to me, in a low voice, 'He turned into oncoming traffic. It was – close.'

John pointed at the occupational therapist's face. 'She's got it in for me! I didn't do anything!'

'I'm sorry,' she said again.

'It's okay, honey,' I said to John.

'Why are you doing this to me?' he said. 'Fucking bastards!'

I ushered John out and into the passenger's seat. I drove him home as he wept with fury, driving past the dense banksias of Kings Park, down the winding Mounts Bay Road, with the limestone shoulder of Mount Eliza on one side, the Swan River stretching pale on the other, and then onto the freeway. I turned onto Canning Bridge, drove him past the places he used to fish as a child, as a teenager. He brightened.

'I was good at fishing,' he said. 'Ma loved me bringing home a catch of bream.'

The tidal Swan River used to teem with fish and seafood before the runoff from manicured lawns created algal blooms that sucked out the oxygen. From the surface, the river still looked the way it always had.

'And you took taylor and gardies to her too, when Annie was little,' I said.

'You're so kind to me,' John said.

It was only lunchtime when we pulled into our driveway. I was due to go back to work. I hoped John would forget the driving test, the way he forgot where he'd just been, or whether he'd taken his tablets, or whether the dog had eaten. He seemed in a better mood, but then he saw his car, Greenie, in the driveway.

'I want to go back to Canning Bridge,' he said.

'We just went there,' I said in the calm and soothing voice I tried to use at all times now.

'Can't I drive my Greenie?' he said.

'I'm sorry, honey, they said you can't.'

'But there's nothing wrong with my driving,' he said. 'Those people were fucking idiots. I've never had an accident. I'm a good driver.'

'I'll see if Shaun can take you,' I said. 'I've got to go to work now.'

'This is awful!' he said. 'It's awful!'

I ushered him outside, feeling panic rising in my throat. I wanted to get away, to be around normal people doing normal things. I didn't want to take my fifty-two-year-old husband to have his licence taken away. I didn't want to have to enlist our daughter to make sure he took his medication. I didn't want to wonder what state the house was going to be in when I got home, whether the sink would be flooded or glass smashed on the floor or shit from the garden trailed through the house. I didn't want to be arguing with government services to get them to provide us help which, when it came, was not even close to adequate. I didn't want people expecting me to quit my job and take care of him because I was female. I didn't want people's baffled pity, or their judgement, or their suggestions that John take turmeric to make him better.

It occurred to me that John was just like he had always been – demanding, irritable, and wanting everything and everyone organised to calm him down. Except now, he didn't have his compensatory charm and wit. And now he had dementia, and I shouldn't blame him for it.

I went to work. I saw Nigel, but he was formal, his arms unavailable, withdrawn into the messiness of trying to work things out with his wife. John phoned, furious, demanding I come home, telling me he'd had the worst day of his life, the absolute worst, and where was I?

That evening, we had our monthly wine club at Parliament. I laughed with my friends and colleagues, and then drank until all I knew was my drunkenness, unmoored from past, present, and future. I drunk-dialled Nigel at 10pm as a friend drove me home, an Ikea bag positioned to catch the vomit that she could tell was soon to follow, but I did not say anything to him. When I unlocked the door, the house smelled as if it had been closed up. There was an empty scotch bottle on the bench and half-drunk bottles of beer. I went to bed with the room spinning, a bucket beside the bed, knowing that all of it would still be there the next day, whether I wanted it or not.

. . .

The same week John lost his licence we were approved to receive our sixteen hours' help a week.

Then began the morning calls from late, sick, or absent carers, or from John demanding to know why these people were in the house, or from the organisation regretfully informing us that a carer hadn't worked out for John. He was lascivious with females, aggressive toward males.

Our Jack Russell, Hecta, took advantage of the situation. Never obedient, he now took to stealing support workers' lunches from their bags and escaping through the front door opened by an unwitting arrival. I would come home from time to time to find John and the carer wandering the suburb, looking for the dog, who darted across roads, in and out of garages, and chased cats. John would cheerfully announce, 'Mr Zoom bolted! He's just gone!'

The dog also got fatter and fatter. Aside from lunch-stealing, he perfected his hangdog look, so whoever was visiting took pity and gave him the meal he was so desperately seeking.

Hecta had always been John's dog. He tolerated Annie and me, but he looked to John as his significant human. But as the John he knew disappeared, suffocated by the plaques in his brain, the less attention the dog paid him. When John finally went into care, Hecta would visit, scouring the floors for dropped food, or jumping up and stealing sandwiches from slack fingers. But the dog never greeted John or responded to his calls. The John he knew was not there. The bone-house was of no consequence.

38

Before long, John's behaviour had deteriorated to the point where I began to worry about leaving him alone even for short periods. With only sixteen hours of care a week, and me working full-time, there was a lot of time left over.

The specialist recommended that I try getting John into respite care, to see how he would get on. He also advised that I should increase my attempts to find a permanent place in a secure dementia facility. Already he was eligible for the highest level of care, according to the government's scale for the severity of his condition. I worried that he wasn't ready to go yet, but the specialist said that he had seen many families – wives, usually, taking care of husbands – who had similarly delayed, and by the time they really needed it, there were no vacancies.

'So what do they do?' I asked.

'They put them in hospital,' he said.

'Are there any other options?'

I guessed the answer to that even before he shook his head.

John's family was firmly opposed to John going into care, even respite care. So we began a roster. I bought a small unit closer to work, where Annie and I took turns getting respite from the house that no longer felt like our own, and when we weren't there his sisters stayed, even though my ex-girlfriend-sister-in-law and I were not on speaking terms. She left her Facebook open on my computer, so I could see exactly what it was she was telling people about me. She left notes around the house in case I was in any doubt, sometimes stuck to my door when I arrived.

Finally, in mid 2014, a vacancy came up. I took John, Annie, and Hecta to the care home several times. John was happy there, liked having other people to whom he could repeat things. So I booked him in and began making arrangements to sell the house.

When his family discovered what I had done, they were furious. I knew they would be furious, but I was beyond caring. I was exhausted, Annie was struggling. I'd changed jobs from Usher of the Black Rod to an advisory officer for the Council's committees so that I could manage the evenings better, but it wasn't enough. Sure, his family was angry, but what could they do?

Plenty, as it turned out. Just as John was due to go into care, they put in applications to revoke my guardianship and enduring power of attorney.

An urgent hearing was called at the State Administrative Tribunal. I was forbidden from placing John into care or selling the house, but I was still required to pay for everything. His family also still wanted me to stay there, taking care of John. It was the only thing I could refuse, so I refused it.

Over the course of a series of hearings, the state was given guardianship and responsibility for all decisions to do with John's care, and responsibility for all financial decisions. Annie, although she was nearly eighteen, was not asked about her views on anything concerning her father or his care. I was ordered into a financial settlement, which meant that the meagre asset pool was drained by having to pay two sets of lawyers before the pool and my superannuation were split between us. I felt as if I were being punished for my own misfortune, and that everything I had endured and tried to do to manage the misfortune that had been visited upon me, upon Annie, had been disregarded. There was no protest I could make. There was no waking up from it.

I still saw John. I saw him in his day group, where adults coloured in and stared at the mysterious outline of puzzle pieces, and when he was out with carers in Fremantle. He was happy to see me wherever I turned up but did not inquire as to why I was not at home. I left Hecta with John, to guard over him for the few months he was cared for by his sisters and support workers before the inevitable happened and orders were made to place him into a secure dementia unit.

From time to time I wondered what would have happened if the situation had been reversed, if it were me with dementia, and John expected to take care of me and Annie. He always professed his devotion to me and Annie, said he would do anything for us.

But I also remembered when Annie was four and I'd been taken to hospital, haemorrhaging. I lost so much blood that I began to faint when I lifted my head, and I needed a blood transfusion. Even though I didn't want Annie to see me in hospital, vomiting or passing out, John brought her in for the five days I was there. When he collected me to take me home, he was full of tamped-down fury. He told me how difficult Annie had been, how unmanageable she was. And then a vehicle cut him off as we drove down Railway Parade toward home.

John had floored the 1982 Volvo and sped off after the driver who, once he realised he was being pursued, veered off down the leafy streets of Shenton Park and tried to lose us through turning this way and that. We followed, me holding onto the seatbelt so it didn't cut into my surgery-distended stomach. John – who abhorred tailgating in others – drove so close to the other car, leaning on the horn and shouting abuse out the window, that I could see the man's alarmed eyes in the rear-view mirror. When we pulled up alongside him, trapped at a stop sign by arterial road traffic, John made me unwind my window while he yelled, 'I've got my wife and child in the car, mate! You could have fucking killed us, you fucking cunt!'

I was glad the question of what John would have done, had the situation been reversed, was theoretical.

You cannot be on the bottom of the wheel of fortune forever, a friend said.

The wheel of fortune felt alternately like a rat-wheel in which I was sprinting to avoid tumbling, like the lone undie at the bottom of a dryer, or else, on tricky days, more like a grindstone on which I tried to keep my footing as it turned, running lest I ended up pulped with the grain.

...

In all this, Nigel was steady and comforting and uncomplicated. He left his wife in the middle of 2012, and after that we moved slowly together, testing whether this unlikely pairing could become a union. In 2013 we drove from Broome to Perth down the long black tongue of Highway 1, following the winding Indian Ocean, which we could smell behind plains of red pindan dirt and spinifex. We walked along shallow beaches threaded with the dolphins that humans had now learned should not be tamed; we saw the skewbald pattern of sharks in the shallow hypersaline waters at Shark Bay as we perched on quad bikes on the towering dunes; we kicked our flippered feet hard to keep ourselves in place in the tidal flow of Coral Bay, floating over fish great and small, coral frilled like doilies, and undulating rays, their bellies flat to the sandy floor. Occasionally we were eyed by reef sharks we were told would not bite.

On our trip, Nigel never became impatient, or angry, or tense. I realised how entrenched my watchfulness of male mood had become only when the need for it fell away. We talked and talked. I fed him pieces of my past, to test the waters. He was thoughtful and accepting. He told me about how his mother had contacted the birth parents of both her adopted children, so that when they were eighteen they could decide on what relationship they wanted with their biological families. He described how unexpectedly becoming a father at twenty-two had given him direction in his life he had hitherto lacked, catalysing him to work hard and to accept the marriage he might not otherwise have chosen. He talked about going to Sydney for his Tongan birth father's funeral. It was the first time most of his father's family knew of Nigel's existence. As he was on his way from the church to the cemetery, Nigel was informed that, as his father's only son, he would be required to give a speech at his father's graveside. During the funeral, he met his half-sister for the first time. She had only learned of Nigel's existence upon her father's death. Even though she wasn't expecting this particular development at her father's funeral, neither was she entirely surprised. 'He always kept things to himself,' she'd said.

When we were together it was easy and comfortable. It was only everything else in my life that seemed hard. I often wondered where I would have been if I hadn't been brave enough to proposition him that night, if it hadn't worked out. He was the cushion for me amid my freefall existence elsewhere.

I was occasionally tormented by fears that something would happen to him. He smoked and rode a Ducati, both potentially life-limiting activities. Each time he rode somewhere, I insisted he text me upon arrival. His birth father had died of melanoma left untreated for too long. I anxiously asked after his medical check-ups and their results. I reasoned with myself that my anxiety was likely due to the health-related catastrophe that had already befallen my other relationship.

Still the anxiety persisted. I could not imagine how anything was possible without him. But he remained hale and whole, regular and reliable. If I had a glimmer of anything else – the strain of the financial pummelling he took during his divorce, or the stress surrounding the arrangements for his son's November 2014 wedding – I did not notice it. He might have seemed quieter, but it did not seem noticeably different from his usual mildness.

Once, we had attended a parliamentary lunch in honour of a visiting Islander Speaker. The Western Australian clerks and presiding officers had done their usual best to be charming, witty, full of stories of other parliaments and their prodigious travel, their own experiences of Fiji or Kiribati or the Solomons. The speaker listened and offered only occasional, succinct observations of her own. At the conclusion of the meal, someone asked for her views on Western Australia, on our parliament.

'You Australians,' she said. 'You speak too much. We Islanders only say what needs to be said.'

The said Australians tried not to look offended, except for Nigel, who nodded in Islanderly agreement.

So Nigel being quiet – quieter – was not a sign of concern. Besides, I had plenty else taking my attention from someone who, surely, I didn't need to worry about, in the scheme of worrying things.

. . .

John had just turned fifty-five, the last birthday he would spend in the home we'd bought with such hope. When I asked him how old he was, he looked thoughtful. 'Fifty-five sixty-five?'

We sat outside on folding chairs as the sky turned pink while Hecta interrogated the boundaries of the yard for concealed cats. The warm air shuffled the leaves of the overhanging gum and the peppermint tree that cluttered the eaves with its thin foliage. John pointed at the elephant palm fronds and said, 'Look! It's Tony Abbott's ears!'

John used to know the names of all the birds that ducked under the patio, or made nests in the gums, or pecked for ants in the grevilleas and

Albany woolly bushes, or waited at the edges of Bibra Lake, or screeched overhead in flocks. Honeyeaters, terns, shags, mallard ducks, blue-breasted wrens, Carnaby's cockatoos. Now he called black swans 'crows', and all other birds 'ibis'.

On this day I pointed to an unusual bird in the old gum tree. John couldn't see it, so I walked him over, closer. I pointed until his eyes finally alighted on the bird's brightly coloured plumage as it preened itself on a high branch.

'How did that get there?' he said.

FIND YOURSELF AND YOUR NEW PARTNER BEING CHASED DOWN THE STREET BY A PHALANX OF REPORTERS

39

It was a bright summer's Wednesday in February 2015. I woke up in my small but airy unit in Maylands, with Annie in her room and Hecta curled in his basket. The year's first meeting of the Public Administration Committee would be held at 9am. The committee was inquiring into prisoner transport, and today I'd be advising on which prisons and lock-ups to visit, which witnesses to call to give evidence. I couldn't wait. I had a committee chair I got on famously with, and a job that married my love of research and writing with my curiosity about the world. Since I'd left calling the Council to attention as Black Rod, I'd done inquiries into subjects near and far. An inquiry into pastoral leases saw me flying over the striated red plains of the Kimberley in a plane so small I'd had to breathe into a paper bag as it seesawed to land. An inquiry into recreational hunting had taken me to the remote forests of Orange, New South Wales, where I met hunters who hated the industrial meat industry, as well as to Victoria, where I cuddled rescued baby wombats. Now, prisoner transport.

I had reason to believe that the wheel of fortune was indeed moving on and up. I had taken Annie to New York in January, aided by a grant I had got to attend a writing seminar in Vermont at the beginning of February. The distance from our Perth-based woes had been bracing, as had been minus-twenty-five-degree-centigrade Vermont, where the seminar featured children's literature luminaries such as the lovely and erudite Gregory Maguire, and where I had worked on a young adult novel about a teenager whose father develops early-onset Alzheimer's disease, *Before You Forget*. While I was away the guardian had arranged for John to be placed in care, and the sale of the house was in its final throes.

On my first day back from the US, dizzy with jet lag, I had visited John in his new abode, a locked dementia unit his father had also been in. I was worried he'd be sad about not having Hecta there, or that the move would be unsettling. Neither thing appeared to bother him. He greeted me cheerfully and did not comment on my three-week absence. He still knew who I was and was happy to see me. We went out into the beautifully landscaped courtyard. He proceeded to strip the foliage from every bush and deposit the leaves in his pockets. When I left, I told him I'd be back tomorrow and he waved and smiled and turned away, unconcerned. After four very difficult years, it was a relief.

Before I left for work I checked my phone to see if Nigel had replied to my goodnight text the night before. He hadn't, which was unusual, but it had been the first sitting night of the new parliamentary year. Perhaps he was tired or distracted. I sent a good-morning message and got in the car.

Because it was committee meeting day I did not have time to write, as I usually might have. Writing provided me with the optimism inherent in the making of coherence. When I wrote I was no longer at the mercy of the tangled feelings, reactions, hopes, and regrets, the habitual composite of which I experienced as myself. Having watched someone's selfhood dissolve into a morass of reaction, repetition, and anxiety, I also had the dual perception of knowing that Self – anybody's – wasn't solid in the least. At minimum, it was reliant on the possession of adequate myelin, something over which nobody had control, no matter how much sudoku you might play. Neither the witty-lovely-John nor impatient-angry-John I'd lived with were solid or reliable or true: they were the product of electrical impulses in the brain as much as the product of experience. Neither person was the product of such a flimsy notion as choice, it seemed to me. The contemplation of this led to regular existential abysses from which, I often told people, I was only rescued by Nigel.

Because Nigel remained my untainted good thing. No matter the storm that surrounded us, he remained steadily at the helm, navigating me through the chaos of administrative tribunals, the wrath of people whether earned or unearned. He was careful in his reactions, reliable in that his words and deeds exactly matched each other, entirely opposite to the daily volatility I had experienced with John. The ways in which he was exciting – taking me riding on the back of his Ducati, impromptu visits to golf and gun ranges, quad biking and helicopter riding, surprise plane fares to family celebrations and Broome holidays – were perfectly balanced by his calmness, his Islander reserve, focused listening, and unruffled demeanour.

Before I went into the meeting I checked my phone again. Still no text from Nigel. It was unusual, I thought, but I would go and see him at lunchtime in his office, the way we always did on a sitting day. He would be handsome in his bar jacket and jabot, and his kind eyes would be happy to regard me after an absence, the way they always were.

. . .

I was part way through the meeting on prisoner transport when one of the committee staff came to the door and asked for me.

Committee meetings are, generally, considered sacred. As creatures of Parliament, committees have the same powers and privileges as the Parliament itself, with considerably more secrecy attached to their proceedings. If anybody, staff or member alike, broke committee confidentiality, they could be subject to the exercise of the powers of the House, which included fines and imprisonment for contempt.

So being called out of a committee meeting was so out of the ordinary that even before I was at the door I was wondering if somebody had died.

The committee staff member looked worried. She said she was sorry, but two detectives from state security wanted to speak to me. It was about a personal matter. They would not provide more detail than that.

The detectives were wearing the type of plain clothes that announced their membership of the police service as surely as a uniform would have done. They thanked me for agreeing to talk to them. I did not recall being given the option.

It was only afterward that I recalled a video my evidence lecturer had required us to watch as part of our law studies. The video, by a fast-talking US law professor named James Duane, was a forty-five-minute-long explanation of the eight main reasons why you should never, ever talk to the police. I'd won an academic prize for evidence, but I failed to remember its most vital lesson when I needed it.

. . .

The detectives and I were ushered into a spare meeting room. All the other rooms were filled with committees also having their first meetings of the year, it being the first week of the post-summer parliamentary sitting. The room was cluttered with boxes of wine waiting to be picked up by wine club members. I looked idly at the boxes to see if my name was on any of them. I'd get Nigel to pick them up later, I thought.

'What's happened?' I asked after I'd closed the door. I wondered if there had been a plot against a member of Parliament, or an allegation that one of my committee members had breached privilege. I'd been required to provide evidence about possible leaking of certain committee papers before, and forbidden on pain of prosecution to ever mention it. But now the detectives had said it was a personal matter.

The detectives exchanged glances.

'Have you spoken to Nigel Lake this morning?' one asked, while the other got out his notebook.

'No,' I said. 'Is he all right?'

'Physically, yes,' the question-asker said. 'Has Nigel been under any stress lately?'

'Well, he's just been through a divorce. That's up there. Why?'

'Anything else recently?'

I thought about his son's wedding the previous November. There'd been some concern about whether his ex-wife would turn up, and although she didn't, the day and its lead-up had been less than entirely relaxing. But that was months ago.

'No,' I said. 'Nothing comes to mind.'

'What about with you?'

I told them I'd just come back from New York. I told them how it had been hard for Nigel to see what I was going through with John, and the unpleasant messages we'd been getting from around the place – but that as far as I knew, we were fine.

The next question surprised me.

'How do you get on with the Clerk?'

'Me?'

Both question-asker and note-taker were looking at me carefully. 'All right, I guess. I don't really know him.'

This was true. The Clerk and his wife had been at a party we'd all been at the previous December. The four of us had stood together a little awkwardly for a brief time during the evening, and I remembered the Clerk mentioning that he and his wife had also met at work. I wasn't sure if he was trying to be kind or pointing out that he knew the kind of gossip our relationship had engendered.

'And how does Nigel get on with the Clerk?'

'Fine,' I said, beginning to get wary. 'He wouldn't tell me anything otherwise, but they seem fine.'

In order to get to how Nigel or I might have felt about the Clerk, I had to describe to them the process of the Clerk's appointment, from what I knew of it.

So I told them:

In October 2013, the previous Clerk had suddenly announced his retirement after years of ill health caused firstly by a head-on collision, and then by the development of a brain tumour. One sitting night the Clerk left the building and did not return. He did not discuss his departure with Nigel, as would have been customary. Nigel was visited by the President during the dinner break and informed that the Clerk was taking extended leave, effective immediately. Already Nigel knew that something was amiss.

The position of clerks in parliaments are prestigious affairs, rarely becoming vacant. They were jobs for life, with an attractive salary accompanied by conditions unknown in the rest of the working world. They were only ever awarded to those with extensive parliamentary experience, limiting the field to those with the tolerance of late nights, outsized egos, and rumour mills that comprise the lot of the parliamentary staffer.

Nigel possessed the inherent abilities listed above, and his many supporters could easily enumerate the reasons he should win the position. He'd been acting Clerk, either officially or unofficially, for some time due to the previous Clerk's ill health. He'd had twenty-five years' experience in Parliament.

Members of all parties trusted his always considered, practical, and correct advice. In Parliaments, conservative as they are, the road to seniority is long, and deputy clerkship is the prime predictor of appointment as Clerk in any given house if the role becomes vacant through retirement or death.

There were only two impediments to this sensible and, in normal circumstances, expected appointment. Firstly, there was the pesky matter of our relationship. Even though it was now evident that it was a relationship and not a rashly conceived affair, it was not seen favourably by some senior staff. Secondly, and more seriously, the President and Nigel did not seem to like each other. They seemed to rub each other up the wrong way for reasons I did not understand. What I did understand was that the decision of who would be appointed Clerk belonged to the President, and the President alone. There was no legal requirement for the process to be transparent or fair.

Unlike me, Nigel knew before he applied that he wasn't going to be given the job. He'd tried to hide from me the depth of the dislike between himself and the President, although it was obvious enough despite that. But I refused to stop hoping. I liked the President and hoped that fairness would overcome whatever other issues might have come into play.

Fifteen minutes before the commencement of a sitting day at the end of November 2013, I'd spoken to Nigel. After two interviews the previous week he still hadn't been told the result of the selection process – except that the panel had conflicting views. He said he'd heard the President phoning someone to congratulate him on his appointment, and Nigel thought he knew who it was. Surely, I said, the President would have to tell him before the announcement was made in the Legislative Council? He didn't know, but he sounded resigned.

I had closed the door of my office in the committee building and tuned in to watch the live broadcast of Parliament. The Usher announced the President, and the members stood to attention. The President climbed the steps to his carved wooden seat and read prayers. The clerks at the table – Nigel and one of the clerk assistants – took their places in front of the President. Then the President stood to make an announcement. I turned up the sound and leaned toward the screen.

The President first delivered dates, times, processes. He detailed the resignation of the previous Clerk and the advertisement for a new one, the panel that had been appointed, the high calibre of applicants from across the country. And now, he was delighted to announce the new appointment. The name he gave was not Nigel Lake, but another Nigel, who had been working in another parliament. The President described the new incumbent in superlatives, said how delighted he was. He did not have the grace to thank Nigel Lake for his long period of acting, nor his contribution to the Legislative Council during the frequent ill health of the previous Clerk. He only added at the very end that Nigel Lake would be continuing to act as Clerk until the other took up his position the following year.

For the duration of the President's speech, as my fury began to grow, I could see Nigel sitting in the Clerk's seat in front of the President, looking down, looking uncomfortable – especially when members, hearing only 'Nigel', began to congratulate him on the job he had not won. He shook his head at them. Later a member told me that the chamber had become silent, then. Nigel collected the statement from the President's hand, ready to give to Hansard.

I began to yell. At first I was merely yelling at the President, and then I yelled at the general injustice of the world, and then I was reduced to half-yelling, half-sobbing a stuttering one-syllable commentary on the situation and the person I blamed for causing it.

I staggered over the corridor to my colleague who had heard me rail about injustices of various kinds with reasonable regularity.

'Did you see that?' I said. 'Nige was just sitting there – humiliated! How dare he! The President didn't even thank him! Twenty-five years working here and he gets treated like that!' And then I added more expletives to summarise the situation, in case the depth of my affront had not been appreciated.

My colleague's response – wary where normally she would have been sympathetic – and the later response of others suggested that they already knew what I had only just learned and were not surprised. Then I remembered that the new appointee had worked with the Clerk who had retired. I also recalled that he had gone interstate some months after the role of Clerk went to its first and only female appointment. I recalled that he knew a lot of the staff and members already.

My committee manager walked me up and down streets, under the purple-flowering jacaranda trees of West Perth. I ranted at him about the unfairness – this unfairness to Nigel after my own personal unfairnesses was beyond toleration. It was what I felt was the deliberate humiliation of Nigel that upset me the most. His dignified response did not match with the manner in which he'd been treated.

With the Don't Talk to the Police video still inaccessible to my working memory, I gave a summary of the above to the detectives.

'Are you going to tell me what's going on?' I finally asked.

There was a pause. 'Nigel has done something very out of character,' one of them finally offered.

'What do you mean?'

'He's been arrested.'

'For what?'

On this point they demurred. They stood up and asked to inspect my car.

I realised my limbs had turned numb when I went to retrieve my car keys from my office. The ground, my feet, seemed a long way away. As in one of the dreams you have in which the numbers on the phone won't work, or the number won't connect, or any other failure of communication your subconscious devises for you, I called Nigel's number as I went to my bag. His number rang out. I texted him to call me.

And then my numbness turned into panic.

The detectives accompanied me to my car and proceeded to check in and around it. When I asked what they were looking for, they didn't say.

'Where is he?' I asked. 'What's going on?'

They told me he was in custody in the Scarborough lock-up. They handed me the President's card. If I had any queries, the President was the one to call.

'I'm not calling *him*,' I said.

They were sorry, but they couldn't tell me more. Then they disappeared toward Parliament, leaving me to walk on unsteady legs back to my office. As I walked in, the desk phone was ringing.

'Julesy?' Nigel said.

'Are you all right?'

'Not exactly,' he said. His voice was dim and muffled. 'Can you let them know I won't be in today?'

'I think they know that,' I said. 'What's happened?'

'I'll talk to you later,' he said. 'I have to go.'

I don't know how long I sat there. I did not know what to do. I did not want to stay where I was, but I didn't know where to go. I was afraid of stepping outside my office. I sat, staring at the computer screen. An email popped up from the Clerk: Nigel Lake is taking urgent personal leave and will be absent until further notice.

Nobody called me. I stayed in my office until the committee manager came in. My absence from the committee meeting, the strange email. What was going on?

My committee manager had told me, the day before, that while I was in New York, he'd invited Nigel over for dinner. Nigel had been quiet, even by Nigel's standards.

'When he left,' my manager said now, 'I thought, I've never seen anybody so lost.'

He'd thought it was because he missed me. Now we realised that whatever it was, it was much, much more than that.

...

I was driven home in my car by my manager. I went inside my unit and paced, waiting for Nigel to call, to explain. But the phone did not ring.

I phoned the Scarborough police. They said he had been taken to the central lock-up. Still nobody would tell me what he was in the lock-up for. I was told, curtly, to leave a message.

I paced some more, and I considered what I knew about Nigel.

I had been acquainted with him for eight years. What did I know for sure? What did this length of time amount to?

What I concluded, after thinking and pacing, was that I knew three things.

Firstly, Nigel seemed driven to always do the right thing, whatever that thing was. He took no stock, it appeared, of other people's views. If he had reached a conclusion that a thing was right, it was what he would do. It is why he would never talk down his ex-wife to anyone; why he stayed with her until it became impossible. In his work he would not stop until a thing was as perfect, as complete as he could make it. When the new Clerk was appointed, Nigel had congratulated him, even though he wondered if the new Clerk been in on the decision that had been made long before any selection process. He congratulated him because it was the right thing to do, and besides, his beef hadn't been with the new Clerk, the other Nigel.

Secondly, Nigel was always kind to women but he could be harsh with men. He was old-fashioned. He opened doors for women, would not let a woman carry something heavy if he were there, gave female staff the benefit of the doubt. With male staff, he could be different. I'd observed the competitiveness with which men regarded each other in Parliament. Nigel did not brag about his chess prowess, or the fact he could bench press a hundred kilograms, or that he had been a junior tennis champion. Other men were the ones who mentioned these things. I had seen Nigel be abrupt over work matters with men whom Nigel felt should know better; that, combined with his well-built frame and his quietness, made some men wary of him. He had heard male staff in the Legislative Council talk about their opinion of the one and only female Clerk; he was deeply offended by what they said and about the way he felt she had been treated. To have a woman being piled on by a group of men, he'd said, just wasn't right. So I knew, as much as I knew anything, that he would not hurt a woman. But I was less certain of whether the same would apply to a man.

And thirdly, Nigel did not want to hurt me. Even when he was in the throes of his messy separation, he was concerned that it was bad for me. Back then, this concern had been no more than the result of our friendship, developed as it was from our collegiate beginnings. Now, Nigel did not like to see me hurting over John's illness and the conflict with John's family, because his feelings had deepened, and what for a long time was mere fondness had become love. On the rare occasion we'd had a misunderstanding, he was at pains to correct it – he would not dissemble or resile from the truth of his beliefs, but he would check in and keep checking in until it was okay with me. Usually these misunderstandings were to do with things he'd held back from me – previous relationships, personal events – and he held back because they involved other people. While he was constitutionally reticent to speak about himself, he found it even more difficult to talk about other people. Some things were not his secrets to tell, he said.

So that was what it amounted to: kindness to women, and to me specifically; a drive to do the right thing, as he saw the right thing.

I called lock-up after lock-up, but nobody could tell me if he was there or if he'd been there. He had been at one place and moved to another; at the second one they had no record of him. Finally, one police officer told me he'd been released on bail and dropped at his flat in Fremantle.

I grabbed my keys, put the dog in the car, and drove with the summer sun in my eyes up Stirling Highway to Fremantle, wondering what I was going to find when I arrived.

As I drove I replayed the recent weeks, recent months, hoping that replaying would alter the result: that I was here not knowing what Nigel had done, left wondering about the person who had been my constant. But whatever it was that he had done, the end of the replaying remained stubbornly resistant to my most fervent wishes for it never to have been done at all.

40

In 2012, unknown to any of us, it had started with a comment from a senior manager in Parliament. Nigel had taken to sleeping on the couch in his office in the process of separating from his wife. He'd tried staying with his mother, but he needed space and peace, and his mother's small unit and her constitutional anxiety prevented her from providing either. So he started to stay at work late, and then taken advantage overnight of the long leather lounge suite in his office. The office door was locked, and Nigel was up before the cleaners came. But he received an email from the manager, first expressing sympathy for his predicament but then advising it had come to their attention that Nigel was using the office as a hotel room. The email included the phrase that he was being watched.

At the same time, Nigel's ex-wife was communicating not only with Nigel's colleagues, but also with members of Nigel's family, including his birth mother, his godparents, anyone she had even met in passing. She would call people, at first indicating that she was calling to say goodbye, and then launching into her version of what Nigel had done and what kind of a person he was, sparing no detail. Once, he was walking into a café for breakfast on a weekend morning when he was struck on the chest with a fork. He looked around and was met with an infuriated stare from his ex-wife, who was with her sister. Then she launched a barrage of abuse, which the sister failed to quieten. As Nigel was turning to leave, his ex-wife leapt over a planter box and attempted to assault him close up before her sister pulled her off. Nigel responded to this in the way he had responded to everything preceding it, by pretending it didn't bother him and pushing the uncomfortable feelings down in the hope that he was also pushing them away.

Work had always been Nigel's focus and source of pride. Now the relationships there also deteriorated.

Nigel's relationship with the Clerk, whose job he had regularly undertaken, had declined from being one of reliance – when the Clerk had his accident in 2010, Nigel was the first person he called – to one that became increasingly chilly. This was not helped by the way I was being treated at the time. In June 2013, Nigel, as my manager, requested the Clerk that I be moved to a vacancy in the committee office for six months – a slight reduction in pay and leave, but nothing unmanageable. This would allow me more time to care for a rapidly declining John, as well as Annie, who was in Year Twelve and becoming increasingly despondent and angry at her situation. I was told that I would have to apply in an open process for the position. When I was successful in that application I asked for a secondment, which was agreed to by the Clerk but vetoed by the President. If I was going, the move would have to be permanent. At the same time, Nigel found an email on the photocopier indicating that the President, Clerk, and another senior manager had been discussing the issue. Nigel was outraged, feeling that I was being treated badly by the three men, but he didn't say anything, either to me or to them. He pushed the feelings down, down and away.

And then there was the appointment of the new Clerk at the end of 2013. The result didn't surprise him, but the feedback the President gave him afterward did. After suggesting that working in another Parliament might help broaden Nigel's skills, the President said that he wasn't going to discuss Nigel's relationship with the retiring Clerk. He then, in Nigel's view, proceeded to decimate Nigel's professional capabilities before concluding with the observation that Nigel's problems in the Council had started when his marriage broke up. Again, Nigel didn't tell me about the feedback he'd received, nor of how humiliating he'd found it. Down and away.

When the new Clerk started, Nigel was determined to carry on professionally. But Nigel felt that every opportunity he had, the President made things difficult, being polite in front of others and scathing when it was only the two of them. Nigel was cordial with the new Clerk, but the Clerk would say things to him that caused him to wonder what he meant, and whether double meanings had been intended.

In 2014 Nigel began ruminating on everything that had happened. About the men he felt were conspiring against him at work, his ex-wife, the financial stress of his separation, the situation I was in. He began playing *Call of Duty* on nights I wasn't staying with him, staying up late, sleeping badly, getting up late. At work, he began scanning air vents, taping over the camera on his computer, checking over his shoulder. He couldn't shake the increasing conviction that what the senior manager had said in 2012 was true: he was being watched.

He took to cycling long distances on his pushbike at night, dressed in a black hoodie and sweatpants, carrying a black backpack, carrying latex gloves in case the chain came off, carrying a tee-ball bat in case something happened, to defend himself, because he was under attack. He knew that he was being talked about by all of them; he suspected he was being watched. But he would stand up to them. He would take it all like a man. He would park, sometimes, over from the Legislative Council, the lights making the sandstone glow yellow, the flowerbeds always neat, the bollards positioned to stop cars driving into the dining room. Here I am, he would think. Here I am, standing. Despite your best efforts.

You might be watching me, but I am watching you too.

...

When I got to Nigel's apartment in Fremantle on the afternoon of 18 February 2015 he was there, standing next to the table. Papers were strewn everywhere, and his normally calm demeanour was riven with agitation. He was looking for my phone number. They had taken his phone. They had taken my laptop.

He smelled of something bitter and of cigarettes when, after a searching pause, I put my arms around him. I could hear his usually slow heartbeat rapid in his chest. He would not speak in the flat. I didn't realise until later this was because he believed we were being bugged. We sat on the balcony overlooking untroubled people entering and leaving a restaurant, a normal activity that I could never again imagine doing.

And he told me what he had done.

...

Nigel explained how it had happened, how everything had come to a head on the night of 17 February 2015.

For months now he had gone from suspecting to being absolutely certain he was being bugged, being monitored. He didn't know why he was being surveilled. Certain people had it in for him, he thought, especially when he had asked questions about expenditure, or because he believed that the Clerk's job had been arranged far in advance of the previous Clerk's departure, and they thought he had evidence that might embarrass them, something that the Corruption and Crime Commission might be interested in. Or because Nigel knew of the other senior jobs in Parliament that had been awarded without due process, and thought that he might be about to do something with that information, and they wanted to stop him.

So they were monitoring him, wanting to catch him out. Being monitored as a general citizen was one thing, but because it was Parliament, Nigel knew it must have involved the Corruption and Crime Commission or the police. It must also have been done with the President's permission, because such monitoring involved parliamentary privilege, of which the Parliament was so protective. The President hated him, and everyone knew they were trying to get rid of him. It made sense.

Lately he'd been trying to get caught, so he could finally prove it with his trademark logic. After all, if he wasn't under surveillance, how would they know what it was he'd been doing? To this end, he'd let down the Clerk's tyres. He'd played first online chess then porn on his work computer. He'd ordered tracking devices using the identification documents of his son and one of the members of Parliament. He waited for them to confront him. But they wouldn't. Why wouldn't they?

Even though he believed he was being bugged and monitored by the President, by the parliamentary services department, it was the Clerk he saw every day. And, of course, the Clerk must have known about it too. On Friday 13 February, the Clerk had held a morning tea and during his speech had mentioned something about people doing the right things and people doing the wrong things. When he said 'doing the wrong things' he looked directly at Nigel, who made a joke of the other people the Clerk might look at when saying such a thing. Everyone laughed. I laughed, and thought it was nice that they got on so well, that Nigel could make jokes like that. But the comment festered in Nigel's head all that weekend, confirming what he'd already suspected. The Clerk knew what was going on, and the Clerk should have been talking to Nigel about it, not making veiled comments in speeches.

So after the first sitting night of the year, Nigel put on the black balaclava he used under the helmet of his motorbike, a grey hoodie, and tracksuit pants. His backpack – with the tee-ball bat sticking out and the latex gloves inside – was already in his car, and he drove to the quiet, lush streets of City Beach, arriving half an hour before midnight. He parked some streets away from the Clerk's house, the personalised numberplate of his work car clearly visible from the road. And he waited for the car that he knew was coming, because he'd affixed a tracking device to it earlier in the evening. He watched the car approaching on his phone, a flashing dot on a map, coming his way.

It was verge-side rubbish collection week, and nearby there was a wooden shelf among a pile of discarded items. Nigel dragged it onto the road. When the Clerk approached, he would have to stop, and then Nigel would step out and confront him. He was going to stand up for himself. He wasn't going to be pushed around anymore. He was going to bring this thing to a head, once and for all.

The only problem with this plan was that the Clerk's car approached and, without slowing down, swerved around the wooden shelf and continued on, out of sight.

Just when the undisturbed part of Nigel's brain concluded that, even if the Clerk had stopped, his current appearance in the middle of the night might not be the best way in which to extract the information he sought, a police car approached from behind. The police inside spotted a well-built six-foot bloke in a hoodie carrying a tee-ball bat a few streets away from the Clerk's house in a suburb that generally did not have tee-ball-bat-carrying men wandering about it at any time of the day or night. Later someone told us that the coincidence of police was in fact a result of the police tracking Nigel, as he'd suspected. Then someone else told us there was a meth house in the street and the police had been keeping a watch on that.

One undoubtable thing is that Nigel was arrested.

. . .

I took in the information that Nigel was telling me.

If I had not worked at Parliament, if I hadn't known the people he was talking about, known the secrecy with which things were done, felt the antagonism that had been directed toward Nigel from certain quarters, as well as toward me, I might have concluded that he was out of his mind. But I didn't.

The first thing I asked him was, 'Were you going to hurt him?'

I had been married to someone who had threatened to break someone's kneecaps over a kiss, and I'd grown up in a suburb where violence was regularly threatened, often visible, shocking in the moment but thereafter the subject of glamorised gossip. I had hosted more than one party as a teenager where the police had to turn up to break up fights. So if Nigel had genuinely wanted to visit violence on our boss, I wasn't so much horrified at the prospect in general as the fact that Nigel, normally so reserved and calm, was experiencing such strength of feeling. I meant what I'd said in my ill-advised words to the police, that he and the Clerk seemed to get on fine. But I was also aware that Nigel might not have told me otherwise.

Nigel's abhorrence at the idea of hitting the Clerk was immediate and extreme. 'No!' he said. 'I couldn't do that. He's got a wife and kids.'

'Then why did you have a bat with you?'

'Because I needed to protect myself,' he said.

'From who?'

'All of them,' he said.

What he'd said to the police was that he was following a work car because he believed his supervisor was releasing confidential information. He gabbled his explanation of what he was doing, in relief at being caught, in shock at being caught, relief that the whole thing would be over, and the truth would come out. The police remarked, as he talked, 'That doesn't make sense.'

And finally he realised that it didn't make sense.

The police attempted a roadside video interview, but the equipment failed. By the time he got to the lock-up his sense had returned, and he declined to answer the questions put to him at interview.

When they took him to the cell it had a concrete bench on one side and nothing else. He put his fists underneath his head and went to sleep.

. . .

Another thing I asked was, 'Do you think you're unconsciously trying to drive me away? Because if you were, this would be a great way of doing it.'

'No, Julesy,' he said. 'It's nothing to do with you.'

'Are you sure?'

'If you need to walk away, I understand,' he said.

I considered what Nigel had told me, held it against what I knew of him. I don't mean by this that it was an easy decision, but that it was the only one that was right to make.

'If you mean it, that it's got nothing to do with me, I'm not going anywhere,' I said.

I remembered when I was twenty-four and living in a flat in Maylands being roused one evening by the police bashing on my screen door. Through the peephole two uniformed officers ballooned, their capped heads huge and their bodies shrunken. I opened the door with a hammering heart. But they were not there for me. They were there for the previous occupant, whose husband had just been killed in an accident. I wrote down the forwarding address she'd left and sat down. So suddenly, things could happen. So suddenly, the moorings of your life dislodged by rips you cannot see.

. . .

Nigel was charged with being in possession of a controlled weapon; possessing a disguise; and the use, installation, and maintenance of tracking devices. They were all summary offences. That is, they weren't sufficiently serious to have been heard anywhere but in the Magistrates Court. I'd recently completed a unit in criminal law, so I understood this. I looked up all the offences and their penalties, just to be sure. If he was found guilty, he could get two years in prison. He could also be fined, and the fines amounted to $20,000 in total. It could have been worse, I supposed, but I could not imagine Nigel having to go to jail. The very idea of one person going from a parliamentary officer appointed by the Governor to prison as a consequence of losing your mind made me vertiginous.

I knew it wouldn't matter that the charges were relatively minor, once the media got hold of it. The optics, as they say, were terrible.

'Wait till it hits the papers,' I said.

'Why would it?' Nigel said. 'Why would anyone care about this?'

'Clerks behaving badly,' I said. 'Man goes after boss with baseball bat.'

'It was a tee-ball bat,' Nigel said.

'Front page,' I said.

...

I had to go back to work the next day. Nobody knew. I would have to say Nigel was unwell and leave it at that.

I was afraid to leave him alone. I was afraid that, if I left him, the man who claimed he had never had a suicidal thought might revise the desirability of forcing things to their conclusion. I wanted him to go into hospital. But he thought the worst was over. He just needed time to think. He needed time to speak to a lawyer.

I arrived at work early, jittery with lack of sleep, with too much caffeine. Everything appeared the way it always did. The doors glided open when I held my pass up to the black panel. I yanked open the front door that always stuck a bit. I put my things down in my office and walked the long, carpeted corridor to the kitchen. I put my lunch in the fridge and made another coffee. When I got to work my computer was on. Normally I shut it down. Maybe I hadn't. It was hard to remember what I had done. When I opened up Facebook, it appeared somebody had tried to get into my account. But maybe it had been me, in my flustered state.

I waited for a message from parliamentary management. Silence. My committee members asked if things were all right. My manager asked me if Nigel was all right. I said I couldn't talk about it. My other colleagues looked at me warily. There were whisperings already. Something was up.

I messaged my friend Loraine, who worked in the Assembly. I asked if she would walk with me around the block at morning tea.

'Is Nigel all right?' she said.

'No,' I said.

She knew enough to not press. I was about to chair some sessions at Perth Writers Festival. I did not know how I was going to manage this when the floor had fallen out of my world, but I had to do it. It anchored me to the world outside of Parliament, for one. So we discussed the writers I was interviewing, whether she had read this book or that book. The jacaranda trees had dropped their purple flowers, their thick, slippery carpets swept away, and now they sieved the hot blue sky through their twigs.

By the time I got back to Nigel's flat after work, he'd got a letter from the President, dated the day of his arrest. It advised that until more information became available, he was to remain at home and not undertake any work on behalf of the Parliament.

Nigel was agitated. He'd got a lawyer. He wanted to find out the truth, whether he'd been monitored or not. He wanted the lawyer to be able to ask for the papers he needed to prove it. I said that, even if they existed, they would never give them up, because they would claim parliamentary privilege. He knew this too, but he still wanted to know. Once they returned his phone and my laptop, he kept looking up cases, defences, unfair dismissal. He wasn't sure what was coming now, but their silence toward both of us made us assume the worst.

In the week after Nigel's arrest, the Clerk came to our regular staff meeting at the committee office. He never normally came to these meetings, so his arrival caused comment. The colleagues who had known the Clerk during his previous stint in the Legislative Council made a show of going up to him, chatting. He seemed normal. I pretended to be fine. He sat across from me at the curved committee table, sitting where the Chair normally sat. He kept looking at me. Was he sympathetic? Was he glaring? I couldn't tell, but I rushed to get out of the room when the meeting was over. We saw each other in the vestibule. He did not smile. He did not say anything.

I sat in my office, my door shut all day. People knocked. People wanted to know what was going on. I wanted to know what was going on, but I'd still had no communication from senior management. I was convinced they were angling to get me out too. I told my manager I was going to the doctor and getting a sick note. I couldn't eat. My skin prickled in waves starting from my scalp and making their way down my torso to my gut, my fingertips. Every time I woke up after an hour of light, nightmare-ridden sleep, I'd jolt up, trying to work out why my heart was hammering, what had happened. Which thing was it my anxiety was attached to now – my perilous finances? John's dementia? Annie's depression? Oh, and this. This.

41

At 5.05pm on Friday 6 March 2015, Nigel was couriered a letter from the President. The President had formed the view that Nigel's employment should be terminated, and a recommendation put to the Governor to that effect. Nigel was required to respond by 5pm the next Tuesday, otherwise termination would be effected.

'At five on a Friday afternoon?' Nigel said, looking at the envelope.

'The bastards,' I said. Then I looked at the signature on the letter as Nigel opened it. 'Singular.'

On Monday 9 March I walked into Fremantle after lunch and had a massage to try to loosen my shoulders. I told Nigel I'd be back soon. When I switched on my phone afterward, the screen was filled with the red bubbles numbering missed calls, messages to call, messages of support and outrage. Because at 1.12pm, the President had sent an email to all Members and staff, attaching a letter saying Nigel had been arrested and charged with a number of offences, that he had been effectively stood down, and that the President regarded the matter very seriously.

At 2pm the story led the Australian Broadcasting Corporation's radio news. The other radio stations began announcing it in their headlines soon afterward.

'Oh Nige,' I said when I got back to the flat.

Nigel was pacing, frowning, the television on with the sound down, the radio on. His phone kept vibrating with missed calls, text messages. He gestured for me to come over to the computer. He still thought the flat was bugged. He showed me the all-staff email from the President.

'Singular,' I said.

We were agitated, waiting for the news to come on. It was too late for the five o'clock news, but it led the six and seven o'clock bulletins. Wide-eyed female anchors talked of the 'shocking' arrest of forty-nine-year-old Nigel Lake, Deputy Clerk, the official photograph of Nigel from Parliament's website appearing behind them, the photo where he sported the red mark and black eye his ex-wife had given him. Then came the re-enactments. One showed a silhouette of a man carrying a bat, walking down a dark street, menacing chords playing low and long beneath, while the voiceover talked about Nigel stalking his boss and being arrested a kilometre from his home. On the ABC there was footage of Nigel, sitting at the table of the Legislative Council.

'Didn't take them long to get that ready,' Nigel remarked.

On Tuesday 10 March, the President sent another email to parliamentary staff, in which he corrected his previous statement where he had said that the actions Nigel had been charged with were 'alleged'. He also told the media that the Corruption and Crime Commission had been notified. Members of Parliament were doorstopped as they went into the Tuesday sitting. They were all shocked. It was bizarre, the Premier said.

The same photograph, Nigel staring impassively outward, dressed in his gown and jabot, was on the front page of *The West Australian*.

When we went to the small gym in Fremantle the next day, the woman at the desk looked at Nigel for a long time as she checked his pass. Inside, people looked sideways. At the shop, at the service station, walking Hecta to the beach. People glanced, then did not look away for a beat or two longer than usual. I glared at them. Nigel continued on, looking ahead. We held hands and kept walking.

...

In the days and weeks that followed I received messages and missed calls from many numbers. Some were predictable ones from those who were keen to gloat. Some were unexpected kindnesses from Hansard staff, former teachers, Nigel's ex-wife's family, colleagues, my cousins, friends I hadn't seen for some time. There were stalwart supporters who checked in: Loraine from the Assembly, the friends I saw regularly on weekends, my family. Other callers were prurient, fishing for information that could be repeated around dinner tables. These people left breathy messages, telling me how *sorry* they were this was happening, after all the mess with John, and how if there was anything they could do, if I wanted to talk – well, just let them know.

The larger number of people, however, were colleagues who until then had crowded around Nigel for his generosity or for the potential of promotion. They vanished as swiftly as the principles of a new political leader. Nigel was sanguine about this.

'Julesy,' he said, 'it's like a battle in a war. Everyone hits the decks when the shooting starts.'

'But this isn't a war,' I said. 'You've had a brain snap. Is that not patently fucking obvious to them? What about all this bollocks about taking care of people's mental health and all that?'

'It's a war,' he said. 'Trust me.'

...

The first court appearance was 18 March 2015. The date had been mentioned in all the media reports, so we knew, in theory, what would await us at the court.

When the alarm went off that morning, Nigel, who had been up late, did not immediately respond. I got up, turned off his alarm, and went to the bathroom. Neither of us had slept well. I had only just managed to fall asleep when Nigel had come to bed, and his restlessness had only ceased before dawn. I shook him awake when I returned and went downstairs to make us coffee. By the time Nigel made his way outside, his face shadowed with tiredness, his coffee was cool. We sat outside on the balcony in Fremantle, overlooking people walking purposefully to the train station, our phones vibrating with messages of luck for the appearance.

Even though he was only there for mention and to confirm the bail conditions, Nigel had employed a lawyer from a high-end firm to represent him. It was a signal that Nigel meant to defend himself as best he could against the institutions of the police and of Parliament. The lawyer had briefed him the day before, in anticipation of the likely media presence.

'Don't wear sunglasses,' he'd said. 'Don't run, don't respond, don't hide your face. Keep as calm as you can.'

'Okay.' Nigel looked impassive as this advice was given, as if already practising.

'Don't use your work car,' the lawyer had added. 'And whatever you do, make sure you're there on time, or they'll put a warrant out.'

I got ready first and then took Hecta briefly around the block as Nigel shaved and showered. He was in the shower when I left; he was still there when I returned. I checked the various media sites that had announced the imminent appearance. I answered some texts wishing us luck. Then I looked at the time.

'Nigie,' I called, knocking on the bathroom door. 'We're going to be late.'

The shower taps turned off, but still Nigel did not appear downstairs until after we were supposed to leave. It was a half-hour drive to the city, and the later we left, the worse the traffic would be. I tried to hide my impatience.

When he finally emerged, his forehead and scalp were slick with perspiration. He took off the jacket of his smart grey suit. His eyes were joyless.

We drove in silence except for the murmuring of ABC Radio National, which discussed the political and social events of the day in serious voices, while interviews with politicians were distinguished by their more combative tones. Nigel's friend called, giving the location of the carpark he would pick us up from. Our work colleague would pick us up afterward. I texted her, and Nigel's daughter-in-law, and my other friends who were coming in support. When I'd been going through the difficult days with hearings in the State Administrative Tribunal, Nigel had said to me, as he dropped us off for each hearing, 'Julesy, remember that after today you'll be one step closer to all this being over.' I wondered if Nigel remembered his own words now. It seemed trite to repeat them aloud.

Nigel's friend met us at the carpark near the Perth Concert Hall. The carpark was one street away from the Swan River, and morning joggers and cyclists moving this way and that on the foreshore, next to the choppy water, under the blue sky. The anxiety and rigidity in my body, in Nigel's posture, felt particular to us. Nigel put on his jacket and asked me if his collar was straight.

In the car, Nigel's friend was positive and practical as we drove the few streets eastward in the early morning city traffic. There were no alternative entrances to the Magistrates Court, or none that were available to the public, I already knew from my prisoner transport inquiry. No matter who you were or what you had done you had to walk the pavement in front of the courtroom, and up the steps. There was nowhere to hide.

As we approached we could see a few people waiting near the court, including guys in loose-fitting black shirts with their boxy cameras resting on the ground while they scrolled on their phones, others with long conical lenses on their cameras, coiffed young females in heels and full make-up nearby. Nigel's son and daughter-in-law were on the steps with our friends from Parliament. Kitty and Brioni, another friend of ours, were chatting.

'Are you ready?' Nigel's friend said.

Nigel didn't answer. I climbed out of the back seat, and I grabbed his hand as he climbed out.

The slouching cameramen and blank faces of the journalists transformed into a greedy attention as they spotted Nigel. As one, they rushed toward us, forming a clicking, questioning, encircling mob. They asked questions, walking backward, or sidestepping, or thrusting their microphones or other recording devices as close to Nigel as they could.

'Why did you do it?'

'Are you going to plead guilty?'

'Were you going to hurt him?'

'Are you going to apologise for what you did?'

'Is there anything you want to say to the Clerk?'

Their pressing and jostling felt to me like the physical manifestation of the prying and prodding of acquaintances and colleagues over the past month. We moved forward as best we could, being careful not to tread on the shuffling feet so close to ours or those that leapt in and out for a quick shot. Nigel's supporters tried to crowd around but they were pushed to the back by the reporters. I focused on each step, imagining the humiliation that would ensue if I stumbled. I held tight to Nigel's hand.

When we reached the landing, the reporters fell back. We walked through the doors. To the left was another group of people, in which I spotted Nigel's ex-wife.

She stood there, her eyes bright, wearing a fluffy blue pullover and neat pants. She was grinning as she watched us go through the metal detector. We had to take our shoes off; Nigel had to take his belt off. I tried not to look over, wished the conveyor belt would move faster. Once we were finally through, we had to wait outside the court so that Nigel could report he was there, even though proceedings didn't start for another forty-five minutes. The friend who had driven us and his wife found us and told us Nigel's ex-wife was waiting outside another court room.

We returned downstairs to wait in the coffee shop. Nigel bought coffees for everyone, despite everyone insisting otherwise, and we sat on the metal chairs around small melamine tables. The coffee was bitter. Nigel and his friend sat at one table, messaging the lawyer. Annie, who had come before an art class, sat with Nigel's son and daughter-in-law; the rest of us were around a corner. The time went slowly; Nigel got up to go to the toilet. I didn't see where he'd gone, but I was alerted to his return by yelling.

'I'm just offering you my help! I want to help you! You need help, Nigel.'

Nigel's ex-wife was walking close to him. He kept turning his shoulder away from the hand she placed on his arm. She was still grinning.

'You can help by leaving me alone,' Nigel said.

I was on my feet without thinking. I remembered all those emails and messages to colleagues, all the turning up at work, talking to anyone who would listen. I hadn't seen her in all that time, but now I knew what it had cost Nigel, and cost me. I'd forgotten my part in it, my own complicity in her behaviour. I had no room left for self-reflection. So I beckoned her over, away from Nigel. I was furious. Blood rushed in my ears, palms sweatier than when we'd walked through the crush of media.

To my surprise, she came with me. I bent forward and said in a low voice, 'I'm sorry he never loved you.'

The grin was gone. I felt a terrible swell of satisfaction, seeing it. She pulled back her fist and swung at my face. I ducked, moved backwards, out of her reach. Her son leapt up and wrestled her until her arms folded across her chest, and he walked her out. 'How could you take that woman's side?' she was hissing.

It was only when Nigel's son glanced at me as he led his mother away that I felt ashamed.

...

In court we sat in among the other accused and their families. There were people who were appearing for traffic offences. There were young men with lank hair dressed in buttoned shirts pleading guilty to minor drugs charges. One woman was sentenced for breaking into her ex-boyfriend's house and smashing all his crockery and kicking in his plasma television. She was remorseful and received a suspended sentence and a fine. There were live crosses to prisons to set dates for hearings. Some people sat with partners or their families in court if they were there to put in a plea or receive a penalty. Some sat by themselves. Some had Legal Aid or Aboriginal Legal Service lawyers to speak for them, offering mitigations, explaining what their client had done since their arrest to make sure they didn't reoffend. The Magistrate drily commented on their previous incomplete treatment programs, unfulfilled undertakings to get clean or sober. None of the accused looked like Nigel or had Nigel's well-dressed, well-shod group of supporters, but it made no difference to the levelling that takes place in a public courtroom. I was aware of Nigel's ex-wife sitting with her friend behind us, but I did not look at her.

After several hours, Nigel's name was finally called.

Nigel stood up from the gallery and his lawyer from the bar table. He confirmed his name. The Magistrate read out the list of charges. The lawyer requested a renewal of bail conditions. The Magistrate set the next hearing for six weeks' time. His lawyer thanked the Magistrate. Nigel had to wait for the bail slip, and then he was free to go.

Nigel's lawyer ushered him around the corner to speak to him privately while the rest of us stood nearby. Someone walked out with Nigel's ex-wife. I can't remember if it was their son or Nigel's friend. We waited where we were until the lunch break at 1pm, hoping that the media would have got bored and gone away.

'We could wait here until 5pm and miss the deadline for the television news,' I tried to joke, but nobody smiled. Our friend Loraine from Parliament went to get her car. She would text when she was approaching the front.

From inside the court near the lifts we peered out at the street. We saw Nigel's ex-wife talking to reporters. They looked politely interested but were keeping their eyes on the court doors. There were even more cameras than there had been in the morning, it seemed.

'Loraine's on her way,' I said to Nigel, putting my phone back in my bag.

Our friends gathered around us, but the door was only wide enough for two at a time. I reached for Nigel's hand, which had balled into a fist. We made our way down the steps, the same questions being asked again, our grim faces reflected in the lenses pointing at us from all sides. We walked as firmly as we could toward the sedan idling at the kerb.

I had thought Nigel would get in the door on the far side, and I would get in the door closest to the footpath. But even though he was being pressed from all sides, even though it gave them extra seconds to photograph his grim face, to push microphones at his mouth, Nigel pushed my hand from the door and opened it for me, the way he always did.

42

Our lives were strung between court appearances. The second, third, fourth, and fifth involved requesting extensions to the date on which Nigel had to enter a plea. At every one, the media surrounded us as we made our way to the court, as we left the court.

At least the camera-toting media couldn't get in the courtroom, though. The journalists could, of course, their notebooks at the ready, glancing at us as we waited. They, however, were the least of our difficulties. Inside the doors of the court building we usually had Nigel's ex-wife lying in wait, staring at us as we had to put our shoes and jackets through the security check. For Nigel's next appearance, she was joined by the Clerk's wife and their children in their school uniforms. The headline on the *PerthNow* news website on 30 April 2015 read, 'Family confrontation kicks off during suspended WA parliamentary officer's Perth court date' because Nigel's ex-wife had confronted Nigel's son during a break, and she was required to leave the courtroom.

I stayed off work until 13 April 2015. Nigel and I went to the gym, walked around Fremantle, talked and talked and talked, trying to unravel how we were now at this place, how he came to this.

I changed my enrolment from part-time to full-time law studies. I had to feel as if I was going forward, even if only into further debt for an extra degree I didn't really need. It was a counterweight, preventing me from being pulled into a vortex of misery, antagonism, and fear of both what each day would bring and the bleak future. I sat in the front row in a corporations law lecture hall, where our lecturer was the State Solicitor, whose office – and likely the State Solicitor himself, given the profile of the matter – would be giving advice to the Parliament on the potential legal avenues to sack Nigel.

I visited John, who would say, 'The yellow kids, the yellow kids, the yellow kids, all the containers, lemons and limes.' I envied him his lack of attachment to the world of events, intentions, disappointments. He would make semi-operatic wailing noises while Hecta scoured the floors for dropped food. When Annie sang along with her father when his pitch became unbearable to her – 'Aaaagh!' – John appeared to delight at their unison.

'Annie, Annie's beautiful, Annie's beautiful,' he'd say from time to time.

If Annie stood in front of him he smiled but did not seem to connect the person standing before him with the sentence he'd utter about her. Once, she was next to him, holding his hand. He lifted Annie's firm, pale forearm to his mouth. She yanked her arm away.

'Honey,' I said. 'Please don't eat your daughter.'

'Annie?' he said. 'Annie's beautiful.' Then he muttered, 'Gwen. Gwen and Bert, Gwen and Bert. Hi-lo. Hi-lo. Hi-lo milk.'

He got up abruptly, began to walk away on tiptoe, still muttering.

'Oh my God,' Annie said. 'Can we go now? Please?'

...

I got a call from Lencie, a friend from university who had become a journalist. She had been told that Gareth Parker, an up-and-coming journalist working for the state's only daily newspaper, had been speaking to Nigel's ex-wife, parliamentary staff, our colleagues. He was planning to do a profile of Nigel after his trial. She'd heard rumours that profile was of an ambitious man, thwarted by someone getting the job he'd always wanted, and egged on by his nasty new girlfriend. This man had, but for the grace of God, been prevented from wreaking violence on the person who'd taken the job that was rightfully his.

Lencie and I began meeting for coffee on Sunday mornings with our dogs – at Bathers Beach in Fremantle if the weather was fine, and under the protection of the Norfolk pines at the Esplanade if it was not. Away from telephones and listening devices, with the waves and the wind muffling our conversation, she told me the latest things she'd heard.

'But he hasn't even spoken to us,' I said.

'He's formed a picture,' she said. 'It's not flattering. To either of you.'

'Do you think he'll talk to us?'

I'd accepted that the facts of what had happened looked bad enough.

But Nigel's psychology and motivations, even in the best of times, did not lend themselves to tabloid-style explanations. He did not, as I'd learned, look at things the same way I did or the way most people did. His adherence to some behaviours, for example, stemmed from an unshakeable sense of right and wrong, but these could easily look to other people like something different. He stayed with his wife after he suspected her affairs because she was the mother of his child. He had looked askance at male staff members in the Legislative Council because of the way he perceived their treatment of women.

'He's got to get your side of the story,' Lencie said. 'But mate, if you leave it too long, it might be too late.'

'Can you ask him if we can meet?' I said.

'I can't promise anything,' she said. 'But I'll give it a red-hot go.'

The next Sunday morning she handed me a number.

'I'm not sure you're going to get anywhere,' she said. 'But good luck.'

Lencie's dog played on the sand, running and returning to Lencie's side while we watched the waves shooshing on the sand, insensible to the conversations of troubled humans on the shore. Hecta stayed on the lead, the way he had to, having never submitted to being recalled once free. If you let him off, you'd be chasing him for the rest of the day. If you let him off, he'd never come back voluntarily.

...

My inability to sleep reached its nadir. Even with the aid of antihistamines, I would lie awake for hours in the middle of the night, listening to Nigel's breathing, asking questions that had no answers.

Why had Nigel not been able to tell me how he felt?

Why had I not recognised what I was seeing?

Why had the President hated Nigel so much?

Why had they all been so quick to turn their backs on someone who had been so loyal to the place where he worked?

Was it because they thought he knew something?

Was it because he knew something, but didn't recognise exactly what he was seeing?

Was there corruption neither of us knew about? Or merely weak men attacking a strong one?

Why had he given them the ammunition to do what they were doing?

Then I would ruminate on the things people said to me. Some people made a joke of it, me ending up with two men with differently broken minds, the breaking of their minds breaking me along with them. You really know how to pick 'em, I was told more than once. Was this true? Did I? I'd thought I was picking someone so completely different from John, but now I was with a different, perhaps worse, kind of chaos because of it. How did I not see it coming, with either of them, the second even more so than the first? How did I not know, twice?

Then I remembered that this was not the first time, nor the second, I'd watched someone I loved deteriorate, helpless to influence them, feeling responsible and powerless both. I recalled how Gwen had come to visit unannounced, once, in 1999. She had had a strange dream in which she could not move, but she was holding my hand and she was trying to call out to me. Her voice did not work, as they never do in such dreams. She was so unsettled by the dream she wanted to see me. Over a cup of tea she told me her doctor had said her blood pressure was high, and her cholesterol. After that I asked about the blood pressure regularly, until she snapped at me to desist. I worried about the increasing stress that she displayed over her real estate business, the weight she was putting on, the cigarettes she held with increasingly tremoring hands, the unhappiness she seemed not to recognise. I worried about her; she seemed incapable of worrying about herself. Three years later, at the age of fifty-six, she had a series of strokes.

'It must have been something in the water,' she said afterward.

'But the doctor told you about the high blood pressure,' I said. 'You told me about it.'

She looked surprised. 'I don't remember that.'

All my life I'd witnessed my mother's periods of recklessness. The driving off in cars when drunk; the going out and returning home with strangers; the going out and coming home in daylight, shoeless and nauseous; the persisting with smoking after being diagnosed with emphysema. My concern irritated her. Only after an extreme event, such as when she tried to crack onto my cousin's teenage friends at his eighteenth birthday, was I allowed to be furious, and she would be, for a brief time, sheepish and shameful, before forgetting.

I was used to watching the people I loved disappear, consumed with whatever invisible thing drove them, while I waited anxiously for their return. Sometimes they did, changed or forgetful. Sometimes they could not.

I wondered which it would be, this time.

43

Nigel's lease on his Fremantle apartment was up at the beginning of July. I had loved staying there. It was in an old confectionery factory, and its balcony overlooked a restaurant and the casual, cool foot traffic of central Fremantle. It was a block away from the markets in one direction and the beach in the other. But even though Nigel was on sick leave and was still drawing an income, despite constant threats to terminate his employment, we knew this state of affairs was unlikely to continue. Nigel's divorce settlement saw him stripped of all assets, keeping only his superannuation, so the only option that was feasible was him moving in with Annie and me in our two-bedroom unit in Maylands.

Annie was infuriated at this turn of events. It was supposed to have been our place, hers and mine. Plus she'd enjoyed coming to the Fremantle apartment in the same suburb she'd gone to school. She and Nigel had got on well enough, but the extra quietness he developed after his breakdown unnerved her.

'Why does he have to move in here?' she hissed.

'Because he has nowhere else to go.'

'I get he's had a breakdown,' she said. 'But it's not fair.'

'I know,' I said. 'Hopefully it won't be forever.'

Annie had surprised me when I had told her what Nigel had done and why. Her first reaction was sympathy toward the man who did not try to be her father but who treated her in the even-handed way her father never did. Some of the people she knew – from her TAFE art course, her old high school or her hospitality job – asked, wide-eyed, whether Nigel was a monster. Annie was offended by the news footage that led them to ask the question, and then by their thinking that what they saw was truth. She was annoyed at how Nigel was portrayed, about the way people were so ready to vilify him. Unlike some of my friends, she wasn't angry at what I was now having to put up with – first John, now this. She understood depression, and she understood what it was like to feel the foundation of your world fracture. But her tolerance did not extend to bringing a new type of fracturing into her home. She spent more and more time out, either at her usual haven of my dad and stepmother's house with my sisters, or else at her friends' places, just as she had when she was a child.

When Nigel moved in, he brought all the boxes that had been delivered to him from the Legislative Council, boxes he could not bear to open. There was extra furniture that had nowhere to go, extra sets of crockery. The small unit was crammed floor to ceiling with remnants of a past life, adding to the feeling of uncertainty, unsettledness, of camping in a life that did not have enough space in it.

And Nigel did not feel at home. In his own abodes his decoration was sparse, tidy, things always in their place in his fastidious manner. Here, he could not bring himself to unpack. He perched on the couch until the small hours of the morning, playing *Call of Duty*, pretending to be somewhere else. When he wasn't on the couch, he was outside, leaning his elbows on his knees, chain-smoking, muttering to himself. Hecta followed him around. Nigel scruffled his ears.

'Hecta the Protector,' I said to Annie as we watched Hecta sitting, looking up at Nigel as he smoked under the bottlebrush tree in the front courtyard.

'That's what Dad used to say,' she said.

'At least you've got someone to drive you around,' I said. It was true. Nigel's one activity was driving Annie, on request, to her friend's places, to my Dad's, to work, picking her up from nights out.

'He doesn't say anything,' Annie said. 'The whole time. It's weird.'

'He's depressed,' I said. 'His whole life has fallen apart.'

Annie looked at me. 'He's not the only one. Is he?'

. . .

Before, Nigel and I – and often Annie too – had gone out to dinner regularly. Perth's small bar and restaurant scene had been transformed by changes in liquor licensing, and we had been enthusiastic about going to the new places appearing everywhere in the wake of the latest mining boom. Nigel enjoyed being generous, and I was still amazed at having a partner with an income, let alone a decent income. Now we had stopped, and not only to save money. The discomfort of staring staff or patrons or, Perth being Perth, running into acquaintances or colleagues who either avoided us or too emphatically told Nigel they were sorry about what they'd read, was too much. Even going shopping required hypervigilance. One day, by the dairy aisle, I saw Nigel nod uncomfortably to a man with a wary expression.

'Who was that?' I asked.

'My arresting officer,' Nigel replied.

So increasingly we stayed home, and increasingly we became isolated. I would go out with girlfriends, and we went to Nigel's friends' house in the hills, but mostly it was more comfortable to stay in. Annie was working nights in hospitality, so it also gave us time to ourselves. We watched *Game of Thrones*, DVD box sets of *Sons of Anarchy*, *The Sopranos*, *The Wire*, anything to take us away from ourselves and into situations where tension and anticipation were only fictional.

One weekend in 2015, between court appearances, Brioni invited us both for dinner. Brioni's partner was another calm, quiet Islander, and she was an excellent cook, which tempered Nigel's reluctance to go out anywhere and converse any more than he had to. Nonetheless, on the day both of us were feeling deflated and disinclined to company, and I phoned to put off the dinner to another week. But my girlfriend begged me not to, telling me of the ingredients she had worked so hard to procure, the preparations already made, plus she had borrowed her brother's unit for the occasion. So we went, taking the customary bottles of wine – one white, one red – and some flowers. When we arrived Brioni hugged us and drew us through the living room and out the back.

On the patio waited a gathering of a dozen of our friends, assembled around a table filled with candles and an array of home-made spring rolls, fish cakes, soy chicken dumplings, vegan samosas, and dipping sauces. They were holding a long banner on which was printed *All You Need Is Love*. They had managed to remain silent until they saw our surprised faces, then they cheered and hugged us, poured us drinks, put on music, and carried plates to us. They delighted in our surprise and enjoyed recounting the stealth required to pull off such a feat, the neighbouring streets on which they had hidden their cars, our always-late friend almost scuppering the surprise by arriving mere minutes before us.

'Nobody's ever done anything like this for me before,' I kept saying tearfully, in lieu of being able to express the gratitude for the buoying our friends had given me. I say 'me', not 'us', because Nigel was too far into the echo chamber of his own thoughts to be able to be relieved of it by other people. He knew the kindness that was being shown, but he was a long way yet from being able to gain succour from it.

...

Almost as frequent as the court appearances were the visits to various psychologists and psychiatrists, trying to work out what exactly had been wrong with Nigel. He needed this for legal reasons but just as pressingly, he needed them to work out what had happened. Was he a good person or a bad person? Was it his circumstances or something fundamentally lacking that had led him to wander up and down the street that February night? Or was it actually a result of being driven mad by covert surveillance, albeit in a peculiarly maladaptive way?

The problem was that none of the professionals could agree on whether his beliefs about being watched, and his behaviour subsequent to that, could be categorised as delusional or not. They all agreed he'd suffered a major depressive episode. They all agreed he had alexithymia, a limited ability to verbally express his emotions, which in psychological parlance is considered an unconscious defence against distressing underlying emotional states. But on the question of whether he was delusional or not they were split.

One of the psychiatrists, in his report, said that a delusion has three related qualities. A delusion is a fixed belief held on inadequate grounds which is out of keeping with social expectations. This psychiatrist – who was the prosecution's consultant – went on to note that the belief may or may not be false. That is, Nigel may well have been under surveillance, but it was why he thought he was under surveillance that was the issue. So the comment by parliamentary management about being watched, combined with the treatment he was getting from his seniors, combined with the reactions from other colleagues, was not sufficiently detached from reality to constitute a delusion, according to this psychiatrist.

And pieces of information kept coming out that led Nigel to look outside rather than in.

In June 2015, four months after Nigel's arrest, a report by the Parliamentary Inspector for the Corruption and Crime Commission outlined twenty-three specific allegations of longstanding misconduct within the Corruption and Crime Commission's surveillance group. The allegations implicated eight officers, and two of these faced criminal charges. Eventually, two of the former CCC officers were convicted of offences, and one was disciplined. Five officers had their investigations dropped because they had left the Commission, and investigations could not take place with former employees.

But whether the corrupt officers at the CCC's surveillance unit, which had been allowed to run with minimal oversight, were involved in surveillance of members or staff at Parliament was another matter Nigel would never know the answer to. Like the question of whether the police in City Beach the night of Nigel's arrest were, as had been whispered, actually there for him.

I measured the Nigel described in the psychiatrists' reports against the Nigel I knew. Unlike John, whose best self had been the one on display at the tennis club or when bantering with the school mums, Nigel's best self was the one reserved for the few people he loved. He was not a person who followed whims and passions, as I did: he was careful with his private self. I could recognise that the psychiatrists were describing someone in extremis. All of them included reference to his imposing build in their reports. I could see how he might have looked from the outside, and their descriptions of the mental state that led him to wandering around City Beach that night were upsetting to read. The reports, combined with my knowledge of his logical approach, his thoroughness, and his reluctance to speak about unpleasant events or feelings, made sense of Nigel's behaviour I could not have figured out alone. But the psychiatrists did not have the advantage of understanding Parliament the way I did. Unlike me, they did not see the way that it could foster uncertainty and paranoia among senior staff, mirroring the political process by which Parliament itself was formed.

In any case, if believing people at Parliament were out to get Nigel had been delusional, it was a delusion that I shared. I didn't know why they had been out to get him, exactly, but because I had worked there, because I knew the people involved, because I had seen how he was treated, it was the one thing I never doubted.

. . .

When I finally managed, through other journalists Lencie knew, to speak to Gareth Parker at a coffee shop, he was polite but sceptical.

'You're saying it wasn't about him missing out on the job – the job that everyone agrees he'd worked so hard for?' he asked.

'After nearly eighteen months?' I said. 'If that was the case, why didn't he lose his shit when the Clerk started? Why now?'

'He's got money troubles,' Gareth said. 'His ex-wife wants to know what happened to all the money he earned over the years.'

'He walked away with his super and that was all,' I said. 'They sent their son to a good school, supported him through uni, she had nice cars and holidays. They helped other people out. He paid half of their son's wedding. He had a decent wage, but it's not like he was a surgeon.'

Gareth nodded but didn't seem convinced.

'What he did to the Clerk and his family was shocking,' he said.

'I know that,' I said. 'He knows that. He wasn't in his right mind. He's mortified at what he did.'

Gareth nodded again.

'Just talk to him,' I said. 'Please.'

Gareth asked me a few more questions about work, how it was for me. I talked about working in a place that did not have the same legal protections as other workplaces. The peculiarity of Parliament was fine when you were going on professional development conferences interstate and overseas, but less so when something like this happened. I talked about how I was trying to get out.

After we finished our coffees, Gareth handed over his card. 'Ask him to call me.'

'Thank you,' I said.

His expression said I had nothing to thank him for yet.

. . .

When the discovery documents from the prosecution came on 21 July 2015, Nigel was devastated that they didn't contain the thing he most wanted: confirmation that he'd been watched. He had been convinced, despite likelihood suggesting otherwise, that it would have to contain information about him being under surveillance. If he hadn't been, then what did it mean for the rest of his behaviour? If he wasn't psychotic, what was he, at the time?

In an effort to understand how he'd got into such a state, Nigel had, when he was still in Fremantle, been staying up late at night, writing in detail what had happened and what he was thinking. When he finished, he wrote some more, adding more and more detail. He was being given advice by lawyers, by psychologists and psychiatrists, by people offering media advice, and he needed to come to his own understanding. But the process of doing this disturbed him further. The question of whether he was a good person or not racked him. How could a good person have done what he did? How was it he didn't understand what he was doing was wrong? He asked me: I did not know how to answer, except that the asking of the question seemed to me an answer in itself.

He was sure he would be able to think his way out of it, that things would follow their normal logical chain of cause and effect. But this required the cause – him being watched – to be proven.

When it was not, he no longer had a starting point. He was more agitated and unsettled than I'd ever seen him.

On 24 July 2015 he went to his psychiatrist, unable to bear his own agitation, the collapse of meaning wrought by the discovery documents, empty of what he was sure he would find. The psychiatrist admitted him to the psychiatric hospital at which he consulted. Nigel came home, which was now our unit in Maylands, to pack a few things and to tell me.

'Great,' Annie remarked. 'My father's in a nursing home and my stepfather's in a mental hospital.'

We sat on the couch and drank wine together.

'At least we have the place to ourselves,' Annie said.

44

The discovery documents held a different kind of surprise for me.

When the police had spoken to me on 18 February, there had been extensive notes taken. None of these appeared in the discovery documents. What I had said did not fit with their view that Nigel had done what he did out of a deep sense of grievance against the Clerk which had turned malicious, although why the sense of grievance waited for more than a year to manifest itself was not explained. The police's initial theory was that I'd been having an affair with the Clerk, and so Nigel had put tracking devices on both of our cars. That was why they had searched mine on that morning.

But it seemed clear from the materials that they had used the information I'd given them about my own feelings about the Clerk's appointment to frame the way they questioned my colleagues, and then took statements from them. One of my colleagues went into great detail about my fury at the Clerk's appointment, implying that I was either expressing Nigel's view or that my views deepened Nigel's grievance.

I was shocked at the malice in the statements. I'd got the gist of what they were saying from the questions I'd been asked by Gareth Parker, who would not, of course, disclose who had been saying what to him. But now I knew who they were. These were the same people I saw every day, whose offices were near mine. Some were the same ones who had fawned over Nigel when he'd been Deputy Clerk, when they'd been after drinks or favours.

Up until that point I had walked into work every day smiling and polite. Now I no longer smiled.

Because of Frank, or despite him, I had always held the police in high regard. I had listened to the derision of activist friends and others, who railed against the arbitrary targeting by police. I conceded that Aboriginal people had reason for fearing the police, given the history of violence they received at the police's hands. But for everyone else, I had thought, well, if you don't ask for trouble, you don't get it.

Now I formed a different view. I saw them exercising a power because they could, and the weight of the institutions of law enforcement, of prosecutors, was a foot on the chest if they decided you were guilty.

They had already decided about Nigel before they spoke to me on the morning of 18 February. And I, unwittingly, gave them everything they needed to make the case. All they needed were a few disloyal colleagues to fill in the details of the conclusions I'd helped them to draw.

. . .

The hospital Nigel was admitted to was located at the other end of Parliament Place. It was a hospital accessible only to those with private health cover and whose mental illnesses were not too severe or disruptive. Patients saw their psychiatrists from time to time, but the main therapy took place in groups, where sessions were based around developing techniques for dealing with whatever malady, or its symptoms, had landed the person in hospital in the first place.

If you stood out the front of the hospital on tiptoe, you could see Parliament. The only benefit of this arrangement was that I could visit Nigel on my lunchbreaks. Otherwise, the proximity to the source of the difficulties that led him to being there in the first place would have been almost cruel. The two-storey building reminded me of the adolescent hospital I'd once been a patient of, but its residents were more subdued. One time we ran into a colleague on the footpath outside as we were saying goodbye. Her smile was forced, but at least she stopped. Most people, now, would walk past him, the way they walked past me in the corridors of Parliament, on the rare occasions I ventured there.

On these visits Nigel and I didn't say much. We sat on the tastefully patterned sofas, feet on the less tastefully patterned carpet, and leaned into each other. We watched residents displaying various levels of misery in their postures and faces.

'When you're here,' Nigel said, 'you realise things can always be worse.'

. . .

Since his arrest, every action, every piece of correspondence, suggested the Legislative Council was going to sack Nigel. Nigel's lawyers pointed out that he hadn't been found guilty of anything, mentioned heady notions of the presumption of innocence and procedural fairness. Eventually the Privileges Committee – chaired by the President – agreed to receive a statement from Nigel *in camera*.

I too sent a letter to the Privileges Committee, emphasising to them my correspondence was not privileged. I told them that a man should not be judged by his worst day. I'd begged for procedural fairness too, that he ought to be heard by an unbiased decision-maker, at minimum.

I was on a visit to the prisoner transport facilities at the Supreme Court of Western Australia on the morning of Wednesday 12 August 2015 when I got a phone call from a colleague. I had been successful in getting a job in the public sector, but the decision had been appealed by an unsuccessful applicant, and so I was forced to keep going to work for the Council, firstly on half days after my time off, and then full-time. Unlike the week after Nigel's arrest, I now heard from senior managers constantly. They didn't want me to drive Nigel's car into work because it caused staff stress and anxiety, even though I'd been driving it in since April. My past timesheets were reviewed and I was asked to change leave types and resubmit the forms for approval. When I asked to purchase leave, it was denied. When I asked to take a secondment to the Legislative Assembly, it was denied. I was called to task for telling my colleagues in the Council office I was going for job interviews. This might upset morale, I was told.

Now my colleague said, 'Did you know they're going to sack Nigel today?'

'They can't,' I said. 'He's in a psychiatric hospital.'

'They've called an urgent *in camera* meeting of the Legislative Council at lunchtime,' she said. 'What else could it be?'

I got off the phone and walked shakily to one of my committee members. I asked if it were true. She said she couldn't tell me anything, but her expression was a mixture of sheepish and avid.

'Fuck,' I said, and walked out of the Supreme Court to call Nigel.

It is unlawful to terminate an employee in Australia if they are in hospital. To prevent Nigel from being able to sue for unlawful dismissal, the Legislative Council was going to terminate him under parliamentary privilege. Parliamentary privilege prevents anybody outside of Parliament using anything that is said in Parliament as part of a legal proceeding. The idea of privilege is to make sure parliamentarians can speak about issues without fear or favour, but it is not for nothing Parliament is sometimes referred to as Coward's Castle.

I considered going into the Legislative Council after the lunchbreak and making a scene. I knew what they were going to do, and I wanted someone to know what I felt about it, how unfair it was. But I decided it was more important to be with Nigel. The managers obviously anticipated my first consideration, because they sent someone to the Committee office to make sure I didn't head for the President's gallery or the public one. But I was already over the road, at the building from which you could see Parliament if you tiptoed.

Once again I was in front of a computer screen, watching the live feed of Parliament about to deliver bad news concerning Nigel, except this time we were in Nigel's room in the psychiatric hospital. The proceedings were short. The President tabled the report. The Leader of the House moved a motion that the Council accept the recommendation in the Procedure and Privileges Committee report, and then another that the Governor be advised. The report appeared immediately on the website as soon as it was tabled in Parliament. Nigel clicked on the link, read the recommendation, and collapsed forward, elbows on knees, forehead in hands. I put one hand on his back. There was no comfort I could offer.

45

By the end of 2015 – after the court appearances, my change of job, finishing more full-time law studies – I was exhausted. I was exhausted but I had to keep going. Nigel had become more withdrawn, spending days on the couch, muttering to himself. I asked him if he knew he was talking to himself. He did, but it was the way he was trying to sort out the complicated strands of his thoughts, picking them apart, trying to sort them, to set them in an order he could live with.

After twenty-five years of turning up to the same building, day after day, the absence of daily structure precipitated his complete collapse. He did not know if he would ever work again. His criminal record screening showed pending charges, which prevented him from getting even basic manual jobs. He did not know if he would go to jail. Even though I'd taken out a $50,000 loan he promised he would repay, he'd run out of money and didn't know how he would afford the trial that would take place in October 2016. I began to feel, unbidden, the similarities between watching Nigel grapple with what was happening to him as I felt watching John's deterioration. Having to deal with it but feeling excluded from it. Being affected by it without being able to have any effect on it. Except that Nigel assured me he was working his way through things. He just didn't know how long it would take.

I started a legal internship program at Legal Aid in January 2016. I was working in criminal appeals, which meant researching and forming a legal opinion on whether sentencing principles had been correctly applied, defences argued fulsomely, juries directed lawfully. If they weren't, they might be worthy of appeal. I read entire transcripts of court cases and witness statements, listened to recordings of 000 calls while murderous fights were occurring in the background, combed through photographs of evidence: fatal wounds, damaged property, bloody weapons and their locations. I visited one of the few prisons I hadn't already been to when I worked for the Legislative Council, lining up with other agencies such as Centrelink to provide information to prisoners, whose agitation and sense of grievance sometimes made me glad of the prison guards who hovered nearby.

But for me the most valuable part of the internship was going to the Magistrates Court to shadow the duty lawyer. The duty lawyer sat behind perspex while one by one accused men who had been in custody overnight were brought in by a guard. They would explain what they'd done, and the role of the duty lawyer was to provide advice on how to plead, what mitigations there might be, what outcomes were likely once they went before the Magistrate. The lawyer had to control, cajole, and placate each accused, who she often had to interrupt with, 'Have a listen. If you can't listen, I can't represent you. Okay?' They were charged with breach of bail, of receiving, of breaching restraining orders, of possessing child pornography. All of the accused had extensive criminal records, usually on minor matters, peppered with short stints inside when they ventured beyond petty crime. It made me realise what summary charges meant in practice and how unusual it was to be a middle-aged professional man ending up with the set of charges Nigel had.

In the context of Parliament, what Nigel did was considered beyond the pale. In the context of the spectrum of criminality, the oddity of it was striking.

...

Meanwhile John moved from the first care facility in which he had been placed because he was denuding their gardens. There was nowhere else for him to walk, and all he did was walk, all day, so if he was limited to the small area inside he became agitated and aggressive. Dementia units are often designed for the elderly, not for the young and strong. So the guardian was able to get him moved to a facility specifically designed for people with early-onset Alzheimer's. It had a circular design, so residents could wander into similar-looking houses, and a garden designed around a central activities room. The outside area was expansive and peaceful, with little paths winding through a garden so extensive John could strip all the foliage he liked.

Now that I have spent a decade visiting, I see residents cycle through similar behavioural phases to those John did. It seems that the shrinking brain activates the same areas. At first John was content there, smiling at the female staff in particular, saying 'Jules Jules Chris Morgan Shaunie Annie. Annie is beautiful, Annie is beautiful.' Once he saw Hecta relieving himself outside, and he looked at me and said, 'Episcopalian?'

Then came the stage when he became incontinent and began eating his own shit, and/or taking his pants off and sitting on the other residents' beds post defecation. The staff couldn't manage him, so he was transferred to an older adult psychiatric unit. On Annie's nineteenth birthday we visited him at the unit. He was dressed in a women's nylon onesie to stop him pulling his pants down, had shat himself without anyone noticing, and had rubbed sunscreen into his eyes.

John returned back to his usual residence after his behaviour had improved and the care home staff were given training on how to deal with his coprophagia. For a few months he was fine, and then he began becoming easily enraged. He became enraged at showering, lashing out at staff with his still muscular arms.

One day he wanted to walk Hecta and kept asking with a tone of agitation, so I put Hecta on the lead and passed it to him. Without warning he began to yell and yanked on the lead, flinging Hecta into the wall, causing the dog to yelp with pain. John didn't notice, and I had to wrestle the lead out of his hand before retreating into the nurses' office to check Hecta for broken bones and to weep.

...

The barrister who represented Nigel at the trial was cheerful, corpulent, and had a crack-shot mind. He was representing Nigel pro bono and seemed chirpy at Nigel's prospects.

'So,' he boomed when Nigel and I went to see him. 'There's a threshold. It's a yes or no question. Was your reasoning impaired because of your mental state?'

Nigel waited.

'They all agree you had mental impairment – major depression, yes. Paranoid, maybe. Delusional, perhaps. Will it reach the threshold?'

The barrister leaned back in his chair.

'So their guy says you weren't suffering from delusions,' he said. 'Your treating guy and our two guys say you were. All of them, except for one of our guys, say you had a major depressive episode.'

'Nobody can decide which brand of crazy I am, you mean,' Nigel said.

'It'll be between two experts on the day,' the barrister said.

'Worst-case scenario, what happens?' Nigel said.

'Well,' the barrister said. 'You're probably going to get a bunch of fines.'

'Prison?'

'Possible,' he said, 'but unlikely. Still, it depends on the magistrate you get.'

Nigel had spoken to a friend of ours who had been sentenced to six months in jail for dealing marijuana. He'd asked him what it was like in prison, about the daily routine, about the worst parts. He'd said he was prepared, if it came to it. He was a big guy. He'd be all right, he assured me. If it came to that.

'I'll argue for a suspended sentence and a small fine, given your impecunious circumstances. If the threshold isn't reached,' the barrister added.

On the day of the trial, the barrister was undeterred by the phalanx of reporters and photographers jostling for a last picture of Nigel pre-trial. Inside the court, Nigel's son, his son's new wife, my daughter and five of our friends formed a protective circle around Nigel as we sat on connected seats that squeaked every time someone shifted. It was a small courtroom, crammed with reporters with their notepads out. Nigel's ex-wife and her friend were there, and someone who looked so like the Clerk's wife we assumed it was her sister. Nigel looked ahead at the seat on which the Magistrate would shortly be seated.

There were two psychiatrists who gave evidence, one for the defence, one for the prosecution. They agreed that Nigel had been mentally ill at the time of the offending, but disagreed both on what the illness was and whether it rendered him criminally responsible. After their opinions, the Magistrate dismissed the court to consider his verdict.

We escaped to an unremarkable corridor in the court building, hoping to avoid the media and Nigel's ex-wife, then we headed to the city library, where we figured nobody would think to look for us. For two and a half hours we waited. Nigel said nothing as the rest of us tried not to comment on what we thought about the evidence the psychiatrists had given, the Magistrate's questions, the response he had to each of them. The psychiatrist brought in by the prosecution had seemed the more assured, the more certain. The other was less definitive.

When we were called back in, Nigel was ushered to the bar table. He was asked to stand to hear the Magistrate read out his verdict.

I sat straight, had to remind myself to breathe. Nigel was in front of me, his suit tight across his broad shoulders, his hands clasped together. His head was bowed.

The Magistrate said that while there was no argument as to Nigel suffering a mental illness, he preferred the evidence of the prosecution's expert because he had seen Nigel closer to the time of the offending.

'Eccentric behaviour, or out-of-character behaviour,' he intoned, 'does not meet the threshold of criminal insanity. I am satisfied that at the time of the offending, Mr Lake had sufficient awareness of the wrongness of his actions to be criminally responsible.'

He declared that Nigel was guilty on all counts.

My face froze. Kitty squeezed my hand. His daughter-in-law turned to me, eyes wide. In front of us, Nigel's head bowed lower. I did not dare to look around to see the gloating or satisfaction that may have been on other people's faces.

The Magistrate took submissions on sentencing.

The barrister launched into an impassioned argument for a spent conviction, citing Nigel's clean record, his mental illness, the cost already wrought on him with the loss of his career, income, and reputation. The voluminous victim impact statement from the Clerk was passed around to the Magistrate.

The Magistrate asked the prosecution if it opposed a spent conviction. The prosecution did not demur.

The Magistrate was silent for a time, then stated that there would be $2,300 in fines, plus costs. He agreed the conviction would be spent.

A spent conviction meant that the finding of guilty, and the penalties imposed, would not appear on any criminal record check. Nigel would not be legally obliged to disclose his record to future employers.

When we walked from the court, we were followed for the last time by photographers and reporters wanting to know if Nigel had anything to say about his sentence, if he was relieved or disappointed, if he had anything to say to the Clerk and his family.

Everyone agreed it was the best outcome Nigel could have hoped for, aside, of course, from being found not guilty. Being declared insane by a court would have had its own set of consequences. So now we had to keep going. For the first time in twenty-one months there were no trial dates to anticipate, no wondering what was going to happen or whether Nigel was going to jail, or how he was going to find a pro bono barrister.

It should have felt like a relief.

...

On the Saturday morning after the court case I took Hecta for a walk to the service station to get a copy of the newspaper. By agreement, the state newspaper's photographer had taken Nigel down to the foreshore in Maylands the afternoon of the trial, and I had joined them. On the way we chatted about local cafés and living in a suburb that was resisting being gentrified, mixing as it did the houses of the middle class and blocks of 60s flats inhabited by low-income workers, refugees, people with mental health and drug issues. Gareth Parker had briefly appeared to get some final quotes for the article he would, after nineteen months, be able to publish.

'It wasn't a very satisfying trial,' he said.

I watched his face to see if it indicated anything else, but he was carefully neutral. He'd checked quotes with me, and I'd had to provide proof that John did indeed have dementia and was in care, so I knew he was going to mention the nature of the beginning of Nigel's relationship with me, at minimum. But I did not know what tone he would take or how sympathetic he was going to be.

Since meeting with Gareth the previous year, Nigel had provided him with all the information he could, including his psychiatrists' reports, and the writing he'd done to try to understand himself. Coming from a man who had such difficulty verbalising his feelings, the writings were surprising:

deeply considered, insightful, and articulate. They'd made more sense of Nigel than I'd been able to, even with all my practice in reading the nuances of human behaviour and my desire to understand human motivation.

In his writings Nigel had explained how, because of the extreme anxiety of his two adoptive parents, he'd learned to keep his feelings firmly to himself, lest he heighten their distress. He explained that he'd grown up with both sets of grandparents living with the family. One grandmother had an anxiety disorder so great she spent her days sitting on the couch, muttering and making repetitive noises. The other was domineering, taking charge of everyone around her; with her, you were either in firm favour or her bitterest opponent. She'd adored Nigel, and had been proud of his sporting achievements, his scholarship to a private school. She was someone who, if you weren't adored by her, you kept away from. He reflected on what that might have meant for the choices he made in future relationships.

The front page of the newspaper featured a picture of Nigel, standing on a spit of sand surrounded by the shallow waters of the Swan River, looking into the middle distance, his hands in his jeans pockets. The headline read 'How my slide to darkness ended in terror' and continued on page four with 'Mental fall's sad aftermath'. I hastily read the reasonably detailed account of 'previously unreleased details of the circumstances leading to Lake's offences', ending with bolded details of how to contact mental health services. There was a brief mention of me, of our affair, and of John's dementia in the final column. I breathed out. Well. That wasn't as bad as I'd been expecting. I thought it was going to include all the details of our affair.

'He must have decided against including it,' I said to Nigel when he got up. 'It's actually all okay.'

Nigel perused the paper while I drank a coffee and tried to breathe out the adrenaline. Then he said, 'Julesy, you saw there's more inside?'

In my haste I had missed an extensive spread in the centre of the newspaper, which captured the detail missing from the front pages. It was titled 'Falling into a fantasy', printed onto the pale blue sky of another photo of Nigel, this time sitting on the jetty, his impressive shoulders and arms barely contained by his cream shirt.

'Oh God,' I said.

And there it was. There were more photos. There was the official photo showing Nigel's black eye, another of Nigel and me surrounded by photographers and cameras, and one of Nigel's ex-wife as she left court. The detail about Nigel's upbringing, family, marriage. The previous affair he'd had before me, his ex-wife's four affairs. And then the blow-by-blow details of ours.

'Well, it's really all out there now,' I said.

'It is, Julesy,' he said.

'And it's pretty sympathetic, even if he doesn't let you off the hook,' I said.

'It could have been worse,' he said.

'At least this will be the last time you're on the front page of the newspaper,' I said.

'Yep,' he said.

'Not an era I'm unhappy to leave behind.'

'Neither, Julesy.'

The public side might have been over, but the private fallout wasn't. When Nigel's mother read the newspaper she was humiliated at being portrayed as highly anxious: not because she wasn't, but because she was worried that people would think Nigel's breakdown was her fault. Nigel explained that the description had come from a psychiatrist's report and that he didn't write the article, but she would not take any reassurance. Before the article she would call Nigel every day, and he spent patient hours listening to her and calming her anxiety. After the article, she stopped calling, even on his birthday. Nigel tried to speak with her, to reason with her, to no avail. He'd believed as a child that expressing his feelings would cause harm to his parents. Now he knew.

And there was more fallout to come.

46

At the end of 2016, the month following the trial, I had a week-long residency at a private school I'd never visited before. It was a co-ed school in the western suburbs, and I had a busy schedule of high school classes, running a series of workshops that developed writing skills for talented students. The new head of English was the husband of one of my former colleagues at Parliament. He'd seen me present in a previous role and was pleased that I could take the time off my new job in health to be at the school.

From the start, something at the school felt wrong. Normally I found it easy to build rapport with teenage students, but after two full days at the school I felt drained. I had been trying and failing to enthuse the classes, and while they were polite, they were strangely diffident. At the end of one class, a boy made a point of asking why I wasn't wearing a wedding ring. I had been discussing *Before You Forget*, which I'd shown the group the proofs of. I responded, warily, that it felt strange to wear a ring when the person I was married to no longer knew who I was.

I was outside texting Nigel about the strangeness of the day, waiting for the school pick-up traffic to clear, when I noticed a woman staring at me. Her expression was displeased. She looked familiar but I couldn't place her.

When I got home I put vegetables in the oven to roast and poured myself a glass of wine. I was sitting, wine in hand, when a sound like a shotgun, followed by shattering, made me jump. The interior oven glass had shattered, leaving glassy chunks through the roast vegetables.

Nigel cleaned up the mess, and I lamented that the extra money I was hoping to save from the week's work would be needed to fix the oven instead. Then I got a phone call from the person who had booked me at the school.

'I'm so sorry,' he said. 'I've been asked to tell you not to come back again this week.'

'What?' I said. 'What have I done?'

I thought back to what I'd said in my presentations, examined any offhand comments I'd made that could have been misconstrued. I was always careful to try to balance being honest about myself with not causing offence. I'd once had a student ask if I were anti-Semitic when I told them that Gwen had worked for a Jewish doctor's family in Melbourne. I explained that I meant quite the opposite, that they'd taken in a young woman in trouble, despite her being Christian, but the incident had made me aware of the different interpretations people could take from your words, and consequently the need for me to use them more carefully.

'Your presence is upsetting to some of the students,' he said. 'I'm sorry, I should have realised.'

I thought about the boy, about the half-familiar woman. About the first court visit, the children in their uniforms. Then I understood.

'Is it the Clerk's kids?' I asked. 'Is this their school?'

'I can't say anything more,' he said. 'It's nothing to do with your presentations. We'll pay you in full, of course.'

'But I haven't done anything,' I said. 'The trial is over. Nigel had a brain snap and he's been punished for it. What has that got to do with me?'

He gave me the number of the principal. She would not say anything more. She would not apologise. I protested the risk to my reputation, what the kids would think, how upsetting it was.

I went to the school early, before it opened, to collect the books and old journals I'd left there. I sat in the librarian's office and talked and cried. Then I went home and looked at the broken oven, at the couch where Nigel was spending his days and evenings after sleeping late.

When I'd taken out the fifty-thousand-dollar legal loan that would take five years to pay, back before anything was public, Nigel had promised me that I would never have to pay any of it. He'd kept his word, eking out the last of his payout for annual and long-service leave he'd got from the Legislative Council. He kept his word, but it meant I was paying for everything else in the meantime.

Before Nigel got up at nearly midday, I'd opened a bottle of wine. I'd looked out at the courtyard with the bottlebrush tree that had already lost its spring blossom, which was now in clumps of puffy red all over the pavement. The fronds of the palm and its yellow seeds had fallen too. Once Nigel would have ensured it was immaculate. Now he didn't see the things he once would have. Or no longer cared about them.

When Nigel emerged he looked warily at the wine but didn't comment. He went out the back for his morning coffee and cigarette, Hecta's claws tapping on the tiles as he followed.

He came back in and sat down opposite me. 'You okay, Julesy?'

'I've managed all of it,' I said. 'The court cases, the looks, leaving my job, the effect on Annie, all of that. But it's never affected my writing before. It was my one separate thing.'

'I know,' he said. 'You shouldn't have to be shouldering any of this.'

'I can't do it anymore,' I said.

'How can I fix this?' he said. 'Tell me.'

'You've got to get a job,' I said. 'I don't care what it is. I can't carry this.'

'I'm trying,' he said. 'What else can I do?'

'You'll have to figure it out,' I said. 'I can't do this again. I can't take care of another man who can't take care of himself.'

Nigel looked pained at being compared to John.

'Okay, Julesy,' he said. 'I'm sorry.'

The statistics for retrenched men over fifty ever becoming employed again gave me no cause for hope. But in the following weeks, through Kitty's daughter-in-law, he got his first job, putting together shelves in a factory. His friend got him some work as a process server. And then, also through his friend, finally, he was offered a job as a trades assistant in a mining equipment factory. He began to get up earlier than me, dressed in hi-vis, like so many workers in Western Australia, the economy of which has only ever thrived on mining.

He came home every afternoon so exhausted he slept on the couch for a while before dinner. Then he started going out for trips to mining sites for days at a time. Annie would come over then, and we would go out to dinner or stay in and talk. We'd talk about John's latest symptom, about her friends at art college, about things that were happening with my sisters. We'd laugh and dance to the latest songs she'd introduced me to, usually with Nicki Minaj, Azealia Banks and Kendrick Lamar on high rotation.

Nigel started smiling more. When people asked what he was doing, he told them and described the machinery the factory made: screens and feeders, industrial sieves with the surface area of ten trampolines that were designed to shake valuable ores from the earth they were buried in. If anybody complained about their desk job, he began to joke, 'You should try getting a real job,' or 'Some of us have actually got to work for a living.'

The final signal that Nigel had returned – not to his old self but to a self that could accept Before, After, and Now – occurred in the back courtyard of our unit.

The unregarded back courtyard served as a toilet for Hecta and an undercover area for smokers. It was not an area I would voluntarily enter without a pressing reason. It had been years since our back neighbour had requested that the tree we'd inherited in the corner of the courtyard be cut back. It spent autumn and winter shedding spiky foliage, and it extended over our neighbour's vegetable patch. The neighbours were polite and did not insist, but for a long time all Nigel had done was ringbark the tree, in the hope its canopy would die. It proved impervious to ringbarking or the occasional prune on the neighbour's side.

One day in 2019 I returned home to find the entire courtyard filled with the sawn-off limbs of the old tree. The pile came to Nigel's chest, so dense that even Hecta could not weave his way underneath without risking an eye. Nigel ordered a skip bin and carried the branches through the unit and out the front, then vacuumed and mopped the floors of the house more thoroughly than I had ever done. He took to the weed-, lichen- and grit-filled pavers with an old kitchen knife, on his hands and knees. He went through the shed, which was where he'd put the boxes brought from the Legislative Council in 2015 after I'd pleaded with him to do so. He sorted through them all, finally, ordering another skip bin to take away the files, folders, parliamentary programs, forgotten coffee machines and coffee pods, and old gym supplies.

A friend had given us newly propagated succulents, and Nigel helped me fill pots with soil and water in the new plantings. We bought modest outdoor furniture, consisting of three chairs with bright blue cushions, low enough for our new rescue dog, Truffle, to launch herself up onto while Hecta mooched around the courtyard, sniffing for signs of rodent life or spilled potting mix, which he was always keen to sample. We could, finally, sit outside in the previously unregarded space, watching succulents of different shapes grow, bloom, and grow pups at their bases. The traffic sounds were distant, and wattlebirds turned up in the afternoon to peck at insect life in the creeper that grew on the trellis. Finally we could sit, not needing to rehash what had happened or speculate on what might. We could sit in silence, remarking only about what we were having for dinner, what antics the dogs had got up to at the dog park that day. We could sit, finally, in peace.

...

The aerial roots of banyan trees hang like ropes, waiting for their macaque Rapunzels to ascend. Their enormous high-gloss leaves enclose the primates, small and large, wending about under the canopy in an atmosphere so humid it necessitates the regular and vigorous application of insect repellent on sweaty skin. At first, the skittering of monkeys makes Kitty and me yelp and hang on to each other; when one leaps up onto Kitty's bag, we pray that it is not rabid and will not bite. In the event, it only wants to try to drink from Kitty's water bottle. Eventually we calm down. The baby macaques leap about endearingly, chasing each other up and down tree trunks, roots, and rocky terraces, and occasionally submit to being groomed by their mothers. Only the larger males appear to have any malevolence to them, and are batted away by keepers with bamboo poles to prevent their suspicion of strange-smelling humans translating into a bite-based message to begone.

I had never been to Bali before. I had associated it with food poisoning, oblivious drunken Australians in Bintang t-shirts, airplane crashes, exploitation of impoverished people, marijuana strapped to surfboards. But I wanted to go away, and so Kitty and I nervously booked flights on Air Asia and accommodation in a new hotel with aqua-blue decor, and a week after Nigel's trial we were ready to board. Nigel was riding his motorbike to the Great Southern, to have time alone to think. Annie stayed home and took care of Hecta.

When we arrived at the airport at midnight, we were greeted by the sweet smell of humid air laden with incense. We drove through the night down winding streets, appearing to be driving headlong into traffic at intersections, but which in the event parted for us. At the hotel we were greeted with a tropical drink and a piece of mangosteen.

In the smoky morning we could make out the outline of Bali's biggest volcano, Mount Agung. When we ventured out, the rank odours wafted up from time to time from open gutters as we dodged lazing street dogs and spaghetti-like clusters of electrical wires hanging at tourist-head-height. We admired the small, beautifully arranged woven baskets of flowers, food offerings, and incense that are everywhere placed and replaced each day to appease various Balinese Hindu gods. The beach was crammed with tourists on rented deckchairs under Air Asia umbrellas, between which hawkers wove, carrying hats, wristbands, and kites. The sand was raked to rid it of plastic debris and other rubbish fed by tributaries of murky runoff, but the rising waves, too big for anyone but the most fearless surfers, were clean and blue, letting off white spume as they broke.

After visiting the monkey forest, Kitty and I found a restaurant overlooking a rice field. We ate sticks of tempeh and tofu dipped in peanut sauce, indulged in glasses of wine that cost more than the food. The harmony sought and practised by the Balinese – between people, with the environment, with the gods – created in me a settling. The humidity slowed us down, and we always had to look where we were walking as we made our way back to town to flag down a ride back to the coast. You didn't want to step on an offering and offend the gods who had been so kind to let you come here.

And whatever it was that led you to come here was now part of the harmony you can hear in the humming of insects invisible, in the susurrations of the broad tropical leaves above, in the softened consonants of Balinese and Indonesian. You walk on soil enriched by the eruptions that formed it, and may re-form it yet.

BORN TO BE ALIVE

47

In 2004 I wrote a young adult novel, published in 2006 as *Bye, Beautiful*, which was based on Gwen's family and dealt in no small part with the consequences of a young woman getting pregnant out of wedlock.

Indeed, I named the main character Frank and made him a country copper in 1966 in a wheatbelt town not unlike the Mukinbudin I knew as a child. I kept the order and gender of the children the same, but I did my best to invent their characters. It said something about their relationship that when they read the novel, both Marlene and Gwen thought the vivacious older sister who gets in trouble was the other. Marlene envied Gwen her quick intelligence, her musicality, her childhood prettiness; Gwen envied Marlene her ability to placate Frank, to always appear to do what was asked of her, and to disguise her impulses so that nobody would even know they existed.

When I finished the novel, my wondering about the brother who was out there, somewhere, sharpened into curiosity.

By this time, Gwen had just had the series of strokes that led to her being hemiplegic for the remainder of her days, and with each hospitalisation her husband, to whom she'd been married since 1990, said, 'Well, I've got her for a bit more yet.'

With this more particular uncertainty about her longevity, I asked her, 'How would you feel if I tried to find your son?'

Gwen blinked at the television. Her swollen feet were on the footrest of her recliner rocker, a new electric one specially designed to tip forward to standing when required.

'He wouldn't want to know me,' Gwen said.

'He might,' I said. 'And, Mum, if you don't try now, you might not get a chance.'

She shook her head. 'It's too late now. Just leave it.'

'But—'

'Just bloody leave it,' she said, her voice rising. 'You have to get my permission, and I say no.'

Not wanting to agitate her into another burst blood vessel, I left it, until my own agitation led me into making quiet inquiries of my own. It turned out that because he was born in the state of Victoria, I was able to search as a sibling, a fact that no doubt would have deepened Gwen's loathing of the place. I knew his birthday because of every year Gwen had mentioned how old he would be on each cold August day. My aunty Marlene, who fully supported my surreptitious searching, was able to supply the name of the hospital he'd been born in.

After some months of form filling, undertaking counselling as required by the department, and waiting, I received a letter indicating the department had located Gwen's son, my brother. He had been adopted into a doctor's family, where he was the youngest of four children, also all adopted, which indicated that he likely knew of his own adoption. He had avoided the genetic lottery of cystic fibrosis and childhood tumours and appeared to be married and a parent to a child in a very nice suburb of Melbourne. Would I like the department to indicate that contact was sought?

For this, I returned to Gwen's house, where I ensured that there was nothing heavy on her side table that she might throw at me with her good hand when she learned of my defiance. I announced I had something serious to share.

'Mum,' I said. 'I have to tell you something. I think I've found your son.'

Gwen appeared not to have heard me at first. She had muted the sound on the television, but sport was playing on the wide screen that dominated the lounge room. Its gel surface was the only thing not coated in the layer of fine dust that cast a slight blur on the collections of salad bowls and platters unused since the 80s, ornaments such as a pair of Dalmatians, polished cuts of Kimberley rock, carved boab nuts, photographs of relatives who became increasingly deceased the longer the photographs stayed there, stuffed and porcelain meerkats, and crocheted doilies. Her sister had attempted to dust during her most recent visit, but Gwen barked at her to stop, so the dust remained, thickening with each passing year.

'Mum?'

I had never before seen the expression that appeared on her face then, which looked as if it would fold into grief but was held in check through the necessity wrought by the previous forty years. That expression was replaced by another: a cautious, unstable smile.

'Really?' she said. 'Christopher?'

But the name she had given him had been changed by his adoptive parents, and so she had to get used to a new name as he crossed from the child she had imagined to the person who now existed in outline in the folder I handed to her.

'So he's had a good life, then,' Gwen said, noting the suburb he'd grown up in and lived in, the composition of the family.

'It looks like it,' I said. 'Do you want me to see if he wants contact?'

This time she said yes.

...

The counsellor whose services were a precondition for contact warned me that adopted children, if they want to know their birth families, usually look before they are thirty-five. Boys are less likely to search than girls. Sometimes the meetings go well; more often they are awkward, nature being no match for nurture. What was lost through relinquishing a child is never restored. He might be angry at being contacted. He might be shocked. He might simply choose not to respond.

Were we sure we wanted to go ahead?

'Please send the letter,' I said. I gave my work contact details as well as my home ones. I wanted him to see that I was a professional, that the mismatch of class and education suggested by our childhood postcodes wouldn't be an issue with me, at least.

For the first couple of weeks I was nervous. I wondered how Gwen might react if my brother refused contact. Was I causing her more distress? What if he was angry with her? What if, despite appearances, his family life had been terrible and he was damaged beyond repair? It happened, and I knew plenty of people it had happened to. But she had already given up her son. It couldn't get any worse than that, could it?

When the weeks became months, I comforted myself by knowing that at least she knew he was alive, that he had gone to a good family, and that it was the best she could have hoped for.

One day I was at work when my desk phone rang. I picked it up, thinking it would be a request for me to complete some task or follow up something I'd inquired about, or, most hopefully, a colleague asking me to lunch. I didn't bother looking at the caller ID, knowing it would only be one of those possibilities.

Instead, the person on the other end asked for confirmation that I was, in fact, Julia Lawrinson. Then he said, 'Hello. This is your brother speaking.'

. . .

Eight-year-old Annie and I were in a mad rush to get from Sydney's North Shore, where we'd been wandering around Luna Park with our luggage, to the airport so we could depart for Melbourne. Lugging our suitcases up the steep slope to the train station while Annie complained about having to leave the fairground so hastily tested both my cardiovascular fitness and my parenting patience.

In my haste I had purchased the wrong train tickets – suburban ones, not ones for the airport line – so when we were required to change at Central, I was sent to the back of a queue I didn't have time to wait in by a railway employee with a blank face. At first I politely explained the urgency of getting to the airport, so that I could meet my long-lost brother for the first time, then explained again more beseechingly, in case he could not keep up with my rapid-fire narrative, and finally, in hope of appealing to masculine protectiveness, pointed to Annie, whose shortness made her look even younger than she was, collapsed over the suitcases with exaggerated exhaustion. When he remained unmoved, the nervousness that had been building over the previous days, plus the fear I had of missing the brother I had waited thirty-five years to meet, sent me into a hysterical frenzy. I yelled, I swore, I wept. I was in Sydney. I would never see these people again. I did not care.

The man also did not care, with or without the scene I was making.

A uniformed woman took pity on me, however, and walked me to a queue-less area to purchase the required tickets, then ushered me through a turnstile, wishing us good luck. We reached the platform as one train was pulling out and, when we finally arrived at the airport, we had to sprint over the shiny, polished floors and were still sprinting as our names were being paged across the terminal.

We scampered through the portal and onto the plane, welcomed by the Qantas staff, eyed balefully by passengers held up by our tardiness.

In our seats, Annie happily donned headphones to watch *Chicken Little*, while I leaned my forehead against the window, using the hour-and-a-half flight to ready myself for the meeting we were flying toward.

When my brother, who I now knew as Rob, first called three months earlier, we had begun speaking as if we were taking up from an earlier conversation. There were no uncomfortable silences. It was, from the start, a warm and wide-ranging discussion of his life, our lives. I asked about his childhood, quelling my envy as he described his comfortable, stable home, holidays in the family's cottage by the seaside, an education at the top private boys' school in Melbourne. All four children had been told, individually, they were adopted, but the subject was never raised again, and nobody outside the family knew. When I asked why he'd never looked for us, he said, 'I always had the sense I'd been given up with love, and taken in with love. I never felt I was missing out on anything.'

Reflecting on our contrasting childhoods, I could only agree.

He'd inherited Gwen's penchant for mathematics and played hockey, as she had. He had once gone on a national quiz show, which Gwen and I were avid fans of. It was strange to think of us watching him without realising who we saw. We talked about books, and about music.

'I don't know why,' he said, 'but I've always loved early Beatles music.'

He had never been to Perth, although one of his brothers lived there. I explained that Gwen had had strokes and could not travel, but I made plans to come, and for him to meet me and Annie and Marlene, who lived on the other side of Melbourne.

So here we were, flying toward this meeting, hoping that our phone and email ease would continue in person.

I took Annie's hand and we shuffled with the other incoming passengers down the aisle and the gangway, heading toward the meeting area. Annie was bouncing around: 'We're going to meet Uncle Rob! We're going to meet Uncle Rob!'

Even if I hadn't known who I was looking for, I like to think I would have recognised Rob because of his similarity to Gwen's brother, to Gwen herself. One thing Gwen's family was skilled at were enveloping hugs; Rob shared this too.

'Jules,' he said, smiling. 'Good to finally meet you. And you must be Annie.'

'Hello!' Annie grinned.

'How was your flight?' he said.

'Mummy was swearing at the man in Sydney,' she said. 'She was swearing and swearing because we were late. But we got here anyway.'

Rob's eyebrows headed toward his hairline.

'Welcome to the family,' I said.

48

In December 2019, Gwen woke up one morning and could not move. My stepfather called an ambulance. That evening he called me. Not long after Nigel and I had hightailed it to the hospital, not long after I was shocked by the contrast between the hot night and the frigid air of the medical admissions unit, I was ushered out of the room so she could be resuscitated.

For eighteen days, every movement hurt her. She held my stepfather's hand while he lifted iced coffee and scotch to his mouth with the other; if he wasn't there, she held mine. When my uncle offered, she took Jesus into her heart. Her lips had become bloodied during the resuscitation she'd needed on arrival at hospital, and she let me swab away the scabs that formed, as well as the mucus that coated her tongue and cheeks as the morphine increased. My cousin's daughters sat around her bed and sang her a song about missing a mother. We cried for different reasons.

On the last day the roads were quiet as I headed for the hills to the hospice she'd been transferred to. When I stepped out of the car, I breathed in the eucalyptus scent the hot morning releases. Out of the corner of my eye I saw birds flitting between the muscular branches of the trees older than I am, or swooping over the ground slippery with gravel and honky nuts. There is a pulse to the shhh sound of the invisible insects, if you listen hard enough.

There are so many things I don't yet know at the moment I step into her hospice room, the summer light too bright to admit, glowing around the closed blind like the silhouette of a doorway.

There are the words my stepfather will say to me before telling me to leave my mother's house.

The drink I will pick up again.

My stepfather snapping at the funeral director, 'I can't hear a fucking word you're saying.' My uncle repeating loudly, 'She wants to know if you want Gwen embalmed or not!'

Cousins who remind me of the women in our family who have always put their heels down when they walk as if they mean it, of Gran and the steeliness under her silence.

My daughter gazing steadily back at the people at Gwen's funeral who eye her tattoos and who display shock or disapproval at my eulogy.

My oldest friend Nobbly saying, 'Welcome to the Fellowship of the Fucked On by Fucked Shit.'

The five decades of my writing collected by my mother, which I find in her bedside drawer along with the school reports she kept, and the newspaper clippings from when I was in the comedy group.

Nigel holding up my phone through the funeral so my brother in Melbourne can see the service by FaceTime, be present to hear my uncle say he should always have been part of our family.

The tuna mornay Nikki brings me, the enveloping hugs brought by Kitty and Claire and Sarah, daily messages from my friend from the adolescent psychiatric hospital.

Telling John that he won't be able to make Gwen laugh anymore, though I know he doesn't understand what I am saying any more than he knows who I am, who his daughter is.

The single picture Gwen took of the moment of Annie's birth, perfectly clear despite her shaking hands, tucked into a photo album of Annie that stopped being added to after Gwen's stroke.

My dad, my stepmother and sisters steadfast, constant and kind.

My friends a solid, colourful block at the funeral and surrounding me as I drink soda water at the wake afterward.

Nobbly also saying, 'You have been your own parent since you were seven.'

And then my uncle bringing me Gwen's piano accordion. The smell exhaled from the concertina gaps as I press in the right side of the instrument drops me straight into Christmas parties, adults and children dancing to 'Skippy the Bush Kangaroo' and 'Roll Me Over in the Clover' with equal abandon, to Gwen smiling as she sings and revels in the joy her skipping fingers unleash. Nobody taught her to play. She taught herself. It isn't my instrument, and I won't learn it. It reminds me of the good times, however long ago. And it would later give me an idea.

But none of these things have happened yet.

On this quiet summer morning, the Christmas fairy lights in the hospice corridor winked as I walked under them, bright decorations shuddering under the air-conditioning vents. I slowed as I approached her room.

She was alone. Her body twitched and jerked, then stilled again. She made the terrible sounds the end-of-life-care brochure assured me was not drowning, no matter what it sounded like. She was making the sounds that Frank had made when she nursed him, which had so reminded her of the sounds I had made when I gave birth. I remembered how her reassurance in the extremes of drugless labour comforted me.

I stood next to her bed and squeezed her hand. She did not squeeze back. I told her I was praying to her long-dead sister to come and help her. The phone reception was poor in the room. I told her I had to go outside to call her husband. I told her I would be back in a few minutes.

When I returned, at first I thought she was holding her breath. I knew what had happened but for what seemed a long time, before anyone else came, I wanted to stay here, standing at her bedside, knowing she'd waited for me to arrive before she would let go, waited for me to go before she would leave. Two days ago, she'd greeted me with, 'Where have you been?' and then grabbed my hand and said, 'Something's going on, Jules. You'll understand.' She nodded at her husband, reading the newspaper in the vinyl chair by the window. 'Something's going on, I think he's involved.' I didn't care that it was a hallucination. My mother needed me again. Something had been restored.

Now, after the long stillness, she made a sound: *aaah*. Her hands began to curl into fists, and I stroked her cooling forehead. I remembered her coming to collect me from Victoria after my accident. I remembered her being there when my daughter was born, so soon after Frank had died. I'd been at her bedside over recent hospitalisations, one after another. We were there, my mother and I, for those moments that held everything else in place.

...

Later, with the few thousand dollars I wrest from Gwen's estate, I buy a cello. I buy it unsure of whether my fingers, after twenty-odd years of rheumatoid inflammation, will be strong enough to hold down the strings, whether my back, still sometimes stiff from horse-riding-related compressed fractures, will tolerate the playing posture, whether my musical ear is up for the task of fingers running up and down the cello's fretless neck.

But when I first draw the bow across the C string, the cello leans on my breastbone and sends its slow, sonorous sound through my heart. I have found my tonic note, the note of beginning and ending, the note that resolves. I may never know where my mother's ashes are, but I recognise the sound I have been trying to find without knowing I was looking. For as long as the sound lasts, I have a resolution.

A Note on Memory, Accuracy, and Completeness

A memoir is not stenography, my mentor Howard Norman regularly advised me as I was in agonies over the writing of the events and people I describe.

There is a lot of reported dialogue in this memoir. Some of it I can remember; some I have reconstructed from perhaps compilations of memory. I may not have remembered the exact words, but rather an approximation of them. I have, however, stayed true to what I remember of what was said.

This is particularly the case where I have reported what was said in court. In 2002 I requested access to the trial transcripts of 1997 and was refused. So I have relied on what I remember and what I wrote down close in time to the events.

After the introduction of freedom of information laws in Western Australia, I was provided with copies of my psychiatric records from Dr Ian McAlpine and Hillview Terrace Child and Adolescent Psychiatric Hospital, before these notes, and the notes of many of my fellow patients, were 'lost' before the 1997 trial. I also obtained my notes from the long-closed Heathcote Hospital. McAlpine wrote my language verbatim in his notes. I was assisted in writing the sections around Hillview by the 340-page *Report of Investigation under Section 7 of the Mental Health Act 1962: Aspects of the Provision of Child and Adolescent Psychiatric Services at the Hillview Terrace Site* by Neil F. Douglas at Minter Ellison Northmore Hale, which was tabled in the WA Parliament in August 1995.

I referred to my diaries during the writing of this memoir. As with all diaries, mine are only ever a partial account, but they have been helpful for ordering what happened and when. My method was generally to record what I remembered first, then refer to the diaries second.

In doing this I also realised how many things I had to leave out. There are events and experiences that didn't fit the shape of the memoir as a whole, from the serious to the ridiculous: other deaths, life-altering assaults, observations that would offend defamation laws, spiritual awakenings, falling into comedy performance, fits of fury, therapies and therapists, ill-advised career or study attempts, ill-advised television appearances, the pleasures of dog parks, the delights of learning languages as an adult, things done under the influence of alcohol, etc.

For example:

One day I was going through family photos with Gwen, some years after her stroke. She pointed to a person in the photos and said in a matter-of-fact tone, 'He fiddled with me.' She then went on to describe her other childhood sexual assaults by other adult males close to the family, including one taking place while she and her siblings were asleep in Frank's vehicle outside a party.

This finally made sense of some of the puzzle of my mother and her behaviour. It was only after the writing of this memoir that I realised I was describing a history of violences of all stripe against girls and the women they grew into by the men who claimed to love them.

It's one reading.

And finally, to be clear, I am not attempting a reconstruction of events, but rather an interpretation of them in relation to my own experience.

...

There have been many things that made my life worth living, in spite of the title of this memoir.

These include the crews who got me, Nigel and Annie to where we are today.

For me, I have been blessed with people who've been there with best advice at the right time, including but not limited to:

My life-changing and/or life-affirming friendships and connections with Dr Noël (Nobbly) James, Kitty Fardoe and Claire Holmes (my amigas), Nikki Jones and Shaunie Salmon, Miss Sarah, Esther Trneny, Brioni Dunstan, Helen O'Brien, Chrissy Wilson, Danae and Zoe, James and Jamie, Morgan Yasbincek, Jane Grljusich, Scarlette, Hooooode.

Special thanks to old school friends Tim and Bev Webb, Tammy (and Lewis), April, Gayle, Graham Bertolini, Brad and Bee, Kel and Neil F., for providing unexpected sources of hope at the toughest times. And even more thanks, Brad, for reuniting me with Shane after all these decades.

My Butler Street housies, Bridget C., Boudicca, Jarrah and Luka – thanks for the Indigo Girls, the protests, the singing, the naked dashing down the street, the gambolling about in ball gowns, the appliance-breaking soy-milk production.

Loraine Abernethie, for her steadfast friendship, great book recommendations, and concert-going company, and for having the courage of her convictions when many did not.

My ever-reliable, droll, Elgar-loving Dad; Olvi, the best stepmother a person could hope for, whose sage advice kept me sane when Annie was young, and whose legendary cooking has been the happy centre of decades of family lunches; and my sisters Luci (and her lovely tribe) and Alice.

My sibling-like cousins, the Adami kids, who lent me their mum when I needed her, who reminded me of the best of my mum and commiserated with me on the rest. The gift of holidays with you guys at Mukinbudin and Busso, and more recently at Lou's legendary gatherings in Yallingup and Dunsborough.

Kylie McShane (my chosen mother), donelle toussaint, Jo, Shelley – thank you for providing support, turning up at court, prompting me to give evidence to royal commissioners, and being general proof of resilience in spite of all we've been through. To other survivors of Ian McAlpine and Hillview's 'care' – your courage is seen.

Lencie's crew: Pip Brennan, Chandrika Gibson, Cait Calcutt, Kate, Leah Knapp, Tess, Emma Young, Anna Takács, Anne McGregor, Roby, Yew Li, Kerry Mace and Cherry (Harry's heroes), for us all doing for Lence what we thought we couldn't, and for the friendships forged in the midst of it.

Kind colleagues in various workplaces – language schools, health, Parliament, WACHS and CAHS, Steve, Meegs, Debbie, Aresh, Kylie, Mel, Kath, Margitta and Ali, Gin, Miss Chris, Ben, Sara, Helsie, Mel, Erika, Sofia, Eileen – who have offered sympathy and tissues, or wine and laughter as required. I hope my Christmas carol parodies were adequate repayment.

My writing and cottage buddies – including but not limited to Deb, Dianne, Frané, Bettsy, Meg, Teena, Cristy, Bec, Amber and Jen especially my Society of Children's Book Writers and Illustrators crew – for their generosity of spirit, deep conversations, unflagging support, and reminders of what matters.

The rocking Danni Carr, Lyndal and my sober tribe – do the fkn work and don't fkn drink, am I right?

My teachers at school, night school and university who opened up new worlds, most notably Mrs Sally Christmass, Mr Genoni (thanks for the reference!), Marion Campbell, Frauke Chambers.

For Nige, thank you to Pat and Donna, Kat and Dwayne, Fred R., Ian and Claire, Steph, and the people (you know who you are) who offered support when it really mattered. And to Gareth Parker, for being fair and getting it right.

For Annie, thank you to our most awesome Egg (Sam Huxtable), Georgia (my Bish) Gregory, Isy Otto, Gemma Maxwell, Chelsea Crowe, Millie Norrish, Montaine (Montang) Stewart, Ashleigh and Laura. And to Bec O'Neil, in memoriam.

For John, thank you to Graham, Shaunie and Webbo, Laurie Apps, his tennis club crew, and the Phoenix teachers he so loved to entertain.

And thanks to Rob, for allowing himself to be found, and for being the best tour guide, and thanks Liz, Claire, Grace and Jack for letting me lob up and join your family out of the blue.

For the writing, I want to thank:

Kate Evans, who in Ubud in 2018 first suggested this unlikely undertaking.

The Society of Children's Book Writers and Illustrators crew, who first heard bits of it at Margaret River – thank you for the encouragement when I really needed it.

Thank you to the State of Western Australia for funding the first draft through its Department of Local Government Sport and Cultural Industries, and to the WA Premier's Book Awards for shortlisting this work for a Writing Fellowship.

The readers of my blog gave me incredibly valuable feedback, both from views and through private comments, on early drafts of the beginnings of some chapters.

I am indebted to memoirists who have traversed difficult territory and who have helped give me courage to get this formed: Natasha Trethewey, Natasha Scholl, Kathryn Heyman, to name a mere few.

Howard Norman, my mentor who became my friend, who steered me through the morass of material and memory, and gave me confidence that I could find the right words.

And to Georgia Richter and Fremantle Press for literally being my dream publisher for this most personal of books.

www.ingramcontent.com/pod-product-compliance
Lightning Source LLC
Chambersburg PA
CBHW031420150426
43191CB00006B/337